The Jet Sex

The
Jet Sex

Airline Stewardesses
and the Making
of an American Icon

Victoria Vantoch

University of Pennsylvania Press
Philadelphia

Published by
University of Pennsylvania Press
Philadelphia, Pennsylvania 19104-4112
www.upenn.edu/pennpress

Printed in the United States of America
on acid-free paper

2 4 6 8 10 9 7 5 3 1

A Cataloging-in-Publication record
is available from the Library of Congress
ISBN 978-0-8122-4481-6

For my mother
and
for the stewardesses
who flew during
the golden era

CONTENTS

INTRODUCTION

WHEN WORLD WAR II ended, assembly lines shut down and America's Rosie the Riveters were sent home to start their lives as wives and mothers. It was a new era for femininity, and television's June Cleaver, who dished up casserole in her suburban dream kitchen, set the standard. But not all women wanted to be full-time homemakers and those who were unmarried or needed to work outside the home had limited options: they could be secretaries, nurses, teachers, or sales clerks, but not much else. Then something monumental happened. Millions of Americans started to travel on airplanes—and the stewardess profession was born.[1]

Now, young working women did not have to change bedpans or take dictation; they could travel the world, meet important people, and lead exciting lives. The stewardess position was well paid, prestigious, and adventurous—and it quickly became the nation's most coveted job for women. Scores of qualified young women applied for each opening so airlines had their pick and could hire only the crème de la crème. In order to win a stewardess position, an applicant had to be young, beautiful, unmarried, well groomed, slim, charming, intelligent, well educated, white, heterosexual, and doting. In other words, the postwar stewardess embodied mainstream America's perfect woman.[2] She became a role model for American girls, and an ambassador of femininity and the American way abroad.

This icon of American womanhood showed up everywhere in postwar culture—stewardesses appeared in Hollywood films and national ad campaigns for everything from milk to cigarettes. In 1955 a Disney television series featured an episode titled "I Want to Be a TWA Stewardess When I Grow Up." In 1958 a *Life* magazine cover story reported that stewardesses held "one of the most coveted careers open to young American women." Airlines enlisted stewardesses to pose for publicity shots, to mingle with international dignitaries, and to speak at civic clubs around the nation. These enchanting women cavorted with A-listers at parties hosted by the Guggenheims. They also made appearances on the national political scene. Forty stewardesses decked out in tailored silver-sequined minidresses welcomed guests as the official presidential hostesses at Richard Nixon's inaugural ball. Even the nation's most popular doll, Barbie, appeared in a navy-blue American Airlines stewardess uniform (complete with a jaunty cap and suitcase). This was an era when little girls dreamed of becoming stewardesses.[3]

At first glance, the stewardess appears to have been a reflection of conservative postwar gender roles—an impeccable airborne incarnation of the mythical homemaker of the 1950s who would happily abandon work to settle down with Mr. Right. A high-flying expert at applying lipstick, warming baby bottles, and mixing a martini, the stewardess was popularly imagined as the quintessential wife to be. Dubbed the "typical American girl," this masterful charmer—known for pampering her mostly male passengers while maintaining perfect poise (and straight stocking seams) thirty thousand feet above sea level—became an esteemed national heroine for her womanly perfection.

But while the stewardess appears to have been an airborne Donna Reed, a closer look reveals that she was also popularly represented as a sophisticated, independent, ambitious career woman employed on the cutting edge of technology. This iconic woman in the workforce was in a unique position to bring acceptance and respect to working women by bridging the gap between the postwar domestic ideal and wage work for women. As both the apotheosis of feminine charm and American careerism, the stewardess deftly straddled the domestic ideal and a career that took her far from home. Ultimately, she became a crucial figure in paving the way for feminism in America.

The stewardess, as both icon and individual, challenged the traditional gender roles of the 1950s in two ways. First, this multifaceted icon appeared pretty, feminine, *and* career oriented. The stewardess image in the postwar media conformed to traditional gender norms in many ways, but it also contained porous spaces, which allowed subversive ideas about gender to leak through and to undermine the dominant happy-housewife ideal even during this conservative era. Thus, this icon exposes early seeds of feminism in the popular culture of the 1950s. The stewardess's metamorphosis from the doting, wholesome wife in training of the 1950s (1945 to 1957) to a glamorous, jet-setting career girl by the late 1950s to a seductress who performed in-flight strip teases in the mid-1960s serves as a link for understanding the critical gender transition in America from the dominant domestic ideal of the 1950s to the gender rebellion and sexual revolution of the late 1960s.[4] Her evolution from a wholesome icon into a sex symbol also offers insight into the broader trend in America whereby images of sexualized women's bodies have been increasingly used to sell products.[5]

Second, the profession fostered a budding feminist consciousness among these women long before the American women's movement brought gender inequality into the mainstream national consciousness. Before feminism was a household word, these pretty women had become aware of gender inequality and found ways to resist traditional gender norms. These girdled women conformed to draconian airline beauty codes, but at the same time they also marshaled a powerful rebellion against beauty-based gender inequality in the workplace (such as body weight limits). Using the Civil Rights Act's Title VII, they were among the first women in America to go up against major corporations for gender discrimination of various stripes, and, ultimately, to win landmark victories for working women on issues including equal pay, maternity leave, age limits, and body weight regulations. They also beat the tobacco industry by winning the nation's first ban on workplace smoking. These stewardesses show how gender consciousness burgeoned in one group of women before the rise of mainstream American feminism.

The stewardess also sheds light on how America's identity was being reconfigured as the nation assumed a new role in the postwar world order. When the United States replaced Britain as a world superpower in the postwar international landscape, American national identity changed in important ways. The stewardess came to symbolize America's emerging identity as a middle-class, consumer nation.[6] This beautiful career girl projected an image of America as glamorous, consumer oriented, and technologically advanced—and this potent image would be central to America's international propaganda campaign as the nation aimed to charm and impress the Cold War world. The stewardess became a much-mythologized, international symbol of glamour.

Introduction

At a time when few women traveled internationally, this pretty jetsetter served a broader role as a female diplomat who sold the American way overseas. Popularly dubbed "ambassadors," American stewardesses were on display all over the world—from greeting visitors at the 1958 World's Fair in Brussels to waving from Coca-Cola parade floats in the Dominican Republic to teaching Soviet women how to apply lipstick.

The stewardess's ambassadorship was particularly symbolic in the context of the global political climate of the Cold War. The stewardess rose to fame at a time when the Soviet Union and the United States were embroiled in a tense, long-term Cold War expressed through economic competitions, a nuclear arms race, wars of extension, and technological contests. The rival empires also fought an intense propaganda war, which prominently featured images of women. The question of which nation's women had better lives and whose women were prettiest were recurring themes in the Soviet-American propaganda wars. Pan Am's stewardess training motto of 1960 captured the power of beauty: "An attractive, well-groomed appearance is a social expression of good will and friendship to the world."[7]

These international dialogues about femininity were intricately woven into larger debates about Communism, capitalism, and freedom. In the international image war, American politicians heralded capitalism's superiority based on the abundant lipsticks, girdles, and suburban homes available to American women. On the American side the perfect woman was a dolled-up housewife who lived in a suburban dream home with an assortment of shiny new appliances. The U.S. stewardess encapsulated this very American version of womanhood—one that relied on being a modern, heterosexual, white, middle-class, attractive consumer. She was the ultimate consumer, who knew the latest Parisian fashion trends, wore designer uniforms, applied cosmetics expertly, and lived an enviable jet-setting lifestyle that brought her to five-star hotels in exotic cities around the world. The mainstream American press portrayed U.S. stewardesses (and American women in general) as glamorous, cosmopolitan, pretty world leaders in femininity—they were set in sharp contrast to unflattering portraits of Soviet women, who were depicted as overweight, unfashionable, and generally mannish.

On the other side of the propaganda war, Soviet politicians flaunted their working women as proof of gender equality and a testament to the success of Communism. Soviet propaganda chastised capitalist nations for lagging behind in women's equality by restricting women to unpaid household labor. The model Soviet woman was a worker and loyal party member who participated equally in the nation's economic and political life. Aeroflot stewardesses embodied this archetypal Soviet woman as a model worker, rather than a glamour girl or housewife in training. The iconic stewardess vividly demonstrates how gender, sexuality, race, technology, and beauty were connected to the global culture war between the Soviets and the Americans. Probing how gender and beauty related to broader political debates within the context of Cold War propaganda, this story of the stewardess highlights the ways in which national identity and global politics have been mapped onto women's bodies and how these female bodies were canvases for national ideals.[8]

———

In 1956, when my mother was in eighth grade, she dreamed of becoming the first female astronaut. She went on to become the salutatorian of her high-school class and won first prize in a model UN speech contest that awarded her a month-long, all-expense-paid trip to historical sites around the country. She subsequently earned a B.A. in Slavic languages from UCLA. The Library of Congress Aerospace Technology Division recruited her for her Russian language skills and she moved to Washington, D.C., where she translated Russian aerospace articles on everything from Alexey Leonov, the first person to walk in space, to metallurgy—all of which bored her to the core.

She considered graduate school for international studies but did not have much savings and could not stomach the prospect of living on peanut-butter sandwiches for four years, so, in 1968, she brushed up on her Russian and interviewed for a stewardess position with Pan Am, which had just started flying to Moscow. She was devastated when the airline rejected her, but she managed to win a position with Eastern Airlines and her hometown newspaper chronicled her success. As a stewardess, she moved into a boarding house with Alice Paul, one of the twentieth century's most famous women's rights activists.

While living with Paul, her life was a collage of contradictions. She lobbied on Capitol Hill for the Equal Rights Amendment at the same time that she went to work as a stewardess wearing pale blue hot pants. In 1969, she gave a speech to Congress in honor of the early women's rights activist Lucretia Mott. The topic: gender equality in the workforce. That same year she also competed in two beauty pageants.[9]

She got married, had my sister and me, continued to fly, and spent much of her adult life feeling guilty about being an absent parent. Flying was never really about the money for my mother. It meant freedom from suburban life and office monotony, and participation in a public realm that was usually reserved for men. I rode on flights with her and felt proud—my mother was the stewardess. And since airlines allowed employees to bring their families on flights for free, by the time I was twelve I had traveled to twenty-five countries.

Some of my mother's early stewardess friends went on to get doctorates in chemistry, to work at the Department of Defense, to manage large households of their own, and to become successful attorneys. My mother, however, continued to fly until Eastern went out of business. Without a job at the age of forty-eight, she desperately campaigned for a stewardess position with other airlines. She created a colorful posterboard presentation that read, "I will die if I don't fly" (along with—I'm serious—a song she wrote about her love of flying) and sent it to the American Airlines personnel department, which, after a series of interviews, hired her.

But this was the early 1990s and, by now, being a stewardess had lost its cachet. Around that time, in my early teens, I was interviewing for admission to exclusive New England boarding schools. During one interview that wasn't going particularly well, the pompous interviewer in a tweed jacket suggested that I become a stewardess like my mother—"because of my smile." I knew then I would be rejected. My face burned. I stopped mentioning my mother's profession. It was no longer something to be proud of. It had become an insult.

My fascination with airline stewardesses began with my mother. It began with curiosity about how a talented public speaker who was nearly fluent in Russian and committed to women's rights chose a career that ultimately allowed her to be written off as a vapid sex object and, ultimately, as a low-status service worker.

When I started researching airline stewardesses, I found that the topic made for amusing cocktail party banter. "You're writing a book about that?

Wow, what fun!" Yes, it was fun, but it was also serious history. Pretty women do not fit into what we have come to think of as serious history. Real histories cover topics like Lincoln, World War II, or, frankly, anything involving powerful white males. These are the books that populate the history sections at bookstores and libraries. So why study stewardesses?

As I dove deeper into research, I never admitted my personal connection to the world of stewardesses. I feared that if I divulged my secret backstory, the topic might be dismissed and trivialized as fluffy family history. But as I began to investigate stewardesses of this bygone era, it became patently clear that this mythic icon deserved deep historical research and analysis. The iconic stewardess served as the perfect lens for exploring broader questions about the origins of the women's movement, the relationship between popular culture and social change, and the role of beauty in activism. The stewardess allows us to see beyond our contemporary perspectives that often stereotype women of the prefeminist era as passive victims of gender oppression—by exposing how these women made sense of their lives, why they made their choices, how they felt about the gender norms of their time, and how they came to rebel against gender-based inequality.

This captivating icon also exposes how seemingly innocuous matters like lipstick, girdles, and virginity have unexpectedly—and surreptitiously—been at the forefront of the ideological battles of international politics. Beauty has had serious political, economic, and military consequences. Images of pretty women have structured our possibilities in this shrinking world and they have significantly influenced the lives of American women (and men) in terms of both aspirations and real behavior. Beauty, gender, and sex are not frivolous sidebars to "real history"—they are major forces that have framed global debates and shaped the nation's past. My mother's lasting devotion to her stewardess career drew me to study these powerful, yet often overlooked currents in history.

This cultural history of the stewardess deepens historical interpretations of gender and sexuality in postwar America by considering these iconic women in the context of globalization, Cold War politics, consumer culture, and the emerging romance with glamour in the United States.[10] In order to understand the rise of the women's movement and the sexual revolution in the United States during the 1960s, we need to consider the United States in relation to global politics. Within the context of Cold War propaganda, the stewardess shows how ideas about gender snuck across international borders and changed each nation. The stewardess suggests the ways in which gender, sexuality, and beauty have been powerful elements of international politics. Images of pretty stewardesses have served to install and justify international hierarchies with serious political, military, and economic consequences. Ultimately, some of the most important air raids of the Cold War were waged by pretty women serving champagne at thirty-thousand feet.

The story begins with the miracle of flight. . . .

1

—————

Flying Nurses, Lady Pilots,
and the Rise of Commercial Aviation

WHEN ELLEN Church was growing up in Iowa during the 1910s, her parents took her to county fairs to watch pioneer aviators swoop through the air. Mesmerized by the goggled pilots performing aerial acrobatics, Church let her imagination soar. She wanted to fly. But at the time, aviation was just a fledgling technology and flying was considered a soul-stirring, yet risky, venture for intrepid explorers. The vast majority of Americans had never been on an airplane. Church had no idea that she would come to play an important role in this intriguing new world of aviation, but she did know she was smitten.

Born in 1904, Ellen Church came of age during the unique era of early aviation and her fascination with flight was not uncommon. When Wilbur Wright demonstrated the airplane in the early 1900s, the Frenchman Frantz Reichel summed up his feelings about flight: "Nothing can give an idea of the emotion experienced and the impression felt, at this last flight, a flight of masterly assurance and incomparable elegance." Europeans were so awestruck by flight that, in the 1910s, a group of Italian artists called the Futurists declared the airplane the foundation of a new theory of literature—"aeropoetry"—which expressed all the "feelings, emotions and reactions unknown to those accustomed to crawl on the surface of the earth."[1]

Ellen Church, 1930. Author's collection.

Although this literary trend did not take off in the United States, the airplane did become an important cultural symbol in America. In the first decades of aviation, the American public imagined the airplane as more than a mark of technological progress: it was perceived as a catalyst for a new utopian society, democracy around the globe, and world peace.[2] America was infatuated.

Young women were also part of the airplane craze. In fact, some were so eager to experience flying that they paid pilots at flying clubs and county fairs for airplane rides. One young girl, who later became a stewardess in 1939, recalled that her parents refused to give her the money for a plane ride because they considered it too dangerous—so she stole the fifty cents from her grandmother to pay for the ride.[3]

At the time, women aerial enthusiasts could even earn a living as "barnstormers"—stunt pilots who traveled across the country performing treacherous aerial feats such as plane-to-plane transfers via hanging rope ladders. The illustrious Ruth Law, a particularly successful female aviator, for example, earned $9,000 per week performing airborne stunts. Law's tour de force: climbing out of the cockpit onto the wing.[4]

"I used to gape at Ruth Law and think that she was the most wonderful person I ever saw," Ellen Church recalled. "I thought if there was any one thing I wanted to do it was to fly one of those machines just the way she did."[5]

Even though Ellen Church could not get aviation out of her mind, she chose a more practical route. Nursing was one of the few mainstream professions open to women at the time so Church attended the University of Minnesota's nursing school and, in 1926, after graduating, she took a position at San Francisco's French Hospital. But during her free time, she watched planes take off at the Oakland airport . . . and she pined for the sky. Church's lofty dreams would become a reality a few years later, when she took flight as the world's first airline stewardess.

Women in the Budding Aviation Industry

During the 1920s, the aviation industry's future was yet unknown. Americans anticipated an era of mass-produced personal planes, akin to Ford's Model T car (introduced in 1908). Media buzz forecast an airplane in every garage. In 1926, Ford announced a prototype of a personal plane; and, in 1933, Eugene Vidal, the director of the Bureau of Air Commerce, announced that the government would spend a million dollars to produce a "poor man's airplane," slated to cost $700.[6]

Meanwhile, aerial entrepreneurs struggled to find revenue sources in the burgeoning industry. In 1918, the U.S. Postal Service opened an experimental airmail route between New York City and Washington, D.C. While some private entrepreneurs offered passenger flights as early as 1913, most aviation companies focused primarily on mail and relied on substantial government subsidies for airmail contracts as their bread and butter throughout the

1920s. Ford Air Services was the first airline to combine an airmail route with scheduled passenger service in 1926, but it was a bust financially.[7]

Passenger air travel faced several major hurdles. Even though flight evoked enormous enthusiasm, it was not easy to get Americans aloft. Trains were more comfortable and luxurious than airplanes, and flying was still very expensive. In the early 1930s, coast-to-coast roundtrip airfare cost between $260 and $440—about half the price of a new automobile. The same trip could cost as little as $64 on the train.[8]

In addition to high prices, the public perception of flying was also marred by frequent, highly publicized crashes and fatalities. Pilots were also a PR nightmare for the budding airline industry. During World War I, pilots became known as daredevil hotshots, and by the 1920s aviation was seen as a daring form of entertainment for thrill seekers rather than a viable mode of travel. By the late 1920s, the airline industry had launched a major campaign to revamp this image of pilots and flying in general.[9]

Women were integral to aviation's image makeover. In order to make flying seem safer to the public and to counter the dangerous image of flying, aviation companies sponsored races, record-breaking flights, and other special events featuring female pilots. This strategy mimicked automobile publicity attempts in early car promotions. In the 1910s, car manufacturers sponsored women to drive across country to make cars look easy and safe to the American public; similarly, airline officials used women pilots to prove that flying was easy and safe.[10]

Throughout the 1920s and early 1930s, the peculiar needs of the nascent aviation industry offered more opportunities for women pilots. Although the number of "girl aviators" and "lady pilots" was small, they received substantial national media attention for their aerial feats. The pilots Amelia Earhart, Ruth Nichols, Jacqueline Cochran, and others made headlines with their record-breaking flights. "Lady pilots" earned incomes through air race sponsorships, teaching, and selling airplanes in the private market.[11] In 1929, women pilots founded the Ninety-Nines, an all-women international pilots' organization with ninety-nine original members, to further women's aerial opportunities and to promote the visibility of women pilots.

"Girl aviators" also became popular in the 1920s because they resonated with broader American gender norms of this era. The 1920s was a time when mainstream American popular culture often portrayed women as self-reliant and independent. This was the era of the flapper, a new type of woman, who showcased her bold independence in various ways. After women gained the vote, the flapper surfaced as a potent symbol of women's liberation—she wore short skirts, smoked cigarettes, and bucked conventional gender mores. Dominant gender stereotypes of the era, however, simultaneously catalogued women as more erratic, scatterbrained, and less technologically minded than men.[12] These conflicting gender norms dovetailed with the needs of the budding aviation industry in ways that allowed air-minded women to carve out diverse positions for themselves in the industry throughout the 1920s. But women's opportunities in aviation would soon shrivel as the industry moved in a new direction.

During the late 1920s, aviation began transforming in important ways. In 1927, Charles Lindbergh's solo transatlantic flight garnered international attention and amplified public enthusiasm about flying; at the same time, commercial aviation in the United States entered a substantial growth spurt. During this aviation boom, more than a hundred airlines in the United States carried passengers, mail, and cargo. Meanwhile, U.S. government officials tried to free the airline industry from government subsidies by encouraging airlines to shift focus from mail to passengers. In the wake of numerous mergers and bankruptcies, four major domestic airlines emerged in the early 1930s: United, American, Eastern, and TWA. Pan Am, which operated overseas routes exclusively, also surfaced as an industry leader. At the same time, passenger air travel was on the rise. In 1933, the four major domestic airlines would carry more than half a million passengers.[13] These major aviation industry changes would pave the way for a new role for women.

A New Position for Air-Minded Women

Since early airlines were geared toward airmail rather than passenger travel, when they occasionally carried passengers, they offered no in-flight service. The copilots provided occasional assistance when passengers asked for it. The first flight attendants in the United States were white, male "aerial couriers" employed in 1926 on a route between Detroit and Grand Rapids operated by Stout Air Services. Other airlines began using male "couriers" to serve food, answer in-flight questions, and handle baggage.[14]

But in 1930, when Steve Stimpson, the division traffic agent at Boeing Air Transport (which later became United Airlines), began preparing for the inauguration of Boeing's new twenty-eight-hour coast-to-coast air service, he considered his options carefully. Charged with orchestrating passenger service details and increasing the airline's passenger traffic, Stimpson mulled over in-flight lunch menus and prospective cabin service.

That year, twenty-six-year-old Ellen Church was working as a nurse and taking flying lessons at the Oakland airport on her days off. According to aviation lore, she stopped by the Boeing Air Transport office located at the St. Francis Hotel in San Francisco, where she met Steve Stimpson. Church ended up telling him that she could fly a plane and they talked for hours.[15]

Church still fantasized about becoming a pilot. But while female pilots had been able to earn a living as flying instructors, stunt pilots, and airplane salespeople during the 1920s, female pilots were having a harder time finding paid positions in the cockpit by the early 1930s. Since fledgling airlines did not hire female pilots to fly passengers or mail, Ellen Church did not have many options.

In spite of narrowing opportunities for women in aviation, many young women dreamed about aviation careers. These women found encouragement in "career novels," a popular edutainment genre for teen girls during the 1930s, which featured young female protagonists making their way in careers. Generally ending with marriage proposals, career novels often presented Nancy Drew-like adventure stories with airborne heroines or focused on young women pursuing their dreams of becoming pilots. *The Sky Girl* (1930), for example, chronicled one young woman's ambition to become a pilot. Her father, a former wartime flying ace, initially thwarted her efforts but ultimately permitted her to fulfill her dream and train as a pilot.[16]

Like the heroines in career novels, Ellen Church was determined to find her way into the sky. When she met Steve Stimpson at the Boeing office, she pitched him the idea of hiring female nurses as cabin attendants. Stimpson had been contemplating hiring men. Boeing could have followed other airlines by employing white male attendants. Alternatively, Boeing could have hired African American male attendants, who were typically employed as railroad porters, or young Filipino men, who usually worked as waiters and attendants on ocean liners and in hotels at the time. On February 24, 1930, Stimpson sent a memo on "couriers" to A. G. Kinsman, the passenger traffic manager at Boeing, stating that he had a bunch of "good prospects lined up." Stimpson considered the position so important that he had interviewed some of the prospective cabin attendants six times before deeming them "good men."[17]

However, the same day, apparently enthralled with Ellen Church, Stimpson sent another memo to Kinsman proposing women attendants.[18] Although Stimpson's original memo has been lost, a transcript of it has been photocopied and quoted ad nauseam as the stewardess origination story for airline publicity ever since. In the famous memo, Stimpson clarified that he would not hire "the flapper type of girl," but nurses with "horse sense" who had "seen enough of men to not be inclined to chase them around the block at every opportunity." "You know nurses as well as I do, and you know that they are not given to flightiness—I mean in the head. The average graduate nurse is a girl with some horse sense and is very practical," Stimpson wrote.[19]

Mr. Humphries, a vice president of Boeing, and other higher-ups at Boeing nixed the idea. William Patterson, Boeing's assistant to the president (who would soon become the company's president), originally wanted to hire young boys. Patterson's wife and children, who always got horribly air sick, however, convinced him to reconsider. "My mother and I didn't want young boys holding our hair when we got sick—no customer wanted that—so we told my dad to hire women instead," recalled Patterson's daughter, Patricia.[20] Patterson gave the go-ahead for a three-month trial for women attendants.[21]

Boeing executives also had compelling financial incentives for hiring women attendants. In the first place, women employees were cheaper than male employees. In 1931, female airline ground personnel earned $24.50 per week, compared to male ground personnel who earned $31.04 per week.[22] Also, as the public lost faith in corporate leaders during the Depression, the political climate was turning in favor of labor over management and unions were gaining momentum and power.

Within this context, airline officials hired women partly as an attempt to forestall cabin attendant unionization. Women were considered more pliable than men and executives considered them less likely to unionize. In addition, craft unions in the early twentieth century often excluded women. While some women in service industries, such as waitresses, had started their own unions during this era, female clerical and retail workers had limited success during the organizing heyday of the 1930s. When Boeing decided to hire female nurses, nurses had not yet unionized.

Airline executives' apprehension about unions intensified when transportation unions garnered more muscle with the Railway Labor Act (RLA) of 1926, which granted the government power to force employers to negotiate with unions and instituted elaborate mechanisms for government intervention to forestall interruptions in transportation. Airline executives suspected—and feared—that airlines soon would be covered under the RLA. Sure enough, these premonitions would come true in 1935, when the Air Line

The original eight stewardesses, 1930. © Boeing.

Pilots Association (ALPA) successfully lobbied Congress for an amendment to the RLA, which placed airlines under its authority.[23]

Unionization efforts were also brewing elsewhere in the aviation industry. Early airmail pilots had organized strikes to protest being forced to fly in bad weather and had organized the Air Mail Pilots of America in 1920, which advocated better conditions and higher salaries. In the late 1920s, most pilots were members of the National Air Pilots Association (NAPA), which tried ineffectively to negotiate with airline officials, but most pilots remained dissatisfied with their salaries and conditions. In 1930, the same year that Boeing officials decided to hire women cabin attendants, Boeing pilots were organizing a new union, the Air Line Pilots Association (ALPA), which was officially formed in 1931 and would go on to become a fiercely powerful force in the airline industry.

Regardless of Boeing's motives for hiring her, Ellen Church carved out a new role for women in aviation and she would be widely credited as the world's first female flight attendant. Church in turn was charged with hiring seven other nurse-stewardesses. Stimpson sent a memo to the Boeing vice president Mr. Humphries on April 8, 1930 reporting on Church's progress finding candidates: "She says that they are all of the very highest type, well educated, all between 25 and 30 years of age, thoroughly accustomed to discipline, and of the wholesome type. They are also all very enthusiastic, and anxious to tackle the job."[24] The first stewardesses were required to be registered nurses. They had to be no more than 5'4" tall (to accommodate low airplane ceilings), between the ages of 20 and 26, weighing less than 118 pounds, and unmarried.[25]

On May 15, 1930, outfitted in matching dark green wool capes with green berets, the original eight stewardesses began service on Boeing's ten-passenger airplanes serving the San Francisco–Chicago route. The trip took twenty hours and made thirteen stops—in favorable weather. One stewardess flew the leg from San Francisco to Cheyenne; a different stewardess took over for the leg from Cheyenne to Chicago. Lunch was served between San Francisco and Cheyenne. While planes were changed in Cheyenne, passengers received a hot meal at Boeing's airport café, and then another meal aloft between Cheyenne and Chicago. The lunches, according to Ellen Church, were equipped with "lovely china decorated with blue-green modernistic design, dainty silverware and Irish linen napkins." The meals were prepared in advance and served cold. They typically included sandwiches, cold fried chicken, potato chips, cake, cookies, olives, coffee, and lemonade.[26]

Boeing issued a brief stewardess training manual in 1931 that outlined stewardesses' duties, including cleaning cabins, heating coffee, completing reports on passengers and equipment, collecting tickets, caring for airsick passengers, and furnishing pillows, reading materials, cigarettes, and gum.[27] Stewardesses also helped load baggage, refuel the planes, and roll planes into hangars. They adjusted the altimeters so passengers could watch the altitude changes. They were expected to learn each passenger's name, point out interesting geographic features along the way, and answer questions about how the aircraft operated. At times, stewardesses were even called upon to walk onto the wing to help mechanics start the bulky engine.

During the early years of passenger travel, the actual experience of flying was more of a white-knuckled adventure than an easy, pleasant experience. In the early 1930s, the Ford Tri-motor, nicknamed the "Tin Goose" after its corrugated metal exterior, was commonly used for commercial passenger travel. It was not insulated and had no air conditioning. To make matters worse, the interior reeked of hot oil and the disinfectant used to clean up after airsick passengers because it had no circulation system. Another popular plane of the era, the Boeing 80, was slightly more comfortable with forced-air ventilation and hot running water.

Pressurized cabins had not been invented yet, so planes had to fly at low altitudes, rather than above the clouds, through inclement weather. Turbulence was standard fare as planes bounced in wind and weather. Airsickness was common. These early ten-to-twelve seat airplanes were also designed for mail service, rather than for passengers, so they had cramped interiors with low ceilings. Plus, planes were so loud and rattly that stewardesses often had to communicate with passengers by speaking through small megaphones. The typical Ford Tri-motor engine roared at nearly 120 decibels during takeoff—loud enough to cause permanent hearing loss.

Air travel was also very unpredictable and slow.[28] Airplanes had to land frequently to refuel, and they were often delayed due to bad weather—sometimes for days. In 1935, Mr. Knutson, the president of Central Public Utility Corp in New York, wrote a letter to William Patterson, the president of

United Airlines, about Knutson's recent trip: "The going out was rough as we entered the storm area in Indiana and had to come down in an emergency field. We trained into Chicago and then went out at midnight. This threw my schedule off 24 hours. The going was rough all night, and we lay over in salt lake [*sic*] three hours waiting for the weather to clear. We got off in the afternoon, but had five hours of very rough going over the mountains, during which everyone was very sick and pretty well knocked to pieces."[29]

"We were getting stuck at whistle stops in the Great Salt Lake area of Utah all the time," Ellen Church recalled. "We received reports of storms ahead, so we might be grounded for days at some little weather station with an air strip before the clouds rolled away."[30] During these unexpected layovers, stewardesses escorted passengers to railroad stations for meals.

Young women flocked to apply. United received fifteen thousand applications from prospective stewardess between 1930 and 1935. In 1939, American Airlines interviewed fewer than one hundred of five thousand applicants. They hired twenty.[31]

Stewardesses received a base pay of $100 to $125 per month to work a minimum of one hundred hours. Their salaries were similar to those of hospital nurses, but less than private-duty nurses. They made more than what white women typically earned in industrial, service, and clerical jobs, and about the same as women in feminized professions such as teaching and librarianship. (In 1931, women working in manufacturing, for example, earned about $60 per month, which was roughly the average income for female wage earners in America.)[32] During the Depression, the popularity of the stewardess position was bolstered by the widespread unemployment of private-duty nurses, who were eager to land stewardess positions.[33] Stewardesses also received paid vacations, insurance, free air travel, and expense allowances for layovers. Plus, the position allowed young, single women to have a measure of independence and to travel without a chaperone.

But it was not just the economy that made the position desirable. Many women simply longed to fly. "The sky was my home, my love," said Mary O'Connor after her first flight in a Tri-motor Ford plane. "I knew I would give it my very best, but first of all my whole devotion in whatever form might be required. I found that I loved flying."[34] O'Connor became a stewardess for United in 1933 and did not retire until 1960.

The idea of female stewardesses caught on. By 1935, Eastern, American, Western, and TWA had all hired female stewardesses. Airline executives, however, were unsure of how best to market them. In 1931, the editor of the *American Journal of Nursing* wrote a letter to Robert Johnson at Boeing to say that she was "disturbed" by the term "stewardess" because it was "less dignified than nurse."[35] Aviation uniforms and terms (such as "steward" and "captain") were derived from maritime transport, but for several years Steve Stimpson of Boeing had debated what to call these new attendants. In 1936, he was still considering alternate terms, including courierette, airette, attaché, skipperette, attendant, and escort.[36] But Stimpson never settled on a satisfactory alternative so "stewardess," "hostess," and "sky girl" were most commonly used.

Further, Boeing officials were unsure of how to deal with the nursing credentials in their marketing campaigns. Airline publicity materials (written after the fact) claimed that airlines hired nurses in the 1930s as a publicity move to make flying seem safer to the public. However, stewardesses were conspicuously absent from airline ads during this era. In fact, Harold Crary, Boeing's director of traffic, advertising, and publicity, asked Ellen Church not to publicize that stewardesses were nurses because he feared it might exacerbate fears that flying was dangerous enough to merit nurses. In an interdepartmental memo, dated November 19, 1930, he wrote to Ellen Church about suppressing the nursing credentials in publicity: "Mr. Johnson has authorized us to go ahead and give publicity to the stewardess service. In our general publicity, for the present at least, we will refer to them as institutionally-trained young women." The memo mentioned that it was only acceptable to note that stewardesses were nurses in nursing journals.[37] In 1935, the airline's president, William Patterson, received a letter from a businessman passenger that reflected the airline's tack on stewardesses: "I would soft-pedal the fact that the stewardesses have to be RN's. There is no reason why you should invite attack from other means of transportation, namely that the riding is so rough that they have to carry Registered Nurses."[38]

In fact, airlines did not use stewardesses in advertising. During the 1930s, airline ads primarily focused on routes, prices, and technology. Designed largely to lure wealthy businessmen away from trains, these early ads claimed that airplane travel was more economical than railroad travel because it saved time. In the prewar years, airfares were not regulated, few airlines served the same route, and there was a wide disparity in technological equipment between the airlines. Airlines competed with each other in these fields by boasting lower fares, promoting particular destinations, and trumpeting technological advances. These early ads rarely mentioned stewardesses, but this would radically shift after the war.[39]

Even though airlines did not use nursing credentials to sell air travel to the public, airline officials believed that having nurses aloft would help reassure passengers in-flight. Given how rough flying was at the time, airlines needed attendants who could work long hours in difficult circumstances without appearing ruffled. Nurses fit the bill. The nurse-stewardess uniform design reflected this. The original stewardesses wore two different uniforms: a "field uniform" to be worn outside the aircraft (and often in publicity photos), which included a jaunty green wool cape and beret, and an onboard uniform—a grey smock and a traditional nurse hat.

Airlines hired nurse stewardesses because they suited particular industry needs and reflected a respectable image of working womanhood during the 1930s. Nurses conjured an image of hard work, caretaking, and discipline. During the 1930s, airlines (following the lead of nursing schools) preferred young women from small towns rather than sophisticated women from urban centers. The small-town recruits were supposedly more likely to have a "good moral standing" and were purportedly accustomed to hard work and discipline. During the 1930s, numerous Hollywood films centered on nurses; these nurse heroines, who promoted idealism and self-sacrifice over personal desire, were potent female icons during the Depression years. Reflecting this feminine ideal, popular culture in the 1930s similarly promoted a vision of stewardesses as self-sacrificing heroines who bravely saved passengers' lives.[40]

Airlines also cultivated a stewardess image that reflected the gender ideals of the 1930s. The Depression had prompted widespread debates about the appropriateness of women working outside the home. The question about whether married women should perform wage work became a heated topic and a broad popular consensus agreed that women's access to wage work should be based on family need. In 1936, a Gallup Poll revealed, "82 percent of those surveyed (including three-fourths of the women) believed that wives of employed husbands should not work outside the home."[41]

At a time when America disparaged married women's workforce participation, airlines hired unmarried women and required stewardesses to resign upon marriage. By defining stewardess work as a temporary step between school and marriage, airlines circumvented the larger cultural debate over women's right to work outside the home. (And, of course, by hiring a short-term, female labor force, airlines also attempted to keep salaries low and forestall unionization.)

Airlines cast the women in this new aerial role as wholesome, respectable professionals.[42] Prohibiting tipping was one way that airlines distinguished the cabin crew as professional. Ocean liner stewards and Pullman porters received tips from passengers, but tips marked porters and ocean liner stewards as lower class. Velma Maul, one of the first American Airlines stewardesses, noted in her flight diary of 1933 that she collected tips: "My tips have been running between $3–5 every trip. . . . Mr. —— the inventor of the cigarette lighter was on board. He gave me a $5 tip. Made $8.00 all together." It is unclear whether American Airlines stewardesses were permitted to accept tips initially or whether Maul was breaking the rules, since she mentioned fearing being fired. But by 1936 American Airlines had expressly prohibited stewardesses from collecting tips. Rule 47 of the manual stated: "Stewardesses shall not accept 'tips.' The stewardesses of American airlines comprise a group of professionally trained young ladies and the position of stewardess is not to be classed as menial service."[43]

Airline officials also tried to create a sexually respectable stewardess image by setting boundaries for intimacy levels between stewardesses and male passengers and pilots. The first Boeing stewardess circular to the original eight stewardesses in 1930 noted: "One's personal conduct, especially with relation to members of the crew and other Boeing system employees, will be watched most closely at all times, and any slight deviation will spoil the whole thing."[44] The 1936 American Airlines manual instructed: "Unnecessary conversation should be avoided . . . the impression should be given that the stewardess is ready and willing to give information or assistance, but in a courteous, brief and business-like manner, and that duties do not permit a prolonged or aimless conversation. . . . Visits to the cockpit should be made only when absolutely necessary and should be as brief as possible."[45]

During the 1930s, stewardesses used professionalism as a way to navigate the thorny cultural implications of a job that allowed informal (and potentially inappropriate) contact with men. As single women who traveled independently with male passengers and pilots, stewardesses ran the risk of being considered promiscuous. Mary O'Connor, who became a stewardess during the 1930s, responded to criticisms of the profession: "Stewardesses are known for their faultless manners, so no stigma of indecorous behavior has ever been known to touch one. [And] pilots are serious-minded men. If he is single, a pilot may not even date one of the stewardesses while on duty, since this is strictly against company rules." O'Connor, in fact, whacked a passenger who tried to "get fresh." She was not, however, reprimanded by the airlines. Generally, airlines frowned on untoward passenger behavior, which allowed stewardesses to make a living with minimal harassment.[46]

The Airline Industry
and the Rise of Passenger Service

Six years after the inauguration of stewardess service, Douglas Aircraft Company rolled out a sleek new airplane that would fundamentally change the course of commercial aviation. Featuring twenty-four seats, a comfortable, more spacious cabin, and galleys for food preparation, the DC-3 was the first commercially viable plane specifically designed for passenger traffic. With just three refueling stops, the DC-3 could fly eastbound transcontinental flights in fifteen hours—a major improvement over Boeing's twenty-eight-hour coast-to-coast service in 1930. It became the industry standard through World War II and was the first plane to turn a profit just by carrying passengers. Largely due to the DC-3, passenger miles in the United States increased 600 percent from 1936 to 1941. With the advent of this passenger-oriented plane, the airline industry began to focus on passenger service and the stewardess was catapulted to new importance.[47]

With the arrival of DC-3s, United Airlines hired a consultant who had designed kitchens on cruise ships to adapt airplanes for food service. On DC-3s, hot food (cooked prior to flight) was padded in insulated boxes on carts, which were plugged into portable generators. Aloft, the carts were plugged into a 28-volt electric system to keep them warm.[48] By the late

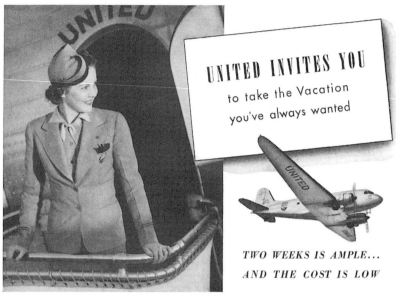

UNITED INVITES YOU

to take the Vacation you've always wanted

TWO WEEKS IS AMPLE...
AND THE COST IS LOW

LEAVE THE ATLANTIC COAST by Mainliner Sleeper this evening, breakfast in Yellowstone tomorrow, see the Park by motor in one or more days; and then fly to San Francisco in 5 hours! Thus you save days for leisurely enjoying the glorious Golden Gate Exposition.

VISIT LOS ANGELES and Hollywood at no extra cost on your United ticket from the East. Go one way to Los Angeles and San Francisco, return another. You see twice as much when you go United. Plan to include the Pacific Northwest at small additional cost. (See map.)

TO THE NEW YORK WORLD'S FAIR — United flies the direct Main Line airway to New York. Only 16 hours from most Pacific Coast cities, 10 hours from Denver, 3 hours 55 minutes from Chicago. United is shortest, fastest, Fair to Fair.

SEE WASHINGTON, Philadelphia, Cleveland, Chicago on your round trip from the West, at no extra cost. Take a side trip to Boston and New England. Consult your travel agent today about your ideal vacation via United.

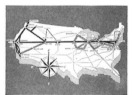

ASK ABOUT UNITED'S low round-trip fares and all-expense tours to the San Francisco and New York Fairs. See your own travel agent, or hotel transportation clerk.

UNITED

AIR LINES

Shortest, Fastest... Fair to Fair

One of the first airline ads featuring an image of the stewardess, United Airlines, 1939. Author's collection.

1930s, most airlines offered some food service, including hot meals served by stewardesses on individual trays. Some even served dinner on Haviland china with sterling silver.

As airlines began to pay more attention to passenger service, American Airlines instituted six-week stewardess training sessions at a hotel in Chicago. In 1939, United began a new stewardess school at the Chicago airport, which used a model of a DC-3 interior for stewardesses to practice serving food.[49] From 1926 to 1938, the number of passengers carried by U.S. airlines skyrocketed from less than 6,000 to 1.4 million.[50] As airlines focused more on passengers, they also rapidly expanded their stewardess corps. From 1937 to 1940, the number of cabin attendants employed by U.S. carriers more than tripled from less than 400 to approximately 1,000.[51]

While most U.S. airlines had hired women by 1935, two U.S. carriers that flew internationally continued to hire men. In 1936, there were 270 stewardesses and 1 male steward on domestic airlines, and 41 male stewards on U.S. airlines that flew internationally. Pan Am, which had a near monopoly on international flights at the time, hired exclusively male stewards throughout the 1930s and early 1940s. Male stewards evoked the European tradition of fine dining served by male waiters, which added a European flair to Pan Am's transatlantic service. But Pan Am executives also hired male stewards because they doubted that women could handle the rigorous, long overseas flights. Since Pan Am flew over water and long distances to small foreign ports, the airline required extensive first aid and seamanship training (including seaplane anchorage, navigation over water, and aircraft repair) for its stewards during the 1930s. But for the most part, cabin service had become predominantly a women's field.[52]

World War II temporarily heightened fluidity in aviation's gender-segregated roles. With thousands of men off at war, women were encouraged to take up typically male jobs and they assumed positions in aviation that had been reserved for men—such as piloting.[53] Peggy Wayne, Sky Girl (1941), a "career novel" for teen girls, depicted a young stewardess who asked, "Why shouldn't women, one day, pilot the big transport planes? Why should the highest goal in commercial aviation be limited to two thousand men?" At the end of the novel, Peggy left her stewardess position to become a transport pilot.[54]

Some actual stewardesses also took leaves to serve in the army. After resigning from a stewardess position, Ellen Church, for example, resumed flying lessons and earned a student pilot's license with "transport pilot" as a special qualification. Church became a captain in the Army Nurse Corps–Air Evacuation Services in 1942, and was one of the first women to earn the Air Medal, an honor awarded to those who distinguish themselves for a heroic act during an aerial flight.[55]

In addition to creating temporary jobs for women pilots, the war also prompted the few airlines that still hired male cabin crews to switch to female stewardesses. In 1944, Pan Am, one of the last airlines to continue hiring male flight attendants exclusively, began hiring female stewardesses. Airlines also dropped the nursing requirements for stewardesses to free nurses for the war.

By the end of the war, women's roles in aviation would be firmly cemented. The Women Airforce Service Pilots (WASP) had employed female pilots during the war, but it was disbanded in the postwar years in spite of the pilots' efforts to remain in service. Since commercial airlines still did not hire female pilots (it was not until 1973 that a U.S. airline would hire a woman pilot), women who had trained as pilots were often desperate to find work in the industry they loved. They often settled for roles peripheral to piloting. Although exact numbers are elusive, it was not uncommon for women who had trained as pilots to become stewardesses because it was one of the few positions in the aviation industry open to women. "Lady pilots" and other air-minded women, like Ellen Church, were now funneled into stewardess positions.[56]

By the end of World War II, several new conditions would radically shift the airline industry. A boom in the air travel market, new airplanes, and new federal aviation regulations would seriously affect the postwar airline business and propel the stewardess to the forefront of the industry in ways Ellen Church never could have imagined.

2

The Rise of the Stewardess

DURING THE years after World War II, the airline stewardess became an American icon. Heralded as the apotheosis of postwar womanhood, the stewardess was popularly dubbed the "typical all-American girl." An expert at doting on men and serving meals, she represented an airborne incarnation of the much-mythologized American homemaker of the 1950s—a paragon of feminine virtue, a virginal girl next door, and a model wife-to-be. Of course, the reality of the stewardess's life and work was different, but this image was a powerful tool in the promotional arsenal of the fledgling airline industry.

This was an era when most Americans had not yet flown and many young women longed to experience flight. At the time, the majority of American women became full-time housewives, secretaries, nurses, retail clerks, or teachers; and most young women lived at home with their parents until marriage because moving away to college was not yet a common practice. In 1950, only 10.9 percent of single, white women between the ages of fifteen and twenty-nine lived away from their parents.[1] The stewardess position was a unique call to adventure—it offered young single women a rare opportunity to leave their hometowns, to travel the world, to mingle with celebrities, and to gain some independence. Stewardesses who started flying in the mid-1940s often came from small towns, and many believed they had limited opportunities to leave the town, much less explore the country or the world. As one stewardess put it: "I had an insatiable desire to see far

United Airlines stewardesses, 1939. Image courtesy Flight Path
Learning Center, Los Angeles. Used by permission of United Airlines.

away places with strange sounding names. After graduating from college, I
wished to broaden my horizons and drink deep of all the interesting places
throughout the world."[2] Thousands of young women yearned for the sky.
They dieted, studied foreign languages, plucked, and primped in efforts to
land this highly coveted job.

Winning a stewardess position was no small feat. The competition was
stiff. In 1951, American Airlines received 20,000 applications for 347 stewardess positions.[3] Immaculate-looking women who spoke three languages lined
up to fly—so landing a position meant beating out hundreds of qualified
applicants. The application process was strenuous—it often included multiple interviews, body measurements, weight checks, foreign language tests,
intelligence tests, and personality evaluations. Many successful applicants
were flat-out rejected by several airlines before securing a position; others
were advised to reapply after losing weight, improving foreign languages
skills, or having their teeth straightened. Women who were too short to
meet airline height requirements padded their shoes, stood on their tiptoes,
or fluffed up their hair during the interviews.[4]

Like so many other young American women, Texas native Mildred Jackson had had her eyes on the sky ever since childhood. In the mid-1940s, stewardess candidates had to be twenty-one to twenty-eight years old, unmarried, 5'3" to 5'6" tall, no more than 125 pounds, with good posture and an "attractive appearance," and preferably with some college education.[5] But when the nineteen-year-old brunette first applied for a stewardess position in 1946, she was three-quarters of an inch too tall according to airline height specifications and she was too young. Two years later, after the height limit had been raised, she reapplied and was hired.

During her tenure as a stewardess, Jackson quickly became a media favorite. A representative of the perfect "all-American girl," she was featured prominently in newspapers, on radio shows, and at airline publicity events nationwide. The press featured Jackson's advice on a range of womanly matters, including cooking suggestions for new brides, instructions on how to apply lipstick, tips on pampering men, and advice on eliciting marriage proposals. American Airlines press releases called Jackson "a statuesque brunette, with dancing eyes and provocative dimples," noting "she weighs 123 pounds, stands five feet, six-and-three-quarter inches, and has brown hair. . . . She's fond of horseback riding, swimming and photography."[6]

Looking pretty was her forte. She judged modeling competitions and the *Chicago Sunday Tribune* featured Jackson's guidance on achieving the "transcontinental look," which delineated how to "look your fashionable best always and everywhere."[7] The ever dazzling, poised, and feminine sorority girl had also been voted "class beauty."

The illustrious Mildred Jackson also offered husband-snaring tips. "Any girl could get a husband if she learns what we teach them about human relations," she told reporters. Jackson's secret to husband catching relied on her "formula for soothing the feathers of an angry male": "Do something to pamper him. He'll purr like a kitten."[8]

On first glance, Jackson appears to have been an embodiment of the stereotypical housewife of the 1950s—the consummate airborne June Cleaver, who was good looking, a master at feigning interest in men's stories, eager to land an eligible husband, and ready to abandon her wage work to live out her true feminine calling as a full-time homemaker.

But newspapers also reported that Jackson herself "resisted becoming a marriage statistic because of her fascination for her job."[9] Jackson simultaneously endorsed and undermined the domestic ideal.

Prior to becoming a stewardess, Jackson had, in fact, earned a bachelor's degree from Baylor University in Texas, with a double major in English and business—a noteworthy accomplishment considering the paltry number of women with college degrees at the time. Plus, she had career ambitions from the get-go. In 1949, when American Airlines hosted a contest for all employees for furnishing the most leads to the sales office for potential overseas passengers, Jackson turned in 750 leads and won the prize—an all-expense-paid trip to Europe.

She was also widely lauded—by both the mainstream press and the airline—for her business savvy. She was popularly portrayed as a smart, motivated achiever, a successful career woman, and an American ambassador to the world. The mainstream press extolled her rapid rise up the corporate ladder at American Airlines—a mere fourteen months after her first flight, she became an instructor; three months later, a chief instructor; and a year and a half after that, she became head of American Airlines' stewardess school at the age of twenty-three. *The Chicago Sun-Times* reported: "Behind her statuesque brunette beauty, her engaging smile and flashing on-and-off dimples are a drive and determination that have carried her." Her career success was celebrated in the national press: "Eight Careerists Honored at 2nd Annual Observance" (1957), "She Sets Three Goals and Reaches All of Them" (1956), and "Sky's No Limit for Her (1950).[10]

In fact, American Airlines' publicity department considered Jackson its premier marketing weapon. Commended for her management expertise as well, Jackson lectured corporate executives across fields on how to recruit and train employees. She toured the country with American Airlines' president C. R. Smith—speaking at advertising organization happenings, mugging for press photos, and courting political dignitaries at high-profile events. American Airlines' publicity headquarters sang her praises in an interdepartmental letter to a branch office: "[Jackie] can capture any audience of any age or any kind, from a medical association to a cub scout den. And she'll have your newspaper columnists, TV station personnel, city officials and everyone else she meets eating out of her hand. This gal makes Elmer

Wheeler [the infamous top salesman in the 1950s] look like an amateur."[11] Jackson was, indeed, a tour de force. She demonstrated that women could be both "feminine" and career-oriented. This, however, was a delicate balancing act in postwar America.

This was an era when the birth rate skyrocketed, the average age of marriage dropped, the suburban home was heralded as the apotheosis of happiness, and *Look* magazine coined the term "togetherness" to describe the family. Expenditures on residential construction rose by more than 40 percent from 1952 to 1960. Television shows such as *Father Knows Best*, *Leave It to Beaver*, and *The Donna Reed Show* reflected these conservative gender ideals. Femininity was almost synonymous with domesticity. Postwar advertisements in women's magazines glorified the housewife—featuring women with whiter-than-white teeth and flawless skin, living in suburban dream homes.[12] Domesticity reigned supreme.

At the same time that popular culture heralded domesticity as true feminine fulfillment, gender roles in mid-century America were, in fact, shifting. American women were entering the workforce in large numbers.

A United Airlines stewardess gives smile instructions, March 1956.
Author's collection.

As more families moved into suburban homes in the postwar era, desires for consumer products expanded dramatically and achieving consumer dreams increasingly required women to earn an income. By 1960, about one-third of American women worked outside the home. So, many Americans experienced a disconcerting disjuncture between real-life moms who worked (both inside and outside the home) and television's full-time homemaker June Cleaver.[13]

The stewardess rose to fame as a celebrated icon of American womanhood during the postwar years partly because she bridged the mid-century gap between domesticity and wage work (witness Mildred Jackson). On the one hand, the postwar stewardess appeared to be a submissive housewife in training, whose primary role was to serve her mostly male passengers. On the other hand, she was educated, intelligent, career-minded, committed to self-improvement, successful, and independent. An American Airlines brochure summed it up: "[The stewardess] has come to typify the young American woman—intelligent, attractive, well-poised, friendly, and helpful."[14] This wholesome American idol would become a powerful ambassador of the American way around the world.

Industry Challenges, Marketing Strategies, and the Rise of a National Icon

World War II had changed commercial aviation in several important ways. First, wartime government contracts resulted in major technological upgrades in aircraft design and equipment. Technology developed during the war became available for civilian air travel afterward and it had a significant impact on commercial air travel. For example, Douglas Aircraft Company originally designed a new DC-6 as a military transport plane during the war, but after the war the company reconfigured the plane for passenger air travel.

Introduced commercially in 1946, the DC-6 flew faster than earlier models and could carry more passengers longer distances. It could carry fifty-eight passengers and it could travel ninety miles per hour faster than its predecessor, the DC-4. Moreover, it included a pressurized cabin, which allowed the planes to reach an altitude of twenty-five thousand feet—well above weather to provide a smooth, comfortable ride. With longer ranges of up to three thousand miles, these new planes inaugurated transatlantic flights and nonstop transcontinental flights. The DC-6 was a boon to air travel.

By the end of the war, U.S. airlines were poised for massive expansion. Beyond the introduction of new, faster, more comfortable planes, the postwar era was a time of vast business expansion, and businessmen wanted speedy travel. The economy boomed, and more Americans enjoyed leisure time and higher disposable incomes. Within this climate of postwar prosperity, air travel would become a rapidly expanding business that served growing corporate and individual needs. From 1945 to 1946, passenger miles doubled.[15]

Federal aviation regulations also precipitated major shifts in the airline industry. While airlines had used fares, routes, and technology to compete with each other during the prewar years, by the end of the war the ways airlines could compete had changed radically. The Civil Aeronautics Board (CAB), the policymaking organization established in 1938 that determined airfares and airline routes, started regulating airfares and assigned more airlines to each route. By requiring airlines to charge the same fares for the same routes, the CAB severely limited the ways that airlines could compete. In addition to limiting the means of competition, the CAB increased the competition itself. Immediately after the war, the CAB granted several major domestic carriers permission to serve international routes, which had been nearly exclusively operated by Pan Am. Furthermore, since the military had funded airline equipment improvements through wartime contracts granted to most major airlines, by the end of the war most major airlines also operated equipment of similar quality.

With fares and routes regulated and similar technology, airlines were suddenly unable to compete for customers based on price, destination, or equipment. So, they sought new ways to distinguish themselves in the marketplace. Airlines began to invest more in amenities aloft and increasingly relied on passenger service to woo passengers. In particular, stewardesses became the linchpin of postwar airline advertising and business models. Airlines began to rely on stewardesses to retain existing customers through first-rate service aloft and to seduce new customers through advertising and public relations campaigns, which now focused on the character and caliber of stewardesses.

Passenger service became a central way that airlines competed not only with each other, but also with other modes of travel. In the postwar years, airlines still faced competition from ocean liners, railroads, and automobiles. Domestic airlines, which served primarily wealthy businessmen, strategized to lure these passengers away from surface transportation—particularly, Pullman trains, the luxury train travel that most businessmen chose at the time.[16] Meanwhile, international carriers, such as Pan Am, which served a higher proportion of leisure travelers, competed to attract passengers away from ocean liners. As airlines battled to win passengers away from other forms of transportation, they tried to cultivate a unique allure to flying—casting airplanes as cutting-edge technology with stellar customer service.

Now that customer service was key to selling tickets, airlines amped up their investment in stewardesses. In 1945, U.S. carriers employed more than two thousand stewardesses and that number had doubled by 1947.[17] Airlines not only hired more stewardesses, they also developed new standards for selecting these critical marketing representatives. Airlines had dropped the nursing requirement during the war to free nurses for the war effort and airlines now focused on recruiting young women with education, social graces, and an idealized "American look." The new stewardess corps was a highly select group of young, white, single, college-educated, attractive American women—often from middle-class and upper-middle-class backgrounds with homemaker mothers and professional fathers. In 1946, airlines proclaimed that the ideal stewardess was from "a small-town, cultured, middle-class home."[18] Airlines also administered IQ tests to stewardess hopefuls and preferred applicants with at least two years of college education (a tall order considering the small percentage of American women in college during the 1950s). Some carriers even required fluency in a second language. Airlines could afford to be highly selective because the position was in such high demand.

Airlines carefully calibrated this new stewardess image to align with the nation's emerging postwar identity. America was assuming a new position—it had replaced Britain as a world superpower—and, in the wake of World War II, an ethic of global responsibility replaced isolationist sentiment in America. Within this new world order, U.S. politicians brandished promises to spread democracy and freedom throughout the world.

Airlines tapped this vision of America's role in the world and promoted air travel as a patriotic duty. Airline executives publicized commercial aviation as a tool that, if harnessed by the "right" nation (that is, America), would be a beacon of world peace and democracy. "Travel, like education, used to be considered a luxury. But in an era of low-cost, high-speed transportation, travel takes on an entirely new significance," Juan Trippe, the president of Pan Am, proclaimed in a speech. "For us, foreign travel is a cultural, political and economic necessity, if our country is to fulfill its destiny and new responsibility of world leadership." Airline marketing strategies positioned airlines as vehicles of American democracy overseas, which transferred patriotic sentiment to a consumer purchase. Air travel became a civic responsibility and an essential way to disseminate American ideas and products all over the world.[19]

By defining air travel as a patriotic duty, airlines transformed tourism into a kind of virtuous consumption, which was particularly important for selling tickets during the postwar years. Americans were still devoted to their Depression-era habits of scrimping and saving, so postwar government offices and ad agencies attempted to spur consumption by changing attitudes about spending. In the new ethos of mass consumption, the good American citizen became a consumer and thrift became patently un-American.[20] Airlines picked up on this broader trend and attempted to teach Americans to spend on tickets by marketing air travel as a way to be a good citizen.

Airlines created a postwar stewardess who reverberated with this larger advertising strategy by pitching her as an emissary of the American way. Designed to embody postwar visions of the "typical American girl," the new stewardess icon derived from a popular female archetype in advertising campaigns of the era—"the girl next door." Postwar modeling agencies selected and groomed their models to fit this ideal by selecting "college girls, daughters of professors, young debutantes," "society girls, graduates of a fashionable finishing school, popular debutantes," who showed "breeding, intelligence, and naturalness." The ideal girl next door, according to modeling agency manifestos of the era, also went to Smith or Vassar College, was listed on the Social Register, and was a member of the Junior League.[21] The "typical American girl" was also, perhaps most importantly, a wife to be.

Chapter 2

Sky Kitchens and Manly Cockpits

Gender roles from mainstream American culture were overlaid onto airline marketing. First, airline ads tapped an image of masculine strength by attaching their corporate images to the air force and by emphasizing their roles in America's military victory in World War II. Airlines dressed flight crews in military-style uniforms in order to link flying with an image of strength. Airlines projected this virile masculinity onto their pilots, but instead of casting pilots as icons of out-of-control masculine strength, they marketed them as strong, rational, and scientifically skilled men—a vision of masculinity that cultivated an aura of safety for fearful fliers. A stewardess career handbook of 1953 described pilots as "the controlling powers behind each safe, comfortable flight." Airline publicity and popular culture also contrasted the daring intrepid birdmen pilots of the 1930s, who "lacked scientific knowledge and skills," to "modern" pilots, who were versed in technology and "specially selected for their superior judgment."[22]

The postwar pilot was also a "solid citizen and family man" who was typically married with children. This "family man" was contrasted with rebellious forms of postwar masculinity embodied by James Dean, the Beat poets, and *Playboy* magazine's bachelor.[23]

This particular brand of pilot emerged during a "masculinity crisis" in American culture. In postwar America, an outpouring of literature written by journalists, public intellectuals, psychologists, sociologists, and novelists bemoaned the "feminization" of American men, and anxiety about faltering manhood ran high. Postwar writers blamed the perceived phenomenon on various factors, including conformity, suburban life, bureaucratic white-collar work, and domineering women. Philip Wylie's popular *Generation of Vipers* (1942) blamed the debasement of American men on pampered, overbearing modern American women, who controlled the nation. An article in *Reader's Digest* in 1949 titled "What's Wrong with American Men?" lamented that the American man had become "so soft in his white-collar job" that he was "losing masculinity." The female author demanded: "give us aggressive men whose real masculinity allows women to bask and glory in their true femininity." This masculinity crisis was personified by the popular icon—"the man in the gray flannel suit"—an effete white-collar bureaucrat and suburban breadwinner. As anxiety around manhood escalated, postwar writers proposed ways to revitalize masculinity. Rodeos and Westerns, which evoked traditional means of masculine self-definition (such as going to the frontier or to war), became trendy again.[24]

The soft American man was not just a trivial problem—he was also popularly perceived as a threat to national security. Cold War politics contributed to fears of declining manhood and projected contradictory ideals for American manhood—requiring "hard" masculinity in defining the nation's boundaries, yet insisting on "soft" masculinity as the basis for responsible home life.[25]

Airlines sold air travel by settling these larger cultural anxieties. They cast the pilot as the apogee of postwar middle-class masculinity, yet a reinvented version of manhood that resolved postwar concerns and appealed to male passengers' desires to rejuvenate manhood. The pilot icon embodied both middle-class suburban breadwinner and tough cowboy. He was the quintessential all-American, "family man" of the 1950s (white, middle class, corporate) who simultaneously reclaimed manliness through frontier language and imagery.

Airlines portrayed the airplane cabin as a reinvented kind of suburban home—sans the domineering women—where masculinity could be revitalized. One stark example of this was when United Airlines introduced flights exclusively for male passengers in 1953. On the "executive flights," men were invited to indulge in a host of "masculine" pleasures, including cigars, cocktails, poker, steak, and "party jokes." In 1955, *Playboy* magazine presented these flights as playboy-style bachelors' clubs aloft, designed to "restore the inner man" through an "atmosphere of masculine informality" and "male camaraderie." United's logic for these flights: tired male executives needed to "relax" in a "manly fashion." *Cosmopolitan* magazine applauded the flights for upholding traditional gender roles.[26]

Women played a special role in this manhood-restoring space. *Playboy* heralded the flights as an opportunity for men to loosen their ties without "female passengers to raise penciled eyebrows in disapproval." Women appeared only to light their cigars and serve "man-sized steak dinner[s]." The "only girls aboard are a couple of unobtrusive stewardesses who encourage him to relax and even provide him with a pair of comfortable knitted slippers."[27] Stewardesses represented the best of female servitude by allowing men to behave as men. This vision of female submissiveness was particularly comforting considering the broad cultural fear about domineering women who purportedly feminized American men. United's PR brought gender difference into plain view—marking planes as masculine technologies where men could "be men" without female interference. By painstakingly portraying stewardesses as submissive women and pilots as manly men, airlines restored the traditional gender order that was slipping into disarray in American culture.

Of course, not everyone lauded these male-only flights. Some female journalists called them "male supremacy crates," suggested "safety belts lined with nice sharp thumbtacks," and compared the male-only policy to racial segregation. In 1957 United's onboard magazine ran a story by a female *Los Angeles Times* reporter who had snuck onto a flight by masquerading as a stewardess. Disgusted that male passengers were served steak by "willing handmaidens lathered with United-approved smiles," she called the flights "the greatest invention for men since kiss-proof lipstick. But in this best of all possible male worlds, they're a giant step back for feminine rights. . . . All these attentions make men perfect passengers, but awfully poor husbands. The comparison with home life must be fearful." As a remedy, she called for an all-female flight with handsome male stewards, loose girdles, French champagne, Russian caviar, and roses. But United published the article in its magazine, which was designed for passengers, because it considered the feminist rebuke good publicity.[28]

The flights received even more national attention when the airline refused to sell a female executive a ticket. She protested and registered a complaint with the CAB. The story was reported nationwide.[29] But since most airline passengers were male, United's publicity department relished (and magnified) feminist outrage about the flights to highlight stewardess submissiveness as a selling point.

Dottie—This Is Delta, a promotional film produced by Delta in 1951, also reinforced traditional gender boundaries aloft. The film tells the story of Dottie, a chipper budding pilot who asks her flying instructor for a job so she can earn more flying time for her pilot's license. He suggests she get a job with the airlines. She reminds him that airlines do not hire "girl pilots."

He clarifies—he meant a stewardess position. Without even a flicker of disappointment, this pilot in training applies to become a stewardess. Cut to Dottie in stewardess school learning that "it's important to make a good landing with the tray, just as the pilot does with the plane." Dottie watches with awe as the mechanics inspect aircraft engines. She finds the cockpit "fascinating" but notes that it is far more complex than she thought—apparently too complex. When she flies a simulated flight as a pilot, she learns that her flying is "erratic." Clearly women were better suited as stewardesses.[30]

Gender stereotypes were also mapped onto the airplane's physical spaces. The cockpit was an arena of technology, science, power, and rational decision making. Called the "male" space and the "real office," the cockpit was designated as the pilots' domain. Meanwhile, the airplane kitchen and cabin area were the "home" or female domain. A career guide of 1953 proclaimed that passengers, "basking in the spacious ease of the luxurious cabin, relax as completely as they would at home." The guide also celebrated the well-appointed aircraft galley: "No wonder this is called the 'stewardess dream kitchen.'"[31]

This was an era when mainstream American consumer dreams revolved around the suburban home filled with modern appliances. The suburban home had become the bedrock of the postwar mass consumption economy—the home became an expensive commodity for more consumers than ever and it spawned demand for a panoply of household accessories. Home was now the epicenter of visions of the good life in America. Moreover, as Cold War anxieties swelled, the home came to be perceived as the cornerstone of safety from the Communist menace.[32] Airlines capitalized on these fantasies by likening airplane cabins to suburban homes. The illusion of the airborne living room was completed by furnishing passengers with a soothing wife/mother in the form of a stewardess. In this way, airlines reconfigured airplanes from frightening wartime weapons into safe, consumer-oriented spaces.

Careful not to emasculate male passengers by overdomesticating air travel, airlines recalibrated the airborne dream home as a space where submissive women doted on male passengers and encouraged men to "be men." While the suburban home threatened masculinity in postwar America, airlines resolved this cultural tension by presenting air travel as a remasculinization zone. Aloft: men could be *real* men and women could be *real* women.[33]

In 1945, TWA adopted the term "air hostess," marking the rise of a new vision of the stewardess. "Air hostesses," according to one vocational guide, treated passengers like "guests in their homes" and "call[ed] the skies their home." An American Airlines press release noted, "[The stewardess's] attitude is that people are her guests, and she wants to make them as comfortable as possible, so that they enjoy their visit aboard the Flagship cabin which is her home in the clouds."[34]

Airlines also exploited mainstream gender norms to train stewardesses in customer service. They taught new recruits to think of the job as a training ground for their future roles as wives and mothers. Popularly called "finishing school[s] of the air," stewardess training schools celebrated and cultivated supposedly inherent feminine qualities—such as anticipating men's needs and serving with a smile. Airlines coached stewardesses to

TWA ad, 1952. Author's collection.

treat male passengers as their own children or husbands. The American Airlines stewardess manual of 1954 instructed stewardesses to care for the vituperative or hostile passenger by "loving him anyway."[35] One vocational guide summed up this vision: "Welding of a woman's touch to the home-like atmosphere of a plane cabin was as natural as combining it in the American home . . . her cabin is her 'sky home' where she reigns as a gracious, serving, considerate, imaginative, sparkling hostess who puts her guests at absolute ease and comfort."[36]

Stewardess personality training taught "patience" and "tact" so that stewardesses could nurture—and manage—male passengers. According to one vocational guide, the stewardess represented a "civilizing" or disciplining voice, but she maintained "cabin discipline by the power of suggestion rather than by force or threats."[37] Instead of blatantly displaying female authority, stewardesses, like mothers and wives, were taught to use a refined performance of feminine tact to discipline unruly men.

In addition to cultivating an appealing consumer fantasy, airlines used domestic language to describe stewardesses in ways that cleverly masked the stewardess's workforce participation at a time when working women were hotly contested. This was an era when visions of the good life in postwar America hinged on a breadwinner husband and a dependent housewife. While government propaganda had encouraged women to join the workforce during World War II, following the war popular media urged Rosie-the-Riveters to abandon their wartime positions to become full-time homemakers because women's workforce participation threatened to emasculate men. An article in *Reader's Digest* in 1949 professed that the "American man's 'successfulness' is in direct proportion to the uselessness of his wife." That same year, another article in *Reader's Digest* proclaimed that American women were "less feminine" because they competed with men in business. Homemaking became the sine qua non of femininity; careers threatened to demolish femininity. According to the journalist Betty Freidan's feminist critique of postwar popular culture at the time, "You could sometimes get away with writing about a woman who was not really a housewife, if you made her sound like a housewife, if you left out her commitment to the world outside the home, or the private vision of mind or spirit that she pursued."[38] This characterization of gender messages in postwar cultural texts captured the tense relationship between women and wage work in postwar popular culture.

Working women, particularly those working in jobs popularly considered to be masculine, were subject to severe criticism in postwar American culture. For example, when the U.S. Army introduced female soldiers during World War II, these women were popularly accused of being too masculine and, consequently, suspected of lesbianism. In order to offset public fears about female masculinity, the Women's Army Corps (WAC) Bureau of Public Relations launched a publicity campaign that constructed female soldiers as feminine by portraying them as eager to become housewives after the war, casting their work as an extension of their domestic duties, positioning them as sexually respectable, and suggesting they were less powerful than male soldiers.[39] Airlines adopted similar strategies to make stewardesses appropriately feminine.

Mid-century debates about women and wage work were also imbued with larger global political significance in the Soviet-American propaganda war. The full-time homemaker and breadwinner husband were served up internationally as evidence of America's successful political and economic system. The American press routinely represented Soviet women as mannish because they performed masculine types of wage work and were not full-time homemakers. According to America's postwar zeitgeist, self-supporting women were unattractive and un-American.[40]

Considering the heightened anxiety over working women, it is not surprising that airline publicity campaigns emphasized stewardesses' femininity to forestall criticism and to circumvent broader debates about women's roles in the workforce. Airlines, for example, publicized stewardess work as appropriate for women by positioning it as a temporary job, rather than a career (which might have been popularly deemed "too masculine"). Airline managers hired only single women, portrayed the work as training stewardesses for their future role as wives, and required stewardesses to resign upon marriage. In 1954, American Airlines (and other major airlines) even implemented an age maximum of thirty-two for stewardesses, which forced them to resign instead of turning the position into a long-term career.[41] The airlines also emphasized feminine professionalism, which airline instructors called "proficiency but not at the expense of femininity."[42]

Best bill of fare in the air

Go ahead, feast your eyes . . . and wish you were on a TWA Skyliner! Food like this makes dining with TWA a different, delightful interlude and one of the high spots of your Constellation flight. It's fun being TWA's guest because there's no standing in line, no tipping and no check. You stay right in your comfortable seat, and a whole wonderful meal like this is brought to you with TWA's compliments, on all regular-fare flights at mealtime.

Where in the world do **you** want to go? For information and reservations, call TWA or see your travel agent.

Fly the finest . . . FLY TWA

TRANS WORLD AIRLINES
U.S.A. · EUROPE · AFRICA · ASIA

TWA ad, 1953. Author's collection.

Stewardesses also publicly portrayed their jobs as extensions of women's domestic roles. The Braniff stewardess Miss Webb, who won the "Miss Skyway" title in 1956 as the "ideal airline stewardess" in an airline-wide competition, traveled the nation speaking on "the value of stewardess training as a preparation for future wifehood." After all, flying was "one of the best ways to learn to be a good wife."[43]

In 1951, an article in the *Los Angeles Times* read: "Are you looking for a job that has . . . almost a 100% chance for a husband in two years?" According to an American Airlines press release, the stereotypical stewardess was in the market for marriage: "Some day she will meet what she believes to be the most interesting person and settle down." Airlines announced that they ran a virtual screening service for men seeking wives, professing that airlines selected stewardesses who made first-rate wives. Airlines even claimed that the divorce rate was lower among ex-stewardesses than any other former career women.[44]

Airlines also required stewardesses to be unmarried and publicly declared that they refused to hire married women because stewardess work "disrupted domesticity."[45] In fact, airlines considered being a good future wife such a critical qualification for stewardess work that they rejected divorced applicants. In an era when femininity hinged on marital success, divorce was considered tantamount to failing at womanhood. Northwest Airlines occasionally bent the rules to hire divorcees, based on an assessment of whether the applicant was at fault in the divorce. A Northwest interviewer noted that one stewardess applicant was divorced, but "she does not appear to carry any grudge for mankind in general/should be a good stewardess prospect on basis of personality, looks, poise."[46]

But while stewardesses were popularly imagined as perfect wives in training, they were also publicly lauded for their career achievements, "determination," and "drive." Magazines also played up the rigorous, professional, and scientific nature of stewardess training. One career guide of 1953 called the stewardess "the present-day career girl . . . the symbol of a new era—the picture of a determined and capable young woman."[47]

Airlines also expected stewardesses to be more than just pretty servants. Mildred Jackson summed up this ethos: "a mannequin is pretty to look at, but men and the airlines want a gal who says the right things when she opens her mouth." Airlines hired intelligent, educated women. An American Airlines press release of 1945 announced stewardess qualifications: "tact, courtesy and diplomacy, well-groomed, neat and attractive. Beauty is not necessary. She must be up on current events and have the ability to talk intelligently on a wide variety of subjects." American Airlines deemed the ability to converse intelligently "the essence" of stewardess work; the airline's stewardess training manual's rule #3: "Don't be uninformed." "A good conversationalist is inevitably a good listener and is seemingly charmed while listening to an expansive businessman tell of his rise to success," advised one stewardess vocational guide. American Airlines boasted: "[Stewardesses] all read the newest books and discuss them. They read *Life, the Sat Evening Post, Mademoiselle, Time, Colliers, Readers Digest*, because they must be well-informed and able to discuss almost anything with passengers."[48]

Airlines also preferred college-educated women. Considering the era's low number of female college students, this preference narrowed the applicant pool to an elite group of women. In 1946 approximately 4 percent of American women ages twenty to twenty-four were enrolled in college (compared to approximately 18 percent of men in the same age group). From 1945 to 1957, 50 percent of stewardesses hired by Pan Am had some college education (more than 20 percent were college graduates). Some postwar stewardesses had attended local two-year colleges; others had graduated from elite colleges such as Vassar and Smith. Pan Am, the largest U.S.-based international airline, also required fluency in at least one language other than English and many applicants were rejected on the basis of insufficient language skills. This requirement narrowed the stewardess pool to an even more select group.[49]

Stewardess training was also arduous—with strict rules, fifty subjects (including flight physics, emergency procedures, radio navigation, and meteorology), and a series of intense exams.[50] It was not uncommon for stewardesses to be expelled from training school for failing exams, for violating rules (such as staying out past curfew), or for lying on their applications.

The profession also created a space for these women to see themselves as more than just wives in training. The position offered them a unique opportunity to identify as ambitious, determined career women. Even getting the job was a badge of honor.[51]

Nineteen-year-old Linda Peddy, who had just finished two years of college in her hometown in Arkansas, traveled to Tulsa, Oklahoma to interview with TWA. Her father took her to the interview and waited in the hotel lobby. Dressed in her best, Peddy was wearing new navy pumps she had purchased for the occasion. Peddy, who had never before stayed in a hotel room, flew to Kansas City for a second interview, where the interviewer told her eyeglasses were prohibited. She was fitted for contact lenses and called TWA for another interview. Peddy did not hear back so she flew to Texas to interview with Braniff. The airline rejected her. Another aspiring stewardess in the waiting area gave her a hot tip: American Airlines was also interviewing at a hotel in town. Peddy took a cab over to apply. She was weighed and her height was measured—all standard stewardess interview procedures. American hired her. "It was such an honor to be hired for this profession," she said. Peddy went on to work as a stewardess for forty years.[52]

Twenty-year-old Detroit-native Diane Johnson, who finally scored a position as an American Airlines stewardess after being rejected by several airlines, wrote home nearly every day when she moved away from her family to the stewardess training school in Texas: "Did I tell you that they have 18,000 applicants for these colleges a year and only 800 are accepted? I'm in that 800 for 1960. They can afford to be choosy, can't they?" In another letter home during stewardess training, Johnson wrote: "Nothing is beyond the best of my ability. I'll never say I can't do something again." "Mom and Dad, you would have been so proud of me if you could have seen me serve my first flight! I was so proud and happy, my heart was singing!" she wrote.[53] Although airlines portrayed stewardesses as temporary workers in pursuit of eligible bachelors, in reality most stewardesses considered flying an opportunity for fulfillment outside of marriage.[54]

Stewardesses were smitten with the sky. "I was too young and too wild about flying. [Therefore] I was never sick and never afraid. I loved it," said a former Delta stewardess. To these women, flying was more than a pit stop on the way to marriage—it was a love affair. One former Pan Am stewardess, who had trained as a pilot in a small, piston-powered Cessna, recalled: "We were all adventurous. We were going to fly! And that was the big adventure!" As aviation lovers, stewardesses were knowledgeable about different airplane models and spent hours chatting about which planes they worked, which ones they adored, and which ones they missed. In 1953, a newly recruited Pan Am stewardess wrote in her journal: "There's simply no way to express how I felt. It was an unbelievable dream come true . . . what a feeling I had walking in that building, knowing I belonged there."[55]

In 1942, twenty-year-old Connie Bosza, who had just finished her second year of college, applied for a stewardess position. She managed to wrangle an interview at United, which had just dropped the nursing requirement, but it turned out she was four months too young and 1¾ inches too short. The supervisor kindly advised her to tease up her hair for the height measurement. Even though United required stewardesses to be at least twenty-one years old, managers made an exception and offered her a position four months before her twenty-first birthday. An opportunity to soar through the clouds for a living was too enticing to pass up—so she dropped out of college to fly.

When Bosza took the job, she was wildly in love with flying. She chose the profession because she found flying magical. Prior to the mass democratization of air travel, most Americans were unfamiliar with the sensation of flight and flying was still an enchanting experience. "Fascinated by the twinkling lights of little cities down below and heavenly bodies up above," Bosza wrote about her first flight. "I wanted to stay up in the cockpit for just a little while and take in all the wonders of the night from up there, where the visibility was so unlimited."[56]

But just a few years into her career, Connie Bosza, like most stewardesses, would be forced to resign from her treasured position. These young aviation lovers faced draconian airline policies that threatened to thwart their career ambitions. In spite of stewardesses' career zeal, in 1955 the average length of service was only twenty-seven months, and 99 percent resigned for marriage. Many of these women desperately wanted to continue flying after getting married, but airlines forced them to resign.[57] In addition to the marriage ban, airlines required stewardesses to resign once they reached the ripe old age of thirty-two or if they became pregnant. Plus, airline beauty policies "grounded" and fired stewardesses for appearance infractions such as gaining a few pounds, not wearing the right hairstyle, or not wearing a girdle. This was a bitter pill. The deep desire to keep flying would ultimately drive these women to circumvent, challenge, and protest anything that got in their way.

Chapter 2

Inventing All-American Sex Appeal

A "dark-haired, long-legged, All-American girl" was how *Holiday* magazine described the stewardess. Stewardesses, according to the magazine, were "good-looking in an unfrightening way: their clothes sit so sweetly on carefully tooled frames; they're 'outgoing' and bubble with a natural friendliness touched up ever so lightly with sex." Postwar airlines bragged to the press about their fleets of pretty stewardesses, but even though these fetching women were designed to attract businessmen, airlines did not project stewardesses as blatantly sexual. Instead, they created a distinctly wholesome stewardess who was sexually appealing without being sexually out of control.[58] This prudish, heterosexual virgin stewardess personified a veiled sexuality that suited the era's cultural taboos and exemplified heightened cultural tensions regarding sexuality in America in the 1950s. She resolved postwar cultural anxieties between the desire for sexuality and constraints around sexuality through an image of sex appeal combined with innocence.

This image of the stewardess derived from the popular archetype of the 1940s: the "pin-up" girl. An issue of *Life* magazine in 1941 coined the term "pin-up" to describe sexualized images of women intended for display in men's lockers, bunks, and fighter planes. During World War II, millions of photographic pin-ups were sent to American soldiers and the American public saluted these pretty women as morale-boosting patriots.[59] The pin-up first appeared in *Esquire* magazine in 1933 as a semi-nude cartoon "Petty Girl" (drawn by George Petty). In 1940, a new style of pin-up girl hit the pages of *Esquire*—the "Varga Girl" (illustrated by Alberto Vargas) appeared patently aggressive about her sexual desire compared to Petty's cherubic pin-ups. Vargas's provocative drawings captured the sexual audacity of female screen stars of the early 1930s, reflecting his background as a portraitist for the Ziegfeld Follies and then for Hollywood studios in the 1930s. Readers criticized the Varga Girl's "hardened and callous" look compared to the baby-faced Petty girl.[60] The Petty-Varga controversy illustrated a larger debate in American culture over what constituted a proper display of female sexuality. This tension escalated during World War II.

The most popular wartime pin-up was the movie star Betty Grable, who blended the innocent face with a leggy, sexualized body. By putting a fresh, angelic face on the half-naked female body, Grable tempered the pin-up's sexuality. She garnered popularity not because she exuded an exotic sex appeal (magazines noted that she "clean[ed] and pick[ed] up around the house" and lacked "sultry beauty or mysterious glamour"), but rather because she served as a model girlfriend, wife, and mother—exemplifying white, middle-class American womanhood. Her sex appeal sprouted from this wholesome image, which established her as a principal icon of moral obligation—the cherished "girl back home."[61]

During the postwar years, this wholesome version of the pin-up became more palatable as mainstream America became increasingly concerned about reigning in sexuality. By the end of the war, various authorities bemoaned America's sexual immorality; mainstream media warned of the dangers of extramarital sex; and campaigns against sexual psychopaths, prostitutes, homosexuals, and pornographers proliferated. In spite of the nation's sexual taboos, in 1948 a study of American sexual behavior (known as the Kinsey report) that sold more than three-quarters of a million copies revealed that the vast majority of American men violated mainstream culture's prudish mores by engaging in extramarital sex. Showcasing the cultural schizophrenia regarding sexuality, American women adopted neo-Victorian full-length skirts with skin-tight sweaters.[62] At a time when anxieties about sexual pandemonium ran wild, childlike sexuality became a dominant expression of acceptable sexuality.

Concerns about sex dovetailed with Cold War insecurities. While connections between American sexual behavior and national stability had been drawn in the past, anxieties about American sexual decay assumed a new urgency in the Cold War era. American authorities articulated concerns about the nation's future by linking them to American sexual behavior. In 1956, for example, a prominent Harvard sociologist deemed American sexual conduct the "greatest threat to American democracy since the rise of Fascism in Europe." Policing the boundaries of "normal" sexual behavior became a national imperative in the fight against Communism, and extramarital sex (or any sex deemed "deviant") came to be seen as politically dangerous. Experts and journalists described sexual perversion as a Communist plot to instigate political chaos in the United States and sexual deviants were removed from governmental positions during

TWA's pin-up stewardess, 1940.
© Blue Lantern Studios/CORBIS.

McCarthy's hunt for Communists. Linking sexual and political threats offered a language through which American social critics could identify and critique other changes sweeping the postwar nation. At its base, the public fear about American sexual behavior expressed deep concerns about the instability of sexual and gender categories and an undercurrent of dread about the nation's future.[63]

On top of America's sexual anxieties at home, the nation's sex-mad reputation overseas was a major concern for U.S. policymakers. Indications of American moral decay precipitated political humiliation, but more importantly, U.S. corporations and politicians feared that America's lustful image overseas would threaten the nation's key diplomatic and military (and commercial) relationships abroad. American sexuality not only jeopardized American-European relations, but it posed an even more severe risk to Cold War relations. As government agencies disseminated positive images of the United States abroad as part of the Cold War ideological battle, many "cultural diplomacy" efforts were designed to mediate images of the United States as a site of moral decay. A well-known American psychiatrist in the 1950s, for example, objected to the Kinsey report because it would "be politically and propagandistically used against the United States abroad, stigmatizing the nation as whole in a whisper campaign."[64]

The wholesome stewardess was born in the midst of this sweeping cultural fear regarding sex in America. Airlines piggybacked on the popularity of the pin-up girl by incorporating aspects of her style into the image of the stewardess. In the early 1940s, TWA even hired the famous pin-up illustrator George Petty to draw a TWA pin-up stewardess (large-breasted, blonde-haired, blue-eyes, and fully uniformed) that the airline used in counter displays, postcards, calendars, and baggage tags.[65] However, airlines tailored the image of the stewardess to suit shifting notions about respectable female sexuality in American culture. The stewardess was a domesticated descendant of the pin-up who softened the sexual threat of the pin-up. She epitomized a nonthreatening sex appeal that was palatable to postwar cultural mores.

The wholesome stewardess, however, also derived from another important advertising archetype of the 1940s, the girl next door. In the 1940s, the girl next door was considered the secret to effective advertising because she created a desirable world that was not too far removed from the real lives of consumers. Successful advertisements needed to establish a precise distance between the world in the advertisement and the consumer—the world in the advertisement was idealized and removed but not so far out of reach that consumers could no longer identify with it. This distance translated into glamour—the invisible force that elicited desire. Thus, advertisers chose models who looked "natural" and "all-American," rather than "too beautiful," so that ordinary consumers could imagine being with these women and buying these products. Ads of this era often painted a portrait of American, middle-class suburban life that was theoretically available to all Americans. The Park Avenue elite was not widely alluring at the time—instead, ads captured the broad cultural intrigue with middle-class suburban life based on an egalitarian philosophy.[66]

Even though air travel was still limited primarily to the wealthy, airlines emphasized air travel's accessibility, rather than its elite status. Airlines promoted a postwar stewardess who was the opposite of "glamour"—she was a girl next door, who was a "typical," middle-class, "all-American" wife-to-be, rather than a sex goddess or a "glamorous" upper-crust social- ite. Airlines mimicked postwar modeling agencies' visions of the girl next door in remarkable detail—from the way they trained stewardesses to apply "natural" cosmetics to the ways publicity materials described their family backgrounds.[67]

The wholesome, typical stewardess was considered a more effective sales figure because consumers could identify with her and imagine themselves consuming the products she advertised.[68] Reflecting this logic, airline publicity materials insisted stewardesses were ordinary. Even though, in reality, stewardesses were an elite group of white, college-educated women culled from thousands of applicants, airlines positioned them as "typi- cal" and distinguished them from overtly sexualized icons like *Playboy* magazine's first centerfold, Marilyn Monroe. A *Flying* magazine feature on stewardesses professed: "Glamour in the Hollywood sense is banned, and paramount instead are traits such as graciousness, presence of mind, good form and common sense."[69] The *Chicago Daily News* reported: "Their glamour is not theatrical. They are typical American girls—good-looking in a wholesome way."[70]

Airline publicity denied that stewardesses were "beautiful" or "glamorous"—claiming instead that personality was key. "Personality and wholesomeness play an intangible but highly important part in selection," reported an American Airlines press release. "Since American Airlines seeks typical, wholesome American girls as stewardesses, a girl needn't be a raving beauty to qualify for the position," another American Airlines press release announced. "Personality and diplomacy are far more important. . . . Most people have the mistaken idea that only glamour girls become airline stewardesses." By emphasizing personality and denying "glamour," airlines designated stewardesses "all-American" (read: sexually respectable) women.[71]

Kelly Flint, a former Powers model who parlayed her beauty expertise into a position as an American Airlines stewardess recruiter, reported, "We're not looking for a raving beauty, a glamour queen or anything like that." But at the same time, Flint expected aspiring stewardesses to be pretty: "too many women are overlooking basic beauty tips that would add greatly to their overall attractiveness." In fact, Flint rejected applicants with "warmth of personality and charm" who "hadn't given enough attention to the basic factors that can enhance any woman's beauty."[72]

From 1945 to 1957, airlines distanced the stewardess from the term "glamour," which had a complex history. The term had been used in the late nineteenth century to denote aristocratic and theatrical elegance, but by the 1920s Hollywood had begun using it as a euphemism for sex appeal.[73] During the 1930s, glamour was associated with Hollywood stars such as Marlene Dietrich and it suggested a bold display of female sexuality.[74] During the 1940s, glamour began to include burlesque stars and semi-nude women. By the 1950s, glamour referred to an upper-class, European, high-fashion look embodied by thin, often exotic models with high cheekbones who covered the pages of *Vogue*.[75] The term also became connected to the sexually dangerous femme fatale/vamp archetype in Hollywood films—often an exotic Eastern European or Asian woman who served as a foil to a wholesome American actress such as Debbie Reynolds or Doris Day.

Airlines eschewed old-style European glamour and wanton sexuality. Instead, they wanted the stewardess to convey the new *American*-style glamour—the wholesome, round-faced, girl next door. Sweet beauty was entirely American. While airline public relations material denied that stewardesses possessed "glamour," airlines were actually trying to cultivate the *right* sort of glamour that would reflect postwar American notions of the desirable life in order to sell seats. The way in which airline advertisements created this alluring image, however, reflected shifting mainstream visions of the nation itself as well as gender and sexuality.

This "typical American girl" stewardess was an object of male desire but also a respectable virgin who rebuffed sexual advances. Airline publicity materials explicitly dispelled the popular myth that stewardesses dated wealthy passengers and pilots. In an article titled "Stewardess Trainer Debunks Theory Flying Leads to Romance," Mildred Jackson told reporters that most stewardesses returned to their "hometown boyfriend" for marriage. Popular magazines emphasized a platonic camaraderie between stewardesses and pilots—the *Saturday Evening Post*, for example, characterized pilots' "avuncular attitude toward the girls." In 1950, *Flying* described one stewardess as "the kind of girl most men turn around to ogle," noting she had lived in a convent and knew how to evade unsolicited male attention. A Hollywood film of 1951 called *Three Guys Named Mike* revolved around an attractive, young stewardess who cleverly deflected three lecherous male passengers by surreptitiously setting them up for a nightcap with each other.[76]

Airlines enforced stewardess respectability through strict policies that controlled male-female interaction on layovers. Stewardesses and male crew were prohibited from entering each other's hotel rooms. Pan Am's pilots' manual of 1945 expressly forbade pilots from "undue familiarity" with stewardesses and instructed them to treat the stewardesses "courteously but impersonally."[77]

American Airlines president C. R. Smith and United Airlines president William Patterson were old-school chivalrous gentlemen who were protective of women and they insisted that airlines protect stewardesses from inappropriate male attention. In fact, when William Patterson's daughter worked as a stewardess during the 1950s, a male passenger appeared at her hotel room and banged on her door in efforts to seduce her. Luckily, she had learned how to handle unsolicited male come-ons during stewardess school. She kept her door locked, informed the hotel desk attendant, then called the captain in a nearby hotel room.[78] Airlines even removed male passengers from flights for making advances toward stewardesses.

Airlines also cultivated the pretty, yet virginal, stewardess image through strict physical appearance rules. "We had silk stockings with seams and we had to keep our seams straight. We had to wear girdles and high heel shoes and always be in full uniform including a hat," said a former stewardess, who started flying with United in 1944. "We had to wear white gloves when the passengers were boarding."[79]

Airlines also outfitted stewardesses in "natural" cosmetics, military-style uniforms with skirt hemlines below the knee, and "professional" hairstyles. Airline uniforms were predominantly light blue, navy, gray, and tan—mimicking military uniforms in both color and style. Flight crew uniform jackets (for pilots and stewardesses) also contained ranking stripes on sleeves—a tradition borrowed from the navy. Like women's military uniforms during World War II, stewardesses' skirts completely covered the knees and jackets were buttoned at all times.[80] Even in 1947, when Christian Dior introduced the "New Look," which accentuated women's waistlines using full skirts and heavy fabrics, the airlines maintained military-style stewardess uniforms that projected wholesome professionalism.

Hairstyle rules also ensured wholesomeness. Upon entering stewardess training, all trainees were shorn to the required hairstyle—half an inch above the jacket collar. Sultry tresses were banned. Natural hair color was also mandated. Hydrogen peroxide produced an artificial-looking bleached color popularly associated with burlesque dancers and showgirls.[81] At the time, dyed blonde hair was associated with celebrities—such as Mae West—who displayed audacious sexuality. "Natural" blondes, however, represented innocent, small town, white womanhood. Brunette hair was, by and large, the mainstream beauty ideal for women in the United States until the mid-1950s.

Prior to the American cultural acceptance of artificial blondes, bleached blonde hair—popularly considered a hallmark of promiscuity at the time— was verboten for stewardesses. In fact, supervisors inspected blonde applicants' roots during interviews to ensure their hair color was natural and rejected those who bleached. In 1955, an applicant for a stewardess position with TWA noted, "[The supervisor] took me to the window where she inspected my blonde hair to make sure I wasn't a peroxide blonde." American Airlines instructed stewardess supervisors: "Avoid dyed hair. It may be suggested to a well qualified applicant to return at a future date for further consideration when hair is a natural color."[82]

Stewardesses were also expected to wear "natural" make-up. "Rouge and lipstick should not be used to excess at any time. . . . Each stewardess shall strive for a natural look instead of a theatrical look," according to a stewardess handbook. At the time, cosmetics could make women look either "artificial" (read: promiscuous) or "natural" (read: sexually respectable). Airlines banned "artificial-looking" cosmetics associated with burlesque and Hollywood—hotbeds of sexual immorality.[83] Modeling agencies at the time also considered naturalness fundamental to the girl-next-door look.[84] "Natural" cosmetics also signified looking "American." In America, cosmetics had become central to expressing both feminine identity and national identity. Beautifying had transformed from a mere grooming habit into an assertion of the American way and cosmetics had become an important means by which to map national identity onto women's bodies.[85]

Airlines articulated a particular logic of beauty that projected American ideals onto stewardesses' bodies. Using the language of equal opportunity, stewardess schools, like popular charm schools of the era, treated grooming as a vehicle for self-improvement and career advancement. American Airlines employed "specially trained experts" who "turned many a plain girl into an attractive product."[86] According to this logic, the self was craftable and anyone could achieve a pretty, wholesome, all-American look. This approach reflected the prevailing American ethos regarding beauty, which constructed attractiveness as a democratic, egalitarian enterprise, available to all women with the help of the right cosmetics.

Casting beauty as a vehicle for individuality was particularly potent within the context of the consumer ethos in America in the 1950s. By mid-century, consumer products had become increasingly integral to personal identity and the logic that individuals could reinvent themselves through buying products was now firmly established.[87] Cosmetics and other feminine accoutrements had become essential tools for expressing gender identity, national identity, and individuality.

But while airline beauty rhetoric used a language of American ideology (that is, equal opportunity, freedom, and individuality), it in fact promoted a single, dominant vision of beauty. For example, airlines prohibited dyed hair, required a certain hair length, imposed strict weight limits, and allowed only selected make-up colors. In fact, stewardesses needed to conform to dominant (and unforgiving) beauty standards, but these beauty norms were masked as opportunities for individual expression, professionalism, equal opportunity, and upward mobility.

Airlines used stewardesses' bodies to display American identity, femininity, and sexual propriety. But while airlines carefully mapped wholesomeness onto stewardesses' bodies throughout the 1940s and the 1950s, one media event foreshadowed that this American icon would morph into a smutty sex symbol. In 1957, *Playboy* magazine showcased its first stewardess centerfold. The spread depicted Miss July, a 5′3″ "brown-eyed beauty" from Dayton, Ohio, nearly nude in white panties, interspersed with photographs of her performing airline duties in full uniform (for an unidentifiable airline). Three outraged airline stewardesses based in Los Angeles protested the centerfold in a letter published in *Playboy*'s subsequent issue, claiming that stewardesses were "trained to dress modestly" and that Miss July made them look like "nothing but a bunch of sex machines."[88]

In spite of *Playboy*'s venture into stewardess indecency, airlines continued to court a prim and proper image of the stewardess. As airlines invented the look of the "typical American girl" stewardess, they negotiated a richly symbolic minefield. Their vision of beauty narrowed the "typical American girl" into a representation of womanhood imbued with broader cultural ideas about race, class, sexuality, and national identity. The stewardess articulates what constituted a "proper" or "typical" representative of American womanhood during the conservative 1950s and this "proper" American woman was distinctly marked as white. In the next chapter, we explore how this American icon was racially coded, and how aspiring stewardesses who did not fit the "typical American girl" mold renegotiated dominant definitions of American womanhood.

3

Breaking the Race Barrier

IN THE summer of 1956, when Patricia Banks was a nineteen-year-old psychology major at Queens College, she had her heart set on becoming a stewardess. Like the vast majority of Americans during this era, she had never flown, but Banks had always been captivated by airplanes. As a child, she dreamed of soaring through the clouds in a sleek plane and she fantasized about becoming a pilot. She also had a passion for learning about different cultures and she wanted to travel. Banks was a go-getter, determined to make her dreams come true. At the time, she was working full time as a machine operator at Con Edison to pay for college. When she saw an ad for a three-month stewardess training program at the Grace Downs Air Career School in *Glamour* magazine, she took the train to the school and filled out an application. The school administered an aptitude test. Banks scored in the ninetieth percentile and she was accepted. Ecstatic about the prospect of scoring a prestigious stewardess position, she enrolled immediately. She managed to put herself through the pricey $225 stewardess school on an installment plan with her wages from Con Edison (approximately $24 per week). She stayed up late many nights studying for her evening college courses and stewardess school exams.

Banks was a remarkably well-qualified stewardess applicant and she knew it. When she graduated from stewardess school with a 95 percent average, she beamed with confidence. She was knowledgeable about airplane models, emergency procedures, meteorology, time zones, geography, charm, and other stewardess essentials. Beyond acing stewardess school, she was college educated and she spoke French and Spanish, scored high on intelligence tests, and played the violin. Plus, she was attractive. She was 5'6" tall, 120 pounds, and her figure measured 33-26-36 (nearly perfect according to airline standards). Wide-eyed and enthused, she believed she was on the path to getting her dream job. She was the perfect candidate. There was just one problem—she was African American. In 1956, when Banks applied, no U.S. airline had ever hired a black stewardess.

Even though airlines did not have explicit written policies against hiring African American stewardesses and airlines publicly touted their diverse stewardess corps (each purportedly had a "unique" look), they barred black applicants in subtle ways—particularly, through beauty requirements. Airlines created rigid physical appearance regulations for new recruits and required aspiring stewardesses to include photographs with their applications. Supervisors meticulously scrutinized applicants during interviews—often measuring their waists, hips, wrists, and ankles. Even the Fair Employment Practices Commission (FEPC), an organization created by President

Patricia Banks in her Capital Airlines uniform. Courtesy Patricia
Banks, author's collection.

Franklin Roosevelt that was charged with ferreting out discriminatory workplace practices, ruled that physical appearance was a legitimate occupational qualification for the stewardess position. Airlines' strict appearance requirements, however, were subtly embedded with a white aesthetic. For example, a 1954 American Airlines supervisor manual expressly disqualified applicants with "broad noses" and "coarse hair."[1]

Airline management also instructed supervisors to hire women who looked like the "all-American girl." But broader mid-century cultural norms constructed a vision of typical American womanhood that was implicitly white. Supervisors, consciously or unconsciously, hired white women to match dominant cultural images of the ideal American woman. In this way, airline beauty requirements mapped mainstream ideas about national identity onto women's bodies.

Emblematic of how racial discrimination operated in American corporations during the 1950s, the process through which African American women were excluded from this iconic position was hidden and amorphous. Even when civil rights advocates and young African Americans entering the white-collar workforce suspected corporations of discriminating based on race, discrimination was difficult to root out and even harder to prove in a courtroom. So, aspiring black stewardesses were up against a tough, yet common, problem in 1950s corporate America and these women would have to find shrewd strategies to expose and to bring down these entrenched discriminatory practices.

African American women applied (and fought) for stewardess positions just as the civil rights movement was reaching a fever pitch in America. In the process, these stewardess hopefuls challenged mainstream assumptions about who constituted the "typical American girl" as they struggled to win this coveted white-collar position that had previously been reserved for white women. The first black stewardesses projected themselves as America's beloved female archetype—the girl next door. The story of stewardess integration tells a broader story about race in America—particularly, it exposes the wily manner in which discrimination operated in American corporations during the 1950s as well as how dominant definitions of the "typical American girl" were renegotiated in twentieth-century America and how global politics contributed to reinventing the ideal American woman as a racially diverse representative of the American way.

Segregated Skies

Patricia Banks, however, was not aware that race mattered in airline hiring practices. She considered herself an attractive, well-qualified applicant and she was sure she would be hired. On August 1, 1956 airline representatives visited the Grace Downs School to interview students. Banks interviewed with Capital Airlines. During the interview, Joy Geddes, a veteran chief stewardess who was responsible for hiring and training stewardesses at Capital Airlines, asked Banks to walk around the room. Banks paraded around the room while Geddes observed her. It was standard for steward-ess applicants to walk around the room while supervisors surveyed their physiques. Geddes told Banks that she liked her "figure" and her "speech." Banks took this as a good sign and she eagerly awaited the news.

A few days after the interview, Banks heard classmates bragging about being accepted for positions at Capital Airlines. Banks still had not heard, so she asked Miss Williams, the director of the Grace Downs School, if she had any news. Williams was evasive—she encouraged Banks to get a ground job. Meanwhile, Banks interviewed with TWA and Mohawk, a regional commuter airline. Weeks went by. Banks still had not heard from any of the airlines. Considering that stewardess positions were extremely selective during the 1950s, Banks began to wonder if she lacked the elusive *je ne sais quoi* that one needed to become a stewardess.

Banks may have been an optimistic young person, but she was not a complete naïf. She was well aware of the intense controversies about race that were sweeping the nation in the mid-1950s. She was a senior in high school in 1954 when the Supreme Court ruled against racial segregation in schools in the landmark *Brown v. Board of Education*. In 1955, when Banks started college, the civil rights movement was in full swing. As a college freshman, she even went down to the mosque on 116th Street and managed to get an in-person interview with Elijah Muhammad, the leader of the Nation of Islam. Even though her friends in college warned against this inflammatory topic, Banks wrote a paper on the organization's philosophies and her attitude about it. (She received an A.) Her brush with the Nation of Islam stirred her sense of injustice and anger at racism, which would later fuel her fight against it.

Banks was also well informed about racial oppression in the South. She read about the school integration riots, boycotts, sit-ins, and marches. Every time there was a murder or a lynching, she was deeply affected. "As a young person, I would hear stories about the South—about Negroes not being allowed to go into bathrooms, about lynching, and about the Ku Klux Klan," she recalled. But that was the South. New York was a different story. Or so she believed.[2]

In New York City and other urban centers, major changes were afoot for African Americans during the 1950s. From 1940 to 1950, with the "Great Migration" to the North, the number of African American urban inhabitants rose by 46 percent. In the 1950s, black consumer spending power grew substantially and black women increasingly entered white-collar positions in the workforce. At the same time, civil rights advocates launched major initiatives for racial integration in various arenas, including employment. Patricia Banks had grown up in Harlem's prestigious Riverton development, home to prominent African American lawyers, politicians, and civil servants. Banks was part of this emerging African American middle class that burgeoned in the 1950s. She would come to play an important role in carving out an image for this new group of middle-class black women in the white-collar workforce.

An ambitious young woman, Banks wondered why she had not been hired, so she approached the school director again. This time, Williams recommended that Banks have her tooth repaired. Banks had a chipped upper molar in the back of her mouth, visible only when she smiled broadly. Determined to eliminate any obstacle that might thwart her ambition to fly, she had her molar repaired. She then returned to the school and asked school officials to arrange another interview with Capital Airlines. They told her that was not possible. Five months had gone by since Banks first applied for a position and she still had not been hired. She was growing despondent. She was confused about what made her an inadequate candidate until she had a conversation with Miss Byrnes that would set her life in a new direction.

Miss Byrnes, a former Capital Airlines stewardess and an instructor at the Grace Downs School, pulled Banks aside in the lobby of the school. Byrnes had seen Banks floundering to get a hostess position and took pity on her. She told Banks that the airlines had a policy against hiring African Americans in flight positions.

Banks was shocked. The teachers at the stewardess school had been friendly and she had not detected any racism. "I had read and heard such horror stories about what happened to human beings in the South. But to have this happen to me, *up North*, that was the shocker. In New York City!" recalled Banks.[3]

In the mid-1950s, when Banks applied for a position, flying was still limited to the upper echelons of American society. Airline passengers were still predominantly wealthy, white businessmen. The vast majority of Americans had never flown and most were not aware of discriminatory practices aloft. Few African Americans traveled by air and those who attempted to buy airline tickets were sometimes refused. Black travelers who did fly systematically encountered different treatment from white passengers. American Airlines even trained ticketing agents to mark tickets sold to African American passengers with a code, E-111. Airlines required black passengers to sit in separate rows on the plane and white stewardesses often treated them rudely.[4]

White stewardesses were also often reluctant to serve black passengers. A white United Airlines stewardess, Connie Bosza, expressed her sentiment toward African American war veterans on her flight in an unpublished memoir written in the 1950s. Bosza reported that when she passed out magazines, coffee, and sweet rolls on the flight from Seattle to Portland, the black passengers did not thank her. This angered Bosza. She wrote: "I don't think any other stewardess would have started out talking to them in the friendly manner I did. . . . Well, my suntanned load deplaned at Oakland and I wish you could have seen the face on the passenger agent that opened the cabin door and watched them climb out. . . . There were only six of them but they were surly, heaven sent. . . . I wanted to air out the cabin. . . . There are just as many dirty and impolite whites running around but I haven't had them concentrated as a lot in an airplane."[5]

White stewardesses' racist attitudes contributed to airline executives' motivation to exclude black stewardesses. Northwest officials admitted that they were "uncertain about the acceptance of a negro stewardess as a roommate by white stewardesses when the girls are required to share hotel rooms at turn-around points." More importantly, airline managers feared that the stewardess position would lose its glamour to white stewardesses if they hired black women.

In-flight discrimination was covered in the African American press, but it rarely received coverage in mainstream media outlets. A few celebrity cases of discrimination in air travel, however, received national attention. In 1954, the famous jazz singer Ella Fitzgerald sued Pan Am for discriminatory treatment that stranded her in Hawaii for three days. She won seven thousand dollars in damages. The actress Mariana Cortina also sued (and won) a discrimination lawsuit against Delta Airlines when white stewardesses treated her rudely.[6]

Beyond discriminating against black passengers, U.S. airlines did not hire any African American women in stewardess positions throughout the first three decades of stewardess service. Wilfred Leland, the executive director of the FEPC, noted, "While Northwest Airlines employs Oriental stewardesses on their Pacific flights, no negro or other non-white workers have ever been employed as stewardesses or in other flight positions within the continental United States."[7]

Airlines in the United States found certain nonwhite stewardesses useful for cultivating the right image aloft. During the 1950s, after American soldiers returned from World War II and Korea with war brides, images of Asian women as subservient wives and "geisha girls" became common in Hollywood films and American culture. American airlines with routes to Asia exploited American stereotypes of submissive, obedient Asian women to sell an image of stellar customer service. These airlines used Asian American stewardesses on flights to Asia as a way to highlight exotic spectacle and to bolster company prestige. Airlines ostensibly hired Asian American stewardesses on flights to Asia for their language skills, but in fact most of these women only spoke English and had to receive airline language training for the flights.[8] But while Asian American women served airlines' marketing agendas, African American women did not.

Airline executives did not openly admit to racist hiring practices, but they did confess that they feared hiring black stewardesses for business-related reasons. In addition to fearing that their primarily white in-flight labor force would resign or demand higher wages if the glamour of the position were marred, airline executives worried that black stewardesses would affect ticket sales. Airlines catered predominantly to wealthy white passengers during the 1950s, and airline executives worried that integrating the stewardess corps—amid the intense national controversy over racial desegregation—would incite controversy.

Donald Nyrop, the president of Northwest Airlines, confessed his position to investigators of the FEPC: "the time is not yet ripe to integrate Negroes into stewardess positions." Northwest Airlines officials told the FEPC that they were "fearful that racially prejudiced passengers, particularly those from the South, might react unfavorably to the presence of a Negro in the position of stewardess."[9]

More importantly, airlines were deeply invested in hiring stewardesses who projected the right corporate image because these women served on the front line of advertising. Airline executives hired white women because they wanted to cultivate an image of air travel that relied on broader cultural assumptions about race. Airlines used white stewardesses to convey an image of airplanes as a "modern" (and safe) technology, distinguishing air travel from rail travel, where African American cabin attendants had been the norm.[10] Airlines also used white women to tap the image of the "happy homemaker" from the 1950s, which translated into a vision of doting, stellar customer service aloft. Hiring African American stewardesses threatened to tarnish airlines' image of airborne luxury—which hinged on the ideal American woman catering to every whim. But airline discriminatory practices (and the logic behind them) were not widely known.

When Patricia Banks found out, she was livid. She was blindsided by the news. "All of my anger about how Negroes were treated in the South came to a head because it was happening to me in New York. I knew right away that I wasn't going to allow this to happen. I was going to fight it to the end. I wasn't going to allow this to exist," Banks said. "Nobody was aware of it. I knew the only way to overcome it was to bring it to the attention of the public. People had to know."[11]

She was infuriated but unsure of how to proceed. She called the nation's largest civil rights organizations—the National Association for the Advancement of Colored People (NAACP) and the Urban League—but neither organization offered her much assistance. She called an influential friend, who encouraged her to talk to civil rights advocate Congressman Adam Clayton

Powell. She met with Powell, who suggested she submit a complaint to the New York State Commission against Discrimination (SCAD), responsible for enforcing antidiscrimination law. Lawyers at the SCAD took her case.

But the case had its complications. First, the statute of limitations had run out on TWA and Mohawk airlines. So, Capital Airlines was their only hope. But Capital claimed that the state of New York had no jurisdiction because the airline was headquartered in Virginia. There were other considerations. Capital was a southern airline, so if Banks did win the case, which could take years, she would have to fly into the segregated South. Did she still want to pursue the case? Did she want to fly southern routes? Her lawyers asked. Banks assured them that she wanted to fight the case to the end—however long it took. On February 1, 1957, Banks filed a complaint against Capital with the SCAD.

Since racism operated in slippery, masked ways, the task of proving discrimination in the courtroom was exceedingly difficult. In spite of the conspicuous absence of African American women from stewardess positions, airline managers claimed to be personally unbiased in their stewardess hiring practices.[12] If explicit orders barring black applicants were ever issued, airline executives were careful not to leave a paper trail documenting such orders, making it difficult, even now, to say how racism operated systematically in U.S. corporations during the 1950s.

Patricia Banks's lawyers understood what they were up against, so they began an in-depth investigation of Capital Airlines. They interrogated supervisors, poured through hundreds of stewardess applications, and reviewed handwritten interview notes. They would have to dig deep.

Busting the Airlines

Patricia Banks was not the only young, black woman applying for a stewardess position at the time. Nor was she the only one who figured out that race mattered in airline hiring. Even though airline racial policies were well masked, many young black women suspected discrimination, and some decided to fight back. While Banks and her lawyers were assembling a case against Capital Airlines, a wave of black aspiring stewardesses around the country also filed discrimination complaints against airlines.

In fact, the NAACP was deeply embroiled in a secret project to uncover discrimination in the airlines. Upon the victory in *Brown v. Board of Education* (1954), one of the NAACP's many challenges to institutionalized segregation, the organization set out to integrate various employment arenas. Well aware of the symbolic importance of stewardesses in 1950s America, NAACP organizers aimed to integrate stewardess positions right after the Brown ruling. The organization's youth and college division had launched a covert airline integration project designed to bust airlines for discriminating against black stewardess applicants.

In April 1954, the organization recruited a group of highly qualified African American and white women to apply for stewardess positions at airlines headquartered in New York. The NAACP chose New York to garner the added protection of the Ives-Quinn Act, the first state legislation (passed in 1945) outlawing discrimination in employment on the basis of race, creed, or color. But the division had difficulty finding African American women who met the exacting requirements for stewardess positions. NAACP officials wrote to African American modeling agencies in New York City to recruit women for this project, and they discussed recruiting from historically black colleges. The National Youth and College Division sent letters to its regional and field staff officers seeking qualified African American women for the project and printed a recruitment flier. The division studied airline stewardess requirements and enlisted African American women who met those requirements: a minimum of two years of college, between 5′1″ and 5′7″ tall, weighing from 100 to 135 pounds, perfect vision, and between the ages of twenty-one and twenty-six. NAACP memos show that the organization carefully sought women who were "very attractive and possess[ed] poise and a pleasing personality."[13] By October 1954, the NAACP had enrolled fifty women in the confidential stewardess integration project. This project was underway while Patricia Banks was building her case, but none of these stewardess discrimination cases had yet received hearings.

At the same time, the Urban League of New York, another civil rights organization, initiated a series of conferences with major airlines to end discrimination in hiring practices for stewardesses. In 1956, after three years of negotiations, eighteen U.S. carriers finally handed the Urban League a paper victory by publicly announcing a nondiscrimination policy with regard to stewardess employment. However, in the wake of the new "policy" not a single black stewardess was actually hired by any U.S. airline.

Meanwhile, in March 1957, just a month after Patricia Banks filed her case against Capital Airlines, twenty-four-year-old Marlene White applied to Northwest Airlines. The airline was headquartered in Minnesota, but it recruited stewardesses in Marlene White's home state of Michigan. White met the airline's basic stewardess requirements: she was 5'4" tall, 112 pounds, and unmarried. She had completed two years of college at the University of Detroit, and she spoke Spanish and French in addition to her native English. The daughter of a Detroit magazine publisher, White was also an ambitious young woman and part of the growing African American middle class. She had been the society reporter for a newspaper. Soon after applying for a stewardess position, she would go on to become a cover girl for *Jet* magazine and to receive a master's degree in business administration from the University of Chicago. Like Banks, White was a seemingly ideal candidate—except she was African American.

When White called the Northwest Airlines interviewer after her interview, an airline official told her that the airline did not hire African Americans in flight positions. White filed complaints with the Michigan and Minnesota offices of the Fair Employment Practices Commission (FEPC). The FEPC negotiated a second interview for her on August 7, 1958. She was interviewed by the Northwest supervisor Miss Kearns and given a battery of IQ and personality tests. She was then rejected purportedly on the basis of low test scores. White filed a second complaint with the Minnesota FEPC. The FEPC pressured the airline into granting her a third interview.

Finally, her airline career began to look promising. Northwest offered her a position as a telephone reservations agent. Airline managers had told her that the job could lead to a stewardess position. She accepted. Then, Northwest officials argued that they had resolved White's discrimination complaint by hiring her as a phone reservations agent.

But White was determined to fly. "I want to fly. I want to travel. I want to meet people. This is something many young women want to do. It means a lot to see the world," she told reporters. The FEPC began an investigation. Examining 720 Northwest stewardess application files created between March and August 1958, the commission searched for evidence that the airline had discriminated against Marlene White based on race. It evaluated the hiring criteria to determine whether White was superior to the 625 rejected applicants. White's lawyers continued to build her case.

In spite of the rash of stewardess discrimination cases popping up around the country, U.S. airlines still did not hire a single black stewardess. But the pressure was mounting. The exclusion of African American women from stewardess positions in America became an international media affair. Soviet publications such as *Civil Aviation* and *Pravda* (the leading newspaper in the Soviet Union and an official instrument of the Communist Party) heavily criticized U.S. airlines for barring African American women from stewardess positions. Russia's *Civil Aviation* magazine claimed that America's race problem at airlines was more proof of deceptive American propaganda. The NAACP cleverly picked up on international criticisms of America's racial tensions to bolster the civil rights struggle. In 1958, the NAACP's official magazine, *The Crisis*, reported, "Last year the State Department . . . was obliged to acknowledge that *Pravda* told the truth when it declared that bigotry barred Negro girls from one of the most coveted careers open to women in this country."[14]

The persistence of legalized racial segregation in America was more than a mere embarrassment—it also posed a vexing political problem for the United States during the Cold War. The story of race in America became an important way to compare democracy and Communism in the global contest for political power. In the global propaganda war with the Soviets, Soviet propaganda used America's "race problem" to condemn capitalism and democracy. While U.S. politicians globally projected an image of America as the land of pluralism and equal opportunity, racial segregation in the United States seriously undermined the nation's image overseas and its claims to global leadership. The nation's racial conflict assumed important foreign policy value as the United States pursued global hegemony. As the Cold War intensified during the 1950s, U.S. and Soviet policymakers exerted substantial propaganda efforts to win the political allegiance of the growing number of newly independent Third World nations. Africa, in particular, was strategically crucial to the United States.

In attempts to divert this mounting bad press overseas, the Truman administration adopted a pro–civil rights posture as a component of its international strategy to promote democracy and contain Communism around the world. In fact, the United States was so invested in its global image regarding race that the State Department promoted African American artists around the world to advertise "racial progress" and financed international publicity campaigns to manipulate global ideas about U.S. race relations. The State Department sponsored African Americans to travel overseas to speak on the "Negro Problem" in the United States.[15]

But in spite of bad press domestically and overseas, airlines would not budge. Civil rights advocates and African American stewardess hopefuls were gearing up for a legal showdown. Some had spent several years assembling evidence against the airlines. By 1959, the SCAD was slated to hear seventeen cases against airlines charged with discriminating against black stewardess applicants.

Airlines, however, had crafty ways of thwarting discrimination suits before they even received hearings. For example, the SCAD had charged TWA with discriminating against Dorothy Franklin, an African American stewardess applicant. Franklin's hearing had been scheduled for May 12, 1958. Days before the hearing, TWA hired the airline's first African American stewardess, Margaret Grant, a psychology major at Hunter College. By hiring Grant, TWA management effectively stymied Franklin's lawsuit. Franklin's case was dismissed. But Grant had to pass a TWA physical examination before the airline allowed her to fly. The TWA physician determined that she had a "rare noninfectious disease that would be aggravated by flight duty." Grant resigned before she ever had the chance to work as a stewardess. Upon learning about Grant's resignation, African American media outlets (such as *Jet* magazine) again lambasted TWA for discrimination. The airline claimed that its efforts to hire black hostesses were sincere.[16] And, yet, TWA did not have a single African American woman in its stewardess corps.

Beyond these short-term publicity stunts, no airline actually employed black stewardesses. In December 1958, SCAD finally managed to persuade a regional commuter airline, Mohawk Airlines, to hire Carol Ruth Taylor, who became the first black stewardess for a regional airline. She resigned after a few months. Taylor's short-lived post, however, did not break open the floodgates for stewardess integration. It took more than a year and a half for another black stewardess to get hired with a U.S. airline. TWA had managed to derail several stewardess discrimination suits, but in July 1959 the Urban League and SCAD successfully pressured the airline into hiring Mary Tiller. It is unclear whether Tiller actually worked for the airline or if her employment was merely a publicity stunt designed to stem antidiscrimination demands on TWA. In spite of Taylor's short stint as a stewardess and Tiller's employment, the many black women with pending discrimination cases still needed courtroom victories to get hired in this coveted position.[17]

Reinventing American Womanhood in the Courtroom

Meanwhile, Patricia Banks wondered if her case would ever be heard. It had been nearly three years since she first applied for a stewardess position and the investigation continued to drag on. Finally, she got her big chance. On July 14, 1959, her SCAD hearing began.

Making it into the courtroom was not enough. She had to win—and, winning a discrimination case was nearly impossible because corporate discrimination was well hidden and tricky to expose. When the Banks hearing took place, Capital Airlines employed nearly six hundred stewardesses—none of them African American.[18] Since the annual flight hostess turnover was about 40 percent, Capital had hired several thousand stewardesses from 1945 to 1959. Not one of them had ever been African American. But this fact alone was not enough to prove discrimination and there was no "smoking gun" to prove her case. Banks's lead lawyer, Henry Spitz, could not find a single corporate memo definitively articulating a policy that barred supervisors from hiring black stewardesses. Would he be able to cajole a confession out of a Capital employee?

On the first day of the hearing, the immaculately coiffed twenty-two-year-old Patricia Banks took the stand. She testified that Miss Byrnes, an instructor at the Grace Downs School, had informed her that the "policy of Capital and other airlines was not to hire Negroes in flight."[19] Miss Byrnes, however, had reportedly left the school due to illness and, mysteriously, could not be located for the hearing. When Chief Stewardess Joy Geddes, who had interviewed Banks, was on the stand, she denied knowing of such a policy. So, it was Banks's word against airline officials. How, then, without a single piece of definitive evidence, could Banks and her lawyer build a compelling case against the airline?

As general counsel for the SCAD, the attorney Henry Spitz was familiar with the subtle ways in which employment discrimination operated. During the hearing, Spitz argued that it was "far more likely" that airline management pursued "discriminatory practices in ways that are devious, by methods subtle and elusive—for we deal with an area in which subtleties of conduct play no small part."[20]

Spitz set out to establish a general pattern of discrimination at the airline. He demonstrated that Patricia Banks met all of the airline's stated requirements. First, she was single, twenty-two years old, 5'6" tall, and weighed 120 pounds. But stewardess eligibility criteria were not that simple. Airlines hired women who embodied a particular vision of middle-class American womanhood, and stewardess applicants were meticulously scrutinized in terms of physical appearance, intelligence, education, and charm.

Drawing on mainstream assumptions about womanhood in the 1950s, Spitz aimed to show that Banks conformed to this ideal in terms of education, musical hobbies, and body measurements. Spitz argued that she was a "fine, attractive, intelligent, talented young lady . . . she is talented in music, talented in arts—an above-average girl." When Banks was on the stand, Spitz asked about her college education, foreign language skills, musical skills, artistic talents, athletic ability, and work experience.

Spitz: Do you have any special musical talent?
Banks: Yes, I play the violin.
Spitz: For how long have you played the violin?
Banks: I have taken lessons for ten years.
Spitz: Do you have any hobbies?
Banks: Yes, I do. I sew, I do a little designing. I do a little art work and I play basketball.
Spitz: What type of art work do you do?
Banks: Sketching. I have used oils on occasion.

By representing Banks as a respectable, middle-class American woman, Spitz challenged broader stereotypes about African American women. In

1950s America, mainstream culture highlighted black women's supposed sexual promiscuity, low-class status, and unfeminine behavior.[21] How, then, could a young African American woman be hired to represent the "typical all-American girl"?

Airlines used seemingly race-neutral terms in instructing supervisors to hire women who looked "wholesome," a prized virtue in the America of the 1950s. The virginal look, however, was implicitly white, since African American women were stereotyped as sexually promiscuous in mainstream American culture. Airline supervisors, at times unconsciously, drew on these larger stereotypes about African American sexuality as they assessed black applicants' physical appearances. For example, Northwest Airlines supervisors rejected one black stewardess applicant because "her bust measurements appeared to be abnormally large." (Investigators for the FEPC later determined her bust size to be "normal.")[22]

When Northwest Airlines supervisors assessed Marlene White as a stewardess candidate, they also evaluated her based on stereotypes about black women—particularly, the ways in which she purportedly violated feminine norms. They rejected White because she was "ill-groomed," had "an arrogant attitude," and lacked the "personality" for stewardess work. But in fact, the question of whether White would make a good stewardess hinged on whether she—as a black woman—could claim respectable femininity. Airline officials were conflicted. Supervisors were expected to judge applicants' "femininity" during interviews and Northwest's chief stewardess had checked off "feminine" during White's interview. However, airline officials later described White as "aggressive," "argumentative," and "masculine." Ironically, Northwest's vice president of personnel used White's discrimination complaint as "evidence of an antagonistic attitude," claiming, "such an attitude would constitute a lack of competence to deal with passengers on the airline." White took a personality test for Northwest, which concluded that she was "too masculine." The test measured thirteen personality traits (including "masculinity") on a scale of one to thirteen. "Feminine" women rated below a five. White scored an eight.[23]

Beauty, an aspect of femininity, was also a critical qualification for stewardess work. During Patricia Banks's hearing, her lawyer, Henry Spitz, set out to prove that she was pretty.

Spitz: What is your height and weight?
Banks: I am 5 feet, 6 inches, 120 pounds.
Spitz: What are your overall dimensions?
Banks: 33-22-36.
Spitz: For the record, does that mean bust 33, waist 22, hips 36?
Banks: Yes, sir.
Spitz: What about your calves and ankles?
Banks: My calves are 13½ inches. My ankles are 8 inches.[24]

Banks's measurements constituted a nearly perfect figure, according to an American Airlines supervisor manual, which described a "perfect figure" as "a bust and hip measurement of the same dimension and waist 10 inches less."[25]

Spitz then called Capital's chief stewardess, Joy Geddes, to the stand. (Geddes had interviewed Banks.) In order to establish that airlines considered physical appearance highly important, he interrogated Geddes about the qualifications she assessed in prospective stewardesses—including hair, grooming, weight, and figure. Geddes testified that she did, indeed, consider all of these attributes when hiring stewardesses. Spitz concluded: "General appearance is terribly important."

The next part was a bit stickier. Spitz sought to show that Banks was a pretty woman, which meant challenging dominant beauty norms. African American women were not considered beautiful according to dominant American culture during the 1950s. During this era, the mainstream American press often depicted African Americans with exaggerated physical features—particularly, "kinky hair," broad noses, and large lips. African American women were also still confined to segregated beauty pageants, modeling agencies, and women's magazines. It would be almost twenty years after Patricia Banks applied for a stewardess position that the first black model would appear on the cover of *Vogue* and nearly thirty years later that the first black woman would be crowned Miss America. Magazines catering to the African American population, such as *Ebony*, featured light-skinned models with European features. It was common for African American women to straighten their hair and bleach their skin before applying for white-collar jobs.[26]

A New York civil rights commissioner reviewing a stewardess discrimination case in the mid-1960s would later explain the low number of African
American airline stewardesses as follows: "I am compelled to the opinion
that for too long there has been an underlying 'white esthetic' in the evaluation of physical attractiveness by American industry. The bias . . . [is against]
dark skin complexions and certain hair textures."[27]

This white aesthetic was disguised as seemingly objective standards
of "good grooming" and the "American look." Airlines issued supervisors
detailed instructions for assessing appearance in prospective stewardesses.
These instructions effectively banned women with features that suggested
African American identity in favor of applicants with an "American" look.
Stewardess supervisors were instructed to discern between "inherent" and
"correctible" features in determining which applicants to hire. "Defective"
features that were difficult or impossible to correct were often those deemed
racially identifiable.[28]

A 1954 American Airlines stewardess supervisor manual noted: "Her nose
is as attractive as it fits in with the general scheme of the remainder of her
face. Prominent hook noses, broken or broad noses, of course, are unsuitable."
The manual continued: "of course, lips should not be excessively full" and
hair should not be "coarse." In other words, blacks and Jews need not apply.[29]

But while airlines hired according to a narrowly defined vision of attractiveness, their publicity materials professed that the stewardess beauty
type was democratic. Airline press releases declared that attractiveness was
available to all women and claimed that it could appear in a variety of physical features. Each stewardess purportedly had a "unique" look.

Airline rhetoric about stewardesses' appearances reflected broader American ideals. Over the years, the mass media has promoted a pluralistic ideal
of American beauty. Cosmetics companies have long advertised products
as opportunities for individuality and self-expression by representing a
melting pot of beauty types including Eastern European, Italian, and even
Latina women.[30] This narrative about American beauty as a democratic
enterprise available to all women became particularly compelling in the
wake of Nazism, when visions of beauty as pluralist and egalitarian were
intertwined with American narratives about a melting pot democracy with
equal opportunity for all.

This celebratory vision of American democracy was increasingly potent in the years after World War II, as U.S. politicians justified the nation's emerging status as the leader of the "free world" based on the nation's claim to democracy, egalitarianism, and pluralism. As the Cold War intensified in the 1950s, the ideals of cultural diversity and individual equality became powerful rhetoric for asserting the nation's superiority in the international propaganda war. But with such rhetoric came an obligation to uphold these purported ideals.

Reflecting the postwar celebration of American diversity, second- and third-generation European immigrants, including Irish, Jews, and Poles who had previously been viewed as dangerous races in the early twentieth century, were now deemed racially white and part of the American middle class. Moreover, by the 1950s, physical features once associated with immigrants' inferior status had come to be popularly envisioned as emblematic of the ideal American look. The upturned Irish pug nose, for example, which had been widely characterized as decidedly foreign only a few generations earlier, in the 1950s came to be seen as quintessentially American.[31] However, the traits that characterized postwar American ideals of feminine beauty continued, at least for a time, to be marked as racially white. A typical postwar beauty, the stewardess was expected to lack traits associated with nonwhite racial identity. Airlines press releases celebrated the typical "American" stewardess as an Irish American girl with red hair or freckles.

Countering this dominant image of all-American beauty was no small feat. Spitz sought to reveal that airline appearance evaluations were racially coded. After establishing that appearance was an important qualification for stewardess applicants, Spitz maneuvered to put race on the table. He questioned Chief Stewardess Geddes: "And, sometimes you go into whether her complexion is fair or dark?" To which she replied, "Not that it is fair or dark, but whether she has marks on her skin, complexion problems, that is important."[32] Airline manuals prohibited supervisors from hiring women with acne and Geddes claimed to be referring to blemishes. But her voice wavered. Spitz asked her to speak up. She apologized. Then, he pressed her: "You do observe whether a person has a fair complexion or a dark complexion?" Geddes faltered. Spitz pushed on: "If you looked at me, what would you call me as far as complexion is concerned?" "I guess you are rather light," she responded. Spitz suggested that skin color was part of the "complexion" evaluation—and that it was the only hiring criterion that Banks could not meet.

On the stand, Geddes admitted that she did not know of any black stewardesses working for Capital Airlines, but she noted that there could have been some who passed as white. Geddes fumbled, "No, it is a little hard to tell whether they are or aren't, however. . . . It is not always certain whether one is or isn't." Spitz then probed, "As far as you know, from visible appearance of the person, you never saw a Negro, I take it?" She conceded, "No, not to my knowledge."

Airline supervisors were trained to evaluate "complexion" in the hiring process. An American Airlines supervisor manual offered vague instructions: "Do not highly recommend a girl with a defective complexion. It is one of the most difficult things to correct."[33] The manual did not clarify the meaning of "defective complexion." However, during the 1950s, airlines hired women with tan complexions, tans being considered fashionable when they were not linked to African American identity. Airline ads in the 1950s often depicted stewardesses tanning by the pool at stewardess training schools to contribute to constructing an image of stewardesses' fashionable, leisure-oriented lifestyles.

Suntans had become a popular trend and status symbol in the United States during the twentieth century. While the suntan had previously been a visual cue of outdoor labor, as the population became more urban and less agricultural the tan came to signify leisure time and exotic travel. A journalist in 1957 reported, "Years ago, light-skinned peoples placed a premium on paleness . . . the gibson girl with parasol aloft was a symbol of this. Within the last thirty years or so, however, the suntanned look has become increasingly desirable, whether as a sign of health, an accompaniment to summer fashions or as tacit proof of a good vacation." In 1961, *Life* magazine reported, "In times past a dark tan was the stigma of the working classes. This attitude still prevails in many parts of the world. But in the U.S. the tan has emerged as a status symbol sought after even by ardent white supremacists."[34]

The vogue for tanned skin allowed some light-skinned African American women to claim beauty partly by obscuring racial identity. The first African American modeling agency, which opened in 1946, specialized in models for ads geared at black consumers and sought models described as "brown-skinned" or "tan," while models with darker skin were less desirable. Ophelia DeVore, a model in the 1940s who had Native American, European, and African ancestry, never declared herself African American. She noted, "I found out later that they basically thought I had a suntan."[35] Patricia Banks was also light skinned, which at times allowed her to pass as a white woman with a fashionable suntan. This made her a good candidate for challenging discrimination in the airline industry.

Even though she was an ideal candidate for challenging discrimination, Banks knew that proving discrimination was exceedingly difficult. She awaited the results of the hearing. More than seven months passed. She began to doubt that the case would ever be resolved. Had Capital Airlines found a devious way to thwart the case? Finally, in late February 1960, when Banks was on her way home from college one evening, she walked up to her usual bus stop next to a candy stall on Jamaica Avenue. When the man working at the candy stall saw her, he shouted, "You won!" He held up the newspaper to show her. Banks had been in class all day and she had not yet heard. "I couldn't wait to get home. I think if I would've had the money, I would have taken a cab home that night," recalled Banks.

At the time, she was living in Queens with her mother, her uncle, and her two sisters. Her family had already heard the news. They were thrilled. Her phone was ringing off the hook. Newspaper reporters were calling. Channel 2 News called to interview her. The next morning, her lawyer called to tell her that the SCAD had ordered Capital Airlines to hire her. After a four-year struggle, the SCAD determined that a general pattern of discrimination operated at Capital Airlines. She received letters of support from all over the world. A friend of hers in Vietnam even read about her case in a newspaper there and wrote to congratulate her.

By the time Banks won, she was four years older and she was planning to marry, but airlines required stewardesses to be single. Banks was also months from graduating college. But there was no question in her mind; she was going to take the job. After all, Banks considered this her big opportunity to show the world that a black woman could be the perfect stewardess. In 1960, Banks postponed her marriage and left college to enroll in Capital's stewardess training program. She was exuberant that she had finally won this revered position. But she was also anxious about being one of the first black women in the job, and rightfully so.

Meanwhile, across the country, Marlene White was still deeply entrenched in her fight to become a stewardess. The FEPC had been investigating her case for five years. The evidence looked damning. First, other stewardess applicants were rejected for specific reasons, such as low test scores, being overweight, or having physical defects. White's test scores were on par with other applicants who had been accepted. She was the only applicant who met all the basic qualifications and was rejected based solely on the subjective judgment of the interviewers. Second, the FEPC found that White's application was routed irregularly in Northwest's corporate structure, implying that the company regarded her application as presenting a specific problem to be handled by "special procedures."

In 1962, after a five-year investigation, two years after the Banks ruling, the FEPC determined that White met Northwest's objective hiring criteria and that these standards had been "wholly disregarded" in favor of the interviewer's subjective standards, which were applied in terms of race.[36] The FEPC ordered the airline to hire White as a stewardess. White graduated from the Northwest stewardess training school on August 10, 1962. But her struggle was not over.

Patricia Banks, Marlene White, and the other young black women who filed discrimination suits against airlines influenced the hiring practices of airlines in important ways. After Banks and White won, dozens of stewardess discrimination suits were still waiting to be heard by the SCAD and the FEPC. Case by case, the SCAD and the FEPC mandated changes in individual airline's hiring policies and practices. Beyond ordering airlines to hire Banks and White, they also ordered Northwest Airlines and Capital Airlines to end discriminatory hiring practices.[37] They also mandated that these airlines take positive steps to recruit African American stewardesses. Northwest officials had defended the conspicuous absence of black stewardesses by claiming that they simply had not received enough black stewardess applicants to find any qualified applicants. The FEPC advised Northwest to advertise at historically black colleges and place stewardess recruitment ads in the African American press. Finally, the SCAD and the FEPC ordered these airlines to notify (in writing) all of its interviewers,

HOW NEGROES
REACT TO
CUBAN CRISIS

NOV 8, 1962

Newest
Negro
Stewardess

MARLENE WHITE
Attractive Northwest
Airline stewardess got
job after bias battle

Marlene White on the cover of *Jet* magazine, 1962.

agents, and representatives that all employment practices should be free of discrimination.

But while these changes looked promising, the select few African American women who would be hired shortly after Banks also had to win the positions through discrimination lawsuits. Plus, airlines could still find ways to dodge mandates to employ African American stewardesses. These pioneer black stewardesses would not receive a particularly warm welcome.

When Banks first wore her Capital Airlines uniform (complete with a stylish hat and white gloves), she felt fantastic. "I was dressed to the nines. After all I had gone through, I couldn't believe I was finally wearing the uniform. I had made it. I was going to fly. It was such an accomplishment," she said.[38] Banks basked in the pride of winning a job that was so well respected and glamorous. She was determined to excel, no matter how she was tested.

Perfectly primped, Banks served her first flight, which included a three-day layover in Tennessee. She stayed at a hotel with the rest of the crew. A hotel maid who was cleaning her room asked, in a southern drawl, "You haven't been down here before, have you?" Banks thought nothing of it. She raved about the trip in a letter to her mom: "I stayed at the same motel as everyone else and was treated beautifully." But trouble was brewing. This was the segregated South and Banks had stayed in a white-only hotel. Rumors that the hotel had integrated spread quickly and when Banks returned to Detroit, airline managers were furious. Her supervisor called to tell her that she had nearly caused a riot and instructed her to stay at black-only hotels in southern cities. Her supervisor wrote the names of black hotels in her logbook, so she knew where to stay during trips to the South. "I felt out of place in many instances," Banks admitted.[39]

Once airlines were legally required to hire black stewardesses, *Ebony*, the African American magazine with the largest circulation in the nation, which likely received airline press releases on stewardess integration, cultivated an intriguing image of this integration. The magazine (launched in 1945) typically presented a celebratory vision of middle-class African America, rather than focusing on racial injustice. In keeping with this ethos, the magazine cast the introduction of black stewardesses as evidence of the success of equal opportunity in America. One article described a fictional encounter in which a white male passenger welcomed a new African American stewardess:

A passenger asks her, "Are you by any chance Hawaiian?" The hostess laughs gently. "Oh, no. I'm Negro." The passenger smiles haltingly, inquires again. "Are there any more Negroes in training with TWA or another airline?" "Not to my knowledge." They pause. He smiles warmly, thumbs his magazine, and asks her name. "I'm certainly happy for you," he says. "I'm happy to serve you," the hostess replies pleasantly, and moves on.[40]

Ebony ran several articles that presented a similar vision of harmonious racial integration aloft. An article, titled "Open Skies for Negro Girls," sketched the biography of the African American stewardess Veronica Gonzales, who was hired by United Airlines in 1963. The magazine reported that Gonzales experienced no race-related conflicts on the job and that there was never any "mention of race." A 1964 *Ebony* article on two black sisters hired as TWA stewardesses also displayed this central vision: they loved their work and they encountered no difficulties based on race.[41] *Ebony*'s coverage obscured civil rights struggles by depicting the racial drama playing out smoothly, thus reinventing intense nationwide debates over civil rights as a classic American story about individual achievement in the land of opportunity. These tales of racial harmony were strikingly different from what Patricia Banks and Marlene White experienced aloft.

Banks meticulously stuck to every airline regulation. "I lived the life of Miss Perfect. I didn't want to jeopardize any other Negro's chances of becoming a flight hostess. It wasn't easy living like that," Banks said. "I felt I had to be this impeccable person. I just didn't want to mess this up. It was a fight. I was determined not to make any errors that whole year."[42]

Banks worried that, as an African American woman, she was at an increased risk of being accused of promiscuous behavior. So she stayed to herself. White pilots invited her out for dinner and drinks, but she declined. "It was a very, very cautious time for me. I didn't know if the socializing was a setup. I was worried that if I did go out with someone, they would spread rumors about it," she said.[43] It was not always easy for her to maintain her stewardess smile.

Banks was light skinned, which at times allowed her to mask her racial identity. Even though her case was widely publicized in the media, because she was not dark skinned most fellow stewardesses and passengers did not know she was the famed African American stewardess who had been hired. Banks did not always inform fellow stewardesses that she was black. Some stewardesses assumed she had a stylish tan: "You must be based in New Orleans. You have such a beautiful tan," they would say.

On a particularly turbulent flight, she held the hand of one fearful white passenger. While she was holding his hand, he kept telling her, "You need to visit Montana—no niggers and no winos." Banks reflected, "I was pissed, but I had to be cool. I didn't say anything." Banks remembered another passenger saying, "You look like you're from Northern India." To which she retorted, "No, I'm from Africa."[44] One white stewardess frequently hassled her, saying that she had heard rumors that Banks was paid by the NAACP.

Banks was determined to keep her stewardess position so she bit her tongue. "If someone's making a racist comment, how was I going to respond? In anger? Yes! So, my control mechanisms were in full operation all the time. I was a feisty youngster and I wasn't going to tolerate that kind of behavior, but I knew the consequences if I did answer with anger," Banks recalled. "I had to be a perfect lady all the time."[45]

After a year of flying, she couldn't take it anymore. She was worn out. "I suppressed a lot of emotions by not responding in any way. I had to smile and grin and take a whole lot. It was an emotionally and spiritually draining experience," she said. She figured a year was enough time to prove to the airlines and the world that an African American woman could be a stellar airline stewardess. She had met all the rigorous regulations. She had held her tongue when passengers made racist comments. She had even received a commendation letter for how she handled a flight during a hurricane. "I represented my people to the best of my ability and if the airlines couldn't see that we were just as qualified as anyone else, they never would." In 1961, she resigned and got married. Still, her love of flying persisted and she began taking flying lessons to earn her pilot's license.[46]

Marlene White would have a rougher time. During her probation period as a stewardess, she was given a series of what the airline called "routine checks"—some of which she purportedly failed. On April 3, 1963, just seven months after she began working as a stewardess, Northwest terminated her. But like Patricia Banks, White was determined to work as a stewardess.

Instead of returning to the FEPC, Marlene White approached an even more powerful committee when she was fired by Northwest. In 1961, President John F. Kennedy had created the President's Committee on Equal Employment Opportunity (PCEEO) to end discrimination in employment and hiring practices. White filed a grievance with the PCEEO, which ordered Northwest Airlines to rehire her. She returned to flying on November 14, 1963—seven years after she first applied for the position.

In addition to creating the PCEEO, President Kennedy had contributed to airline integration by pressuring airlines as federal contractors to integrate stewardess positions. As head of the PCEEO, Vice President Lyndon Johnson had made stewardess integration his personal cause.[47] When Johnson became president, he took up Kennedy's torch for civil rights with even more gusto. Both presidents were particularly vested in civil rights partly because such rights factored into America's tarnished reputation overseas. Since stewardesses were major icons in the press who also served foreign dignitaries traveling to America, Johnson recognized their value in revamping America's global image regarding race. During Johnson's first year as president, the image of the United States abroad was badly in need of repair because the nation's persistent "race problem" was making headlines all over the world. The United States Information Agency (USIA) had found that 85 percent of the educated elite in Asian and African countries was aware of racial incidents in the United States. In a study done in 1965, for example, nine out of ten had a negative opinion about U.S. race relations. In designing his civil rights strategy, Johnson was well aware that the issue had serious international consequences. With worldwide news organizations covering the historic moment, President Johnson signed the 1964 Civil Rights Act, which outlawed segregation in businesses and banned discriminatory employment practices. The Johnson administration reveled in the success of the new act and its positive impact on America's image overseas.[48]

The Civil Rights Act also had important repercussions at home. The legislation provided new legal muscle to win stewardess discrimination cases and airlines faced even more political, legal, and social pressure to hire black stewardesses. By the mid-1960s, the SCAD and the FEPC had ordered airlines to include the text "Equal Opportunity Employer" on employment ads, advertise stewardess positions in the African American press, and schedule interviews at historically black colleges.

In 1965, following an onslaught of stewardess discrimination lawsuits, approximately fifty African American women were employed as stewardesses on U.S. airlines, constituting 0.33 percent of the total stewardess workforce of over fifteen thousand.[49] Pan Am, for example, had hired no African American stewardesses from 1945 to 1957. But in the wake of legal action against airlines, 0.79 percent of Pan Am's stewardesses were African American from 1958 to 1969. Pan Am continued to hire a predominantly white stewardess corps, but the airline also hired others: 5.16 percent of the airline's stewardesses were "Hispanic" and served to advertise international flair on Latin American routes; 5.3 percent were "unknown"; and 11 percent were "other," composed largely of Asian American stewardesses, who offered an exotic image on flights to Asia.[50]

Displaying Racial Harmony for the World to See

Beyond legal pressures that forced airlines to hire black stewardesses, new business conditions in the airline industry also prompted a newfound interest in hiring African American stewardesses. While airlines had targeted wealthy white businessmen during the first three decades of air travel, following the introduction of jets in the late 1950s, airlines began directing advertising dollars into targeting a new mass market—which included women, young people, and the growing African American middle class. For the first time, airline marketing teams identified the potential market of African Americans. Black consumer spending power had increased substantially during the postwar years and by the late 1950s many white-owned corporations had recognized African Americans as consumers. Major ad agencies even opened "special markets" divisions to target black consumers.[51] Airlines wanted a piece of this market.

In 1963, Pan Am advertised air service in *Ebony* magazine. This was the first airline ad targeting African Americans.[52] The following year, after Pan Am began advertising to black travelers, airlines began placing stewardess recruitment ads in *Ebony* magazine with the SCAD-ordered text: "Equal Opportunity Employer." The civil rights struggles that resulted in legal mandates to hire black stewardesses in the late 1950s and early 1960s overlapped with the airline industry's capitalist expansion into the mass market, which included African American consumers. Some scholars of African American history have argued that the gains of the civil rights movement resulted partly from white business responses to black spending power, rather than purely to moral transformation.[53] These connections between corporate interests and racial integration in the airline industry dovetailed in interesting ways. Airlines now had a vested interest in publicizing their new black stewardesses to a new market of potential fliers—middle-class African Americans.

While airline management had excluded African American women from the airlines' definition of wholesome, all-American womanhood, after airlines were legally forced to hire black stewardesses, airline marketing departments reinvented black stewardesses as respectable, middle-class, all-American women. Airline press releases about new black stewardesses painstakingly described their backgrounds to signify that they were from typical, middle-class, "all-American" homes: they highlighted that these new black stewardesses had attended college and that they had participated in typical American activities such as school newspapers, glee clubs, pep squads, and civic clubs.[54]

Portraying African American stewardesses as a celebration of all-American diversity was an astute marketing strategy because it tapped a potent cultural narrative that was developing during the Cold War. By representing stewardess integration as harmonious and all-American, airlines obscured the civil rights struggle with a story of equal opportunity. This vision of America was particularly compelling at a time when the Soviets and the Americans were fighting an intense international propaganda war and America's global leadership relied on its image of egalitarianism and pluralism. As the world looked to the United States to live up to its ideals, airlines linked the new black stewardesses to this image of America.

But while airlines professed equal opportunity among their stewardess corps, they also insisted that black stewardesses conform to dominant American images of feminine beauty. For example, the airlines prohibited the Afro hairstyle and TWA even required African American stewardesses to straighten their hair. By the mid-1960s, young civil rights workers were condemning a white aesthetic and wearing unstraightened hair as a sign of

Some people have an instinct for picking the best in everything.

You know the type. Perhaps someone like you. Not *finicky* people. But people with taste and unerring instincts.

They select their clothes, and their restaurants, and their cars, and their doctors, the same way. With care.

And they approach airlines that way, too. So they choose Pan Am.

What sets Pan Am apart is more than the cuisine by *Maxim's of Paris.* Or the 900 helpful offices, 'round the world. Or the expertness of the maintenance and flight crews.

It's all of these things, of course, and so many more they'd fill a book. But above all else, it's a feeling you have. The good feeling that's yours only when you know you've chosen the very best there is. It adds not a penny to your fare.

And it's a feeling you can fly away with to just about anywhere. Because we fly to 118 cities. 83 lands. And all six continents. Just call your Pan Am Travel Agent. Or call us.

World's most experienced airline PAN AM
First on the Atlantic   First on the Pacific   First in Latin America   First 'Round the World

Marva Mitchell is a TWA expert...
specializing in people.

Marva's the nice girl who used to live next door. Remember?

Now she's a gracious hostess, an executive secretary, a superb cook. She knows just the right moment to talk to a first-time traveler, leave a businessman alone, take a steak from the oven. And she knows a lot more . . . mostly about you.

She'll make you feel at home at 30,000 feet – answer questions before you ask – make your trip on TWA a person-to-person experience. All our hostesses are like that – across the U.S., Europe, Africa and Asia. And they all liked people long before they went to work for TWA.

Next trip, see for yourself.

We're your kind of airline.

Nationwide
Worldwide
depend on **TWA**

TWA ad, *Ebony* magazine, 1966. Author's collection.

black solidarity. The Afro became a symbol of black women's resistance to white beauty ideals and *Ebony* magazine began featuring black models with unstraightened hair. In 1969, United fired an African American stewardess for refusing to cut her Afro. *Newsweek* reported that "some whites fearfully see Afro hair-dos . . . as a symbol of anger and rebellion," but the reporter concluded that United's action was "simply a matter of enforcing the airline's traditional standards of good grooming."[55] These seemingly objective standards of "good grooming," however, relied on a white aesthetic.

Jet, a weekly magazine marketed to African American readers that chronicled the civil rights movement, played up black stewardesses' attractiveness. In 1962, one of the magazine's cover stories called the "raven-haired," "attractive Marlene White" "an air-minded beauty" as it recounted the lengthy battle and series of discrimination complaints involved in her "fight for flights."[56] In this way, the magazine reported the civil rights struggle while simultaneously forging an image of black women as beautiful.

Ebony's coverage of stewardess integration, however, portrayed African American stewardesses as women who successfully conformed to mainstream, middle-class American gender norms. *Ebony* ran a cover story on Mary E. Tiller, TWA's first African American stewardess. *Ebony* described Tiller as an "all-American type" who "prove[s] that a pretty, well-trained Negro girl could approvingly represent a leading air line, consider the plane her home, receive its visitors as distinguished guests and make them feel welcome and comfortable."[57]

These representations of African American women contributed to the image of the emerging professional class in black America during the 1950s and 1960s. As African Americans integrated into white-collar positions and black spending power increased, magazines such as *Ebony* disseminated images that celebrated dominant visions of femininity, sexual respectability, heterosexual appeal, and beauty as standards for African American women. Rather than overturning mainstream, middle-class definitions of American womanhood, these images instead suggested that black women could fit into them.[58]

African American stewardess applicants, such as Patricia Banks and Marlene White, marshaled successful legal challenges to airlines' discriminatory hiring practices by claiming respectability, femininity, middle-class status, and beauty—attributes that had been reserved solely for white women. By asserting that they conformed to dominant middle-class gender norms and sexual mores in 1950s America, these black women claimed inclusion in the definition of proper American womanhood. Black stewardesses expanded postwar definitions of typical American femininity, but they also upheld conservative, middle-class definitions of femininity and sexuality. Once airlines were legally required to integrate, they marketed black stewardesses as exemplars of respectable American femininity and a pluralistic, egalitarian America—but this vision relied on traditional gender, class, and sexual norms. As black stewardesses expanded traditional definitions of American womanhood, airlines were reinventing the stewardess icon in ways that would popularize a new brand of femininity in America and usher the nation into a new era.

4

A New Jet-Winged World

ON OCTOBER 26, 1958, the first commercially successful jet made its debut flight. It was a media sensation. Magazines and newspapers proclaimed the dawn of a "new jet-winged world." They praised the majestic beauty of this sleek flying machine and touted its potential to change the world. Heralding the jet age as the new era of "speed" and "glamour," airline press releases generated substantial buzz about jet technology. A stewardess heroine in the novel *Girl on a Wing* (1960) captured the cultural intrigue of jets: "[The jet] looked so majestic, so patient, standing there waiting for us, its wings swept back, its engines thrust forward, its tail tall and sharp against the cool sky. It was like, I thought, some gigantic wild orchid. . . . I loved airplanes, and I shall always love them, and when I'm near one it turns my bones to jelly."[1]

The advent of the jet had, indeed, ushered in a new era of travel. It marked the beginning of major changes in the airline industry, the air travel market, and airline advertising strategies. With the intensification of Cold War rivalries and the emergence of new business conditions (such as larger, faster jet planes and the new prospective air travel market of middle-class vacationers) during the late 1950s, airlines reconfigured their advertising and management strategies in important ways.

In particular, airlines reinvented their key marketing device: the stewardess. While the wholesome homemaker stewardess of the 1940s and 1950s traveled primarily within the United States, the jet stewardess would travel

Esquire magazine, February 1964.

all over the globe and she would become an iconic, cosmopolitan, glamorous "career girl" and an honorary member of the exotic destination-hopping social elite dubbed the "Jet Set" by a gossip columnist in 1960.[2] But the jet stewardess was not a complete departure from her predecessor, the girl next door, nor was she a boldly sexualized icon; she was a transitional figure between the two stewardess incarnations. Being a stewardess was now an opportunity to become elite, worldly, and stylish. Thousands of young women aspired to be just that.

Twenty-two-year-old Clare Christiansen, who grew up in a small town outside of Cleveland, Ohio, was the first in her family to attend college, but she wanted to do something more exciting than become a teacher. She had scored a few modeling gigs, but "then [she] read an article in *Life* magazine about this exotic overseas airline, Pan American, and decided that being a stewardess for an overseas airline would be the most exciting job in the world." When she applied for a stewardess position, she had never been on a plane.

Two years before the advent of jet service, Christiansen wrote to Pan Am in New York to ask if it ever made an exception to the height limit since she was 5'10" and most airlines would not hire women taller than 5'7".[3] A form letter response encouraged her to apply. Meanwhile, she sent her headshots to Eileen Ford, who had just opened a modeling agency in New York City. Ford recommended she lose ten pounds. Christiansen dropped the weight and flew to the Big Apple, where she was promptly rejected by the modeling agency. Now that she was thinner, her head looked too big for her body. Christiansen showed up at Pan Am's headquarters in Long Island City and was instantly enamored with the exotic travel posters that plastered the walls. The personnel manager took one look at her and nixed her for being too tall, but he agreed to send her on for a panel interview as a courtesy. When the panel told her she was too tall, she explained that she would be an asset on the larger jet planes that Pan Am would soon begin flying. Plus, even though she was tall, she was still slim enough to meet their weight requirements. She managed to pass the French exam, then waited to hear whether she had been accepted.

"I called home every day to see if I'd gotten any mail. I remember the day my mother said there was a letter for me and I asked her to open it. My heart was pounding as she opened it, and she burst into tears and said I'd been accepted. She was so upset ... she was certain I'd never return home."[4]

Christiansen relished joining this elite corps of working women. Beaming with enthusiasm, she wrote home nearly every day during stewardess training: "I feel so select—only 17 in the class." Three days later, in another letter home, she wrote, "I just can't believe I got the job. The girls are so qualified—one girl speaks English, German and Spanish fluently."[5]

Sporting Pan Am's jaunty cap, this young midwestern girl went on to see the world. She flew to Paris, Copenhagen, Tokyo, Bangkok, and beyond. Her

Pan Am stewardess Clare Christiansen on a Boeing 377 Stratocruiser
just before the advent of jets, circa 1956.
Courtesy Clare Christiansen.

palate changed. "I became sophisticated. I read a lot and attended theater all
over the world," she said. "We were interviewed for foreign magazines; we
met celebrities on long flights; we were invited to parties in foreign capitals.
It was just plain glamorous." Christiansen wrote to her family on Istanbul
Hilton stationary: "Are you impressed? You should see this place—luxury
plus. There's a terrace off every room! I really had a wonderful time on this
trip—the hotel in Istanbul was gorgeous and they gave us such generous
meal allowance. I lived like a queen."[6]

The stewardess position afforded young women a great deal of respect,
admiration, and prestige. They savored their fame. "To be a Pan Am stewardess in those days was like being a supermodel or a movie star. I felt so very
special," said Christiansen.[7] Stewardesses felt respected by airline management in part because airlines offered them a lavish lifestyle. Stewardess school
graduation ceremonies featured steak, champagne, roses, and limousine
service. Airlines put stewardesses up at opulent hotels during layovers—such
as, the Drake, Chicago's most elegant hotel at the time. "Each step you take
at the Drake is like walking on diamonds," said the actor Peter Ustinov.

Northwest Airlines even housed stewardesses working the Tokyo route at a former princess's estate.[8]

Being a stewardess offered unique access to elite places and styles. One Pan Am stewardess wrote in her journal about knowing when Dior shortened skirts in 1953 before the news even hit the American press because she was in Paris on a layover; she saved newspaper clippings to commemorate this fashion milestone.[9] While some stewardesses came from upper-middle-class backgrounds with professional or wealthy parents, many were from small towns and had not experienced an affluent cosmopolitan lifestyle. For them, the profession offered an opportunity to become a suave socialite. These young women danced at London's world-class Savoy hotel and attended parties with foreign dignitaries, Hollywood celebrities, and international socialites. They shopped all over the world during their twenty-four-hour-layovers. Stewardess scrapbooks brim with postcards from ornate five-star restaurants and the world's most luxurious hotels.[10] Many saved postcards from these ritzy establishments because they found this upper-crust world new and exciting. They parlayed their glamour into personal advantage—using it to gain access to star-studded events and to attract high-caliber dates.

Stewardesses viewed themselves as members of an exclusive sorority and considered their broad cultural knowledge and sophistication critical qualifications for membership in this highly selective group. A former stewardess who flew from 1957 to 1961 said stewardesses were the "crème de la crème, mostly college educated, multilingual women."[11] Becoming a stewardess "was probably second only to becoming a starlet. You could be proud to say you were a Pan Am stewardess. They hired only the cream of the crop," said a former stewardess, who flew with Pan Am for thirty-one years and Delta for eleven years.[12]

The stewardess of the jet age embodied an emerging type of American womanhood that was intimately connected to consumerism. Svelte and stylish, the jet age stewardess spoke several languages, indulged in a luxurious lifestyle, knew her way around Paris, and was up on the latest couture. She displayed a compelling vision of desirability—what the nation should want, which reflected the increasing role of consumerism in constructing personal and national identity in the postwar period. American citizenship has been increasingly expressed through the goods and services people purchase. The jet stewardess embodied this consumer vision—her femininity, individuality, and Americanness were all wrapped up in her lifestyle, fashion, and cosmetics. Airlines painstakingly selected (and decorated) stewardesses' physical bodies to convey this particular consumer-oriented vision of American womanhood.

This jet age stewardess was the apotheosis of a new, more sophisticated, and cosmopolitan image of the nation itself that had global ramifications during the Cold War. As an international ambassador, the jet stewardess articulated America's identity and image overseas, revealing a critical aspect of America's Cold War strategy—an international image campaign that relied on pretty women, glamour, and fancy gadgets. This alluring international icon tells a larger story about the unfolding relationship between consumerism, the Cold War, and globalization—three critical developments in the postwar era.

But it all began with a faster, bigger airplane. . . .

Jets and the Dawn of Mass Travel

During the jet age, air travelers were still predominantly wealthy businessmen. In the early 1960s, air travelers were 70 percent male and 77 percent college educated with median incomes of $15,000 per year. In 1960, only 7.7 percent of the U.S. population had college degrees and less than 3 percent of American families earned $15,000 or more per year, so jet travelers constituted a highly elite segment of the population. The advertising industry magazine *Printer's Ink* reported that business travel constituted 65 percent of the total air travel market.[13]

Jets, however, promised to reinvent air travel. The media blitz was not just hype. Jets could carry 111 passengers over 3,300 miles at 575 miles per hour. They carried twice as many passengers and flew nearly twice as fast as their propeller predecessor, the DC-6. They also offered a much quieter ride with less vibration than piston aircraft, which made flying more comfortable for passengers. By traveling much faster and carrying more passengers, jets catalyzed an era of mass air travel.

Jets also precipitated new business conditions that would pose major challenges for the industry, and airlines would need to find innovative marketing strategies to handle them. First, the enormous seating capacities of jets increased pressure on airlines to expand the air travel market. In 1957, the executives at J. Walter Thompson, Pan Am's ad agency, ominously predicted that the airline's seating capacity would more than double from 1957 to 1961. By the end of 1959, 197 Boeing 707 and 150 DC-8 jets were in service or on order. Even with a hefty annual growth in air traffic, airlines would be hard-pressed to fill the new jets.[14] Airlines had invested heavily in jet technology and they needed to increase ticket sales radically to make an adequate return on the investment.

As airlines struggled to fill jets, the Civil Aeronautics Board (CAB) exacerbated the problem by doling out new route allotments during the late 1950s, which increased competition between airlines because now more airlines served each route. Predictions of plummeting profits swirled. In a board meeting in 1961, Pan Am executives lamented more competitors flying the same routes with equal equipment, food service, and fares. In light of these issues, Pan Am's advertising team declared: "The honeymoon is just about over."[15]

Airlines dreaded an intense battle for market share. By the jet age, airlines had solidly won business travelers from train travel. Businessmen already traveled by air and most marketing teams believed that the possibility of expanding the business air travel market was limited.[16] Targeting business travelers might win a larger share of the air travel market, but it would undoubtedly prompt a tense skirmish between airlines over the small number of existing fliers. Plus, even winning some business travelers from other airlines would not fill jets. Marketing teams had to think bigger.

With a massive increase in seating capacity available on jets, airlines were poised to turn air travel into mass transportation, but they would need to entice more Americans aloft. While wealthy businessmen usually opted for air travel, the vast majority of Americans still took the train or drove. In fact, in 1961, only an estimated 8 percent of the adult population in the United States had ever flown.[17]

By the jet age, airlines' desire to lure the masses aloft overlapped with another significant trend in American society—Americans now had more leisure time and higher disposable incomes. The number of American families with disposable incomes of at least $4,000 annually more than doubled from 1950 to 1956, and was expected to triple by 1959. At the same time, the annual vacation was becoming a common practice. In 1948, only 68 percent of American workers took two weeks of vacation and only 23 percent took three weeks; by 1955, 82 percent took two weeks and 38 percent took three weeks. From 1951 to 1955, the total travel and holiday market increased 22 percent.[18] In addition, the rise of consumer credit in the 1950s contributed to expanding travel spending through travel-now, pay-later programs.

For the first time, airlines were beginning to ferret out this critical emerging market of middle-class leisure travelers. Airline marketing studies reported that new personal travelers had lower incomes and included more women and families, compared to the existing market of wealthy businessmen. In 1958, an American Airlines marketing survey found that rich men were still the majority of air travelers, but it noted a shift toward the middle-income group (earning $3,000 to $7,000 per year), which accounted for half the U.S. population. The report determined that two-thirds of new fliers were from middle-income groups and it advised American Airlines to appeal to both the "mass and class" market.[19] For the first time, airlines recognized that the industry would become increasingly dependent on middle-income vacationers—particularly, women and families.

Plus, more consumers had time and money to travel overseas. While overall consumption in the United States increased 63 percent between 1953 and 1963, American spending on foreign travel grew even faster (89 percent) during that period. From 1951 to 1955, the overseas travel market increased 51 percent.[20]

Jets sparked even more overseas travel because transatlantic jet service took six hours–compared to twelve hours via piston airplanes, and eleven days via ocean liner. With jets, international air traffic ballooned from 3 million passengers carried in 1955 to more than 5 million in 1960. In 1953, Americans made 376,000 trips across the Atlantic; by 1959, that number had doubled; by 1965, the number had doubled again to 1.4 million. Americans traveling to France went from 264,000 in 1950 to 792,000 in 1960. In 1958, airlines surpassed ocean liners in overseas travel.[21]

But even though airline marketing teams recognized the trend toward middle-income personal travelers and the need to seduce the nonflying masses into the air to fill the large seating capacities of the new jets, airlines were still conflicted about whether to divert the bulk of their advertising dollars toward convincing the huge potential market of nonfliers to fly or toward cajoling the existing market of wealthy businessmen away from other airlines.

"A well-aimed rifle shot at the best non-flying prospects could be fruitful," Philip Schaff, an ad man working on the United Airlines campaign, told his colleagues at the Leo Burnett Advertising Agency in Chicago. The agency had just bid for the prestigious United Airlines account and its initial strategizing sessions revolved around the debate over whether to target air travel market expansion or to increase market share. Spearheaded by the illustrious Leo Burnett, a committed creative who was ahead of the curve in the ad industry, the Burnett agency was eager to design innovative ads for United. Burnett's team was aware of the huge potential market of vacation travelers. Philip Schaff believed Americans could finally afford air travel for vacations, but they had not yet been sold on the idea. Another Burnett ad man, James Love, agreed that airlines had not encouraged families to fly, and he considered families the most critical potential market. But the team was divided on whether to funnel advertising dollars into market expansion: while Schaff and Love suspected that personal travel was the biggest untapped market, others feared that attempts to expand the market could be a "trap" that would prove too costly for a single airline if it diverted its ad dollars away from efforts to increase market share.[22] Even though many airline ad teams were not yet ready to pour advertising dollars into the burgeoning vacation travel market, this new market caught their attention and shaped their ad strategies.

Pan Am was the first carrier to take the plunge. In 1958, the airline aggressively directed advertising dollars to the burgeoning middle-class market. International airlines such as Pan Am led the way to targeting the broad middle class, partly because they had always carried more personal travelers than domestic lines. While Pan Am's advertising had previously focused on the wealthy, college-educated market, its 1958 marketing plan deemed this demographic "too narrow." The ad team urged the airline to consider air travel "a normal commodity for sale to all Americans, regardless of income or education." Pan Am executives agreed that the airline's financial future rested in the new market of people who had long desired overseas travel and now finally had enough money to pay for it. In 1958 Pan Am also tried to attract middle-income travelers by introducing a third fare—"economy" class tickets (which were 20 percent cheaper than its "tourist-class fare") and tickets on credit. That year Pan Am also redirected advertising dollars from selective highbrow magazines (such as the *New Yorker*) to middlebrow magazines (such as *Life*) because they reached a larger audience. Pan Am's new advertising campaign was intended to reach 90 percent of the total U.S. population.[23]

But while airline ad teams mulled over how to accelerate the coming of mass air transportation, at the same time they faced new problems from the reality of rapidly expanding air travel. Jets had stimulated a massive boom in air travel: air ticket sales went from 38 million in 1955 to 62 million in 1960.[24] As air travel mushroomed, airlines attempted to handle the swift increase in traffic by adopting popular business practices of the era. At the time, many businesses serving large numbers of consumers had streamlined operations. For example, fast-food chains (such as McDonald's, founded in 1955) that became popular during the 1950s were based on a system of simple menus and assembly-line kitchens that ensured efficiency and consistent products. Airlines followed suit by streamlining efficiency and consistency in service. This business strategy would play out in how they reinvented the stewardess.

With the introduction of jets, cabin service became substantially more efficient and less personalized. Earlier stewardesses had called passengers by name and engaged in casual conversations, but with the introduction of larger, faster planes, stewardesses served more passengers in less time. Partly as a cost-saving measure, airlines employed only 2 stewardesses onboard each jet flight of up to 111 passengers, which did not yield the same level of personalized service they had previously offered on the smaller prop planes. Meal carts were also introduced on jets, so instead of delivering each meal individually on trays, stewardesses began serving meals in efficient assembly-line fashion from a cart on wheels.

The trouble with the larger jet planes, however, was that they promised the democratization of air travel—and, consequently, the decline of flying's allure. Critics bemoaned that flying would no longer be restricted to elites and popular magazines featured images of crass middle-class American tourists acting boorishly among European socialites.[25] These criticisms of jet age travel dovetailed with broader critiques of mass consumption, which had risen to a fever pitch in mid-century American culture. Airlines needed marketing strategies both to sell air travel to the broader public and to reinvigorate its appeal as a lavish, exotic adventure available to a chosen few. Enter glamour.

Beverly Hills Designers, Exotic Lands, and America's Crème de la Crème

At precisely the era when air travel was poised to become mass transportation, airlines began chasing a mysterious thing called "glamour." In 1957, the year that Pan Am's marketing team decided to target the broad middle class, Pan Am's advertising plan aimed to build an "urge to travel abroad even in those who don't go now—to build a potential market for the jets" by placing a "strong emphasis on glamour."[26] In 1958, TWA inaugurated its "Jetstream Glamour" campaign, which created a major stir in the industry. Baffled by TWA's pitch-perfect campaign, the marketing team for American Airlines interviewed nearly six thousand respondents to investigate how to revamp its image. The team determined that TWA was the most popular carrier: it was "everybody's airline—society people's, Hollywood stars' and businessmen's airline." In a section called "TWA's Image and Where It Gets It," the report concluded that TWA's popularity was based on "glamour." Since the airline was admired by inexperienced travelers and criticized by frequent travelers, the team deduced that TWA's popularity was a result of image and advertising, rather than performance. The marketing team's recommendation to American Airlines: add a splash of "glamour."[27]

Since marketing studies showed that those who had never flown selected an airline based on image rather than actual service, airlines began investing heavily in corporate image creation through advertising.[28] Airline advertising budgets skyrocketed. In 1960, eleven domestic lines spent $26 million on advertising, but by 1962 domestic airline ad expenditures had jumped to $34 million.[29] The heart of the new air travel campaigns was the elusive beast—glamour.

But what did airlines mean by glamour and how did they try to create it? Glamour was the invisible, unidentifiable force that could tempt the nonflying public into the air. Even the marketing teams consciously trying to create glamour admitted they did not know what it was exactly:

> TWA seems to have what we would call—for lack of a more precise word—glamour. The ingredients and proportions of ingredients which make up this glamour are hard, at this point, to define. The indications are that it stems from some or all of the following: its world-wide routes, the name and looks of the Constellation, the connotations of the word "Jetstream," Howard Hughes' name, the ambassador Siesta seat flights and the idea that you'll get luxurious service and meet important people. . . . In more general terms, these specifics would seem to add up to "glamour", the components of which are excitement, adventure, the intrigue of far away places and luxury.[30]

This vision of glamour revolved around an image of luxury and personalized service that camouflaged any hint that air travel was on the verge of becoming mass transportation. Airlines promoted an image of glamour that linked technology, consumerism, femininity, beauty, and American identity. While immediate postwar airline ads pitched air travel as practical transportation for ordinary Americans, now air travel was sold as an entrée for middle-income Americans into an exotic adventure.[31] The vacation started when you stepped on the plane. Flying was all glitz.

Technology was a fundamental component of glamour. Airline executives were concerned about keeping up with the latest aviation technology and considered it critical to marketing. The public was, indeed, captivated with jets. Many air travelers knew which model of plane they were traveling on and longed to ride on certain models. An American Airlines study found that nearly 70 percent of passengers on Electras had specifically sought out the Electra plane (as opposed to other models). United's ad team noted that American Airlines was "aggressively trying to create impression of more and more modern jets" by promoting the "fan jet" as cutting-edge technology—even though it was effectively the same as the "astro jet."[32]

America's long-standing fascination with technology gained heightened meaning within the context of larger global politics—particularly, the bitter Soviet-American rivalry. When the Soviets launched the first man-made satellite into space on October 4, 1957, Americans were deeply rattled. The 183-pound object, known as Sputnik, struck a monumental chord with the American public and catalyzed an increasingly nerve-racking "space race" between the Soviets and the Americans. With the specter of nuclear annihilation looming, Americans did not take Sputnik lightly. The Russian craft held potent symbolic meaning and influenced the trajectory of international politics for years to come.[33]

This international technological competition was a central feature of the tense, long-term Cold War between the Soviets and the Americans, which shaped the global political climate for decades. This intense technology showdown between the rival superpowers was not limited to space. Civil aviation also assumed political valence in the global battle for prestige. Shortly after the Soviets launched Sputnik, the Soviet airline Aeroflot, which was funded by the government, announced a massive increase in air traffic and a sprawling new international route system that included key centers in Western Europe. In response, Senator Bartlett of the United States warned that the Soviet advance in passenger jet planes "would be almost as devastating to [America's] national prestige as was the first Sputnik."[34] Authorities in the United States agreed that the airplane was an "essential instrument" for the country's "prestige as a nation" and a way to win "political good will and technological respect" around the world.[35]

Commercial jets were introduced in America a year after Sputnik was launched, in the midst of this technological showdown between the Soviets and the Americans. The jet was, indeed, a very real technological advance that allowed people to travel much further and faster, but its symbolic importance was magnified in the wake of Sputnik. Within the context of American humiliation over Sputnik, jet technology was imbued with amped up global political significance and served as a crucial gauge for national superiority in the propaganda war. American glamour hinged on the availability of a wide array of technologically advanced consumer products. This technologically oriented consumer wonderland was the centerpiece of America's Cold War identity as the nation squared off against the Soviet Union.

Tapping this broader vision of American glamour in the global propaganda war, U.S. airlines played up cutting-edge jet technology. But marketing missives touting technological advances would not alone charm the American public. Garnering international prestige was not merely a matter of rolling out bigger, faster jets; there was another critical ingredient.[36] Airlines converted technology into a desirable consumer product by introducing another integral component to the new glamour campaigns.

This was the advent of a fresh ultra-chic jet stewardess incarnation that revolved around an elite lifestyle, exotic travel resume, stylish consumption habits, and cosmopolitanism. A departure from the wholesome homemaker stewardess of the 1940s and early 1950s, the jet stewardess was a sophisticate with "glamour" and "a Hollywood look."[37]

The stewardess requirements remained largely the same as in the immediate postwar era—candidates still had to be single women, between the ages of nineteen and twenty-seven, weighing less than 135 or 140 pounds, between 5'2" and 5'9" in height, and preferably with some college education. Stewardesses were still prohibited from marrying, and most airlines required stewardesses to resign upon reaching the ripe old age of thirty-two.

But while the employment requirements had not changed much, the stewardess image had changed dramatically. In the first place, the profession had become almost exclusively feminine. By the jet age, the male steward was nearly extinct. In the mid-1940s and the early 1950s, of the flight attendants hired by Pan Am, the last airline to switch over to female stewardesses, 62.7 percent were female. From 1958 to 1969, 98.8 percent of the attendants hired by Pan Am were female.[38]

Femininity was deeply intertwined with consumerism. This feminine profession was all about showcasing a luxurious, consumer-oriented lifestyle, which was now inextricably linked to being an American woman. The jet stewardess was not only a global traveler—she was also a savvy shopper who consumed upscale products. *American Youth* encapsulated the jet stewardess lifestyle: "You can pay frequent visits to Paris, do your shopping on Fifth Avenue, serve dinner to statesman and movie stars and ski regularly in the Austrian Alps—but only if you happen to be rich, or an airline stewardess."[39] A Pan Am stewardess recruitment brochure sold the career similarly: "You lead an exciting life. Your heart is in the clouds . . . your chosen career is stimulating—free from workaday monotony and far, far more than 'just a job.' . . . Your days are filled with the romance of far-away, exotic lands . . . the adventure of our ever-changing world. . . . You enjoy the prestige of a profession that is widely—and deservedly—acclaimed as glamorous. You meet the most fascinating international celebrities."[40]

While airlines had previously portrayed stewardesses as future stay-at-home wives, by the late 1950s airlines were portraying them as glamorous "career girls," and discussions of marriage were intertwined with descriptions of exotic travel and socialite lifestyles. These jet-setting sophisticates had access to prospective wealthy husbands. According to a 1962 American Airlines press release: "When it comes to acquiring a first class husband, stewardesses top the list."[41] National Airlines seduced new recruits with a similar brand of glamour: "So you'd like to be a member of the jet set, live in Miami Beach and wing away frequently to other glamour cities. . . . But you don't have any money. Don't give up hope, if you're an unmarried young lady between the ages of 20 and 25. You can become an airline stewardess. . . . The job is rewarding in many obvious ways . . . you start out as the perfect all-American girl that every man dreams of marrying. National Airlines training will make you even more perfect."[42]

The jet stewardess was also an educated woman versed in global culture and politics. While official education requirements remained the same as before, airlines actually hired more educated women. From 1945 to 1957, for example, 23 percent of the stewardesses hired by Pan Am had high school degrees or less; but from 1958 to 1969, more than 92 percent of the stewardesses hired by Pan Am had at least some college education (and 10 percent had even attended graduate school). Stewardesses were a highly select segment of college-educated women—since, in 1960, only 5.8 percent of American women (ages twenty-five or older) had college degrees.[43]

As part of the glamour campaign, airlines magnified the "college girl" image. In 1957, American Airlines opened the world's first "stewardess college"—a $1 million, ultra-chic campus. Airline ad campaigns publicized the new school as a "resort-like contemporary college" and a finishing school for socialites. The twenty-two-acre campus included a U-shaped building with classrooms, a kitchen, a dining room, a beauty salon, an ultramodern lounge, shuffle-board areas, tennis courts, "spacious bedroom suites,"

"Hollywood style beds," and a pool.[44] The ads featured rookie stewardess learning about aviation technology, cooking, and sunning by the pool—all while looking stylish.

Airlines also concocted glamour by introducing sleek "jet age fashion" to match swanky new jet interiors. In 1958, Pan Am hired the "world-famous Beverly Hills courtier" Don Loper to design jet stewardess uniforms. The Loper uniform appeared in the same "Pan Am blue" as previous uniforms, but it included a pencil silhouette skirt, white gloves, a "jaunty cap" with white piping, and a torso-length four-button jacket that emphasized a defined waistline. The new uniform was "fashionable, feminine and practical."[45] In 1959, United hired the famous industrial designer Raymond Loewy to design jet interiors (complete with "red carpet rooms" aloft) and "Loewy look" uniforms. Oleg Cassini, famous for creating Jackie Kennedy's wardrobe, even designed uniforms for National Airline stewardesses in 1963. This was the first time that airlines hired celebrity fashion designers to fabricate stewardess uniforms. The new uniforms generated publicity whirlwinds as airlines boasted about haute couture designers. These elegant new designs marked a distinct departure from the previous military-style uniforms.[46]

Cleverly, airlines used this glamorous stewardess image to rally huge numbers of well-qualified applicants willing to work for modest wages. In 1957, U.S. airlines had employed approximately 8,000 stewardesses, but by 1967 that number had grown to more than 20,000. In the wake of jet age glamour campaigns, the profession became an even more desirable, prestigious position for young American women. In 1968 more than 266,000 had women applied for 12,000 stewardess openings with U.S.-based airlines, and the Careers Research Corporation reported that senior high school girls ranked the position as the top job they wished to pursue.[47]

But this chic career girl image not only appealed to aspiring stewardesses—it also appealed to women travelers, who dreamed of being this kind of woman. The glamorous career girl stewardess sold an alluring image of a woman with an enviable jet-setting lifestyle who invited middle-class travelers to be part of this elite social world. While airlines had previously only considered women in their ad campaigns because they believed women influenced their husbands' travel choices, jet age airlines became more interested in women as prospective fliers. In 1958, Pan Am hired Jane Kilbourne, the airline's first "women's promotion manager," and in the late 1950s, TWA created a fictitious female travel advisor named Mary Gordon, who appeared in ads offering travel tips for women.[48] The glamorous stewardess was part of this nascent interest in selling air travel to women—a project that would precipitate unexpected new directions in airline advertising.

This career girl stewardess was so captivating to American women because she surfaced just as a new attitude about working women was dawning in American culture. While only 20.6 percent of American wives had earned wages in 1950, that number had grown to 30.5 percent by 1960.[49] In the early 1960s, several women writers anticipated and influenced the nation's evolving gender attitudes by promoting careers for women. In 1963, Betty Freidan's wildly popular *The Feminine Mystique* offered a feminist critique of women's domestic-centered roles of the late 1940s and the 1950s, and urged women to pursue careers. Helen Gurley Brown's bestselling *Sex and the Single Girl* (1962), which celebrated careers and sexual freedom for single women, was a how-to tome for single women aspiring to be glamorous sophisticates. While Brown touted careers for women, calling "career girls" the "newest glamour girl of our times," she did not exactly shatter gender assumptions. Her justification for careerist women hinged on the assumption that women wanted to—and should—get married: a career was the "greatest preparation for marriage." After all, men found "worldly" and "brainy" women even more desirable.[50] Brown soon became the editor of *Cosmopolitan* and went on to promote a vision of glamorous, fashion-centered women through the magazine. The stewardess represented the apex of this burgeoning American icon: the glamorous career girl.

The jet stewardess—who showcased careerist independence, consumerism, beauty, sophistication, and femininity—represented a new aristocratic type of womanhood that was unfolding in America at the time. During the late 1950s, the "aristocratic look" became a popular style in America that could be achieved by anyone with the right consumer products, rather than being a quality reserved for those who had inherited aristocracy.[51]

Another major icon who popularized this emerging brand of American femininity on the heels of the jet stewardess was the wife of the nation's dashing new president, John F. Kennedy. Jacqueline Kennedy, who erupted onto the American cultural scene in 1961, dazzled the American public with her intelligence, charm, and femininity. Not only was she stylish, beautiful, rich, and young, she also spoke several languages, loved art, and read voraciously. She had studied at Vassar, George Washington University, and the Sorbonne. Jackie "made the world safe for brunettes . . . it is now quite all right for a woman to be a bit brainy or cultured," claimed the *New York Times* in 1962. "And hardly anyone considers it affected these days to be able to hold a conversation in a couple of languages." Jackie was the quintessential traditional woman—a consummate homemaker, mother, and wife; but she also worked outside the home. She popularized a new incarnation of American womanhood that was consumer oriented, stylish, elite, smart, and cosmopolitan.[52] But before Jackie made a splash in American culture, the jet stewardess had already hit the cultural scene with a remarkably similar brand of American femininity that enthralled the public.

Like all good aristocrats, the stewardess was cosmopolitan—with especially strong ties to French culture. During the 1950s, when the American middle class chased taste and style, corporations regularly used images of sophisticated Europeans to sell products. U.S. airlines played up their association with French culture as a way to amp up stewardesses' mystique and allure. Paris was still the epicenter of fashion and cuisine, and Americans considered French fashion designers the arbiters of taste. "Frenchness" served as a paragon of high culture—French fashion, cuisine, and champagne were deemed the apex of luxury production. This fascination with French culture filtered into the lives of American stewardesses. Some American stewardesses even sewed French labels into their own clothing.[53]

U.S. airlines heavily publicized French wines, cuisine, and cultural influences. In 1959, U.S. airlines even used a photograph of a French air hostess, Annie Labzine, next to a bust of the ancient Egyptian queen Nefertiti (famous for her beauty), in which the two looked remarkably similar. The image became a public relations sensation in America and the Public Relations Society of America judged the photo as one of the top five publicity photos in 1959. In 1965, National Airlines boasted that stewardesses were trained "to serve and pronounce Quiche Lorraine." The stewardess position was an opportunity to learn "how to pronounce correctly the names of wines like Chateau neuf du Pape" and how to "serve 100 guests with 'cordon bleu' cookery of meals prepared under the supervision of the famed Maxim's of Paris," according to a Pan Am press release.[54]

Airlines in the United States even hired foreign and ethnic stewardesses to bolster the image of an international stewardess corps. During the jet age, Northwest Airlines began dressing hostesses on flights to and from Hawaii in *pake-muu* dresses with long winglike sleeves to create the "Hawaiian hospitality atmosphere." United Airlines began hiring muumuu-clad "island-born" Hawaiian stewardesses to cultivate an exotic, "authentic" experience for travelers. They even provided live in-flight entertainment by singing, dancing the hula, and playing the ukulele.[55]

Pan Am touted its stewardess corps as a "Junior League of Nations," representing dozens of nations around the globe.[56] The airline began hiring Scandinavian-born stewardesses for flights to Europe and publicizing their Nordic physical features. As Pan Am expanded its Pacific routes and anticipated massive jet age expansion, it also hired Japanese American stewardesses purportedly for their language skills. However, in fact, many of the new recruits did not speak Japanese; plus, the airline served so few Japanese passengers at the time that Japanese language speakers were not actually necessary in-flight. Instead, Pan Am used Japanese American stewardesses to bolster the company's reputation for cosmopolitanism. Drawing on stereotypes of Asian women, Pan Am publicized Japanese American stewardesses as subservient geishas, dedicated to pleasing men, who had been specially trained to behave and to look like Pan Am representatives.[57] By the jet age, when airlines were legally forced to hire African American stewardesses, they also publicized black stewardesses as well-trained beacons of multicultural exoticism with all-American feminine charm.

Pan Am hired international stewardesses as part of an exotic spectacle that boosted the airline's reputation for glamorous cosmopolitanism and displayed the airline's mastery of the world. Press releases featured representations of "exotic" women "before" (depicting them standing in indigenous costume) and "after" (depicting them in U.S. airline uniforms). In this way, airlines assimilated "exotic" women into what the anthropologist Christine Yano calls "domesticated otherness." The airline's demonstration of these nonwhite women's professionalism proved that the airline could transform a woman of color into someone equivalent to even the whitest woman.[58]

The new glamour campaign made the American jet stewardess the most cosmopolitan, stylish icon in the world, and airlines attempted to map this new vision of American womanhood onto stewardesses' bodies through strict new beauty standards.

Patrolling Waist Lines, Coiffure, and Girdles

"We had to have monthly weight and appearance checks. . . . We all had to wear girdles," said Peggy Lee Baranowski, who became a Western Airlines stewardess in 1968. "I weighed 102 lbs and I had to wear a girdle!! They checked! They checked every aspect of our appearance and we had to comply."[59]

As airlines rolled out the chic new jet stewardess, they revamped beauty standards to reflect this fresh image. The jet stewardess encapsulated the rising American career girl of the 1960s, who was stylish, upper class, cosmopolitan, and consumer oriented (a la Helen Gurley Brown's vision of the "Cosmo girl"), and these qualities were mapped onto stewardesses' physical bodies. During the 1950s, Italian magazines had depicted American film stars with an elitist chic—an "aristocratic type" embodied by tall, slim, angular women.[60] This glamour girl was elite and knowledgeable about fashion without being sexually available. The jet stewardess represented this aristocratic model of womanhood and airlines tailored stewardesses' physical requirements to convey this new vision. The jet stewardess was taller, slimmer, and more international than her predecessor, the girl next door.

Airlines also became more demanding about crafting an impeccable image of the stewardess. In 1959, the Pan Am "grooming monitor" Miss Roiz sent monthly beauty tip memos to her stewardesses to encourage them to live up to their reputation as the "best-looking stewardesses as well as the best groomed gals in the airline industry."[61] While airlines had maintained strict height and weight standards for stewardesses since the advent of the profession, by the jet age airlines were investing more time and money in standardizing and managing the stewardess look.

In fact, airlines enacted highly specific physical standards and rigorous beauty boot camps to churn out assembly-line women who displayed visual uniformity. Creating a standardized stewardess body was part of airlines' larger strategy to streamline passenger service as jet age air travel ballooned.

Supervisors were given manuals that articulated, in exacting detail, the desirable physical qualities for new stewardesses. Jet-age airlines permitted taller stewardesses, but they also began hiring women within a narrower height range. Pan Am hired stewardesses between 5'2" and 5'11" tall, but by the jet age, the majority of newly hired stewardesses were between 5'4" and 5'7" tall—making the height range a mere three inches.[62]

The stewardess's body became a commodity of sorts that airlines standardized and streamlined, much like their aircraft. For example, airlines drew semiotic and graphic parallels between jet planes and these women's bodies. For example, in 1965, a stewardess grooming manual touted "polishing the appearance of the personnel" as part of the attempt to improve "facilities and equipment." Airline press releases linked the changing heights of stewardesses to technological advances: "as airplanes grow bigger, stewardesses grow taller." American Airlines considered stewardess uniforms a critical marketing opportunity for "the broader story of American's progress and recent product improvements." Its marketing team used new uniforms to showcase technological developments, such as "new galleys, new equipment, [and] computerized maintenance," and to "capitalize on interest in the uniform to call attention to those many other innovations and improvements taking place at the new, modern American." American also organized a tie-in with Ford Motor Company, in which life-size cardboard cutouts of fashionably uniformed stewardesses adorned sixty-five hundred Ford dealerships nationwide. Airlines publicized stewardesses' bodies alongside airplane technology, representing both as visual objects of beauty.[63] By streamlining airplanes and bodies, airlines marketed stewardesses as products with measurable qualities so consumers could expect a consistent service product everywhere (à la McDonald's). Uniformity was key.

Airlines, however, attempted to mask these efforts as they prepared to turn air travel into mass transportation. As widespread critiques of mass culture spread across American society, conformity was criticized as a much-maligned characteristic of mass consumption in such popular literature as *The Organization Man* (1956), *The Man in the Gray Flannel Suit* (1956), and *The Lonely Crowd* (1950). Airlines denied that jet stewardesses exhibited conformity: "This will never mean that we shall have stereotyped, assembly-line cabin attendants all looking and smiling alike, like rows of kewpie dolls in an amusement park. On the contrary, the aim of any program such as this is to develop the personality of each subject as an individual, to make her a more interesting person." Even though airline beauty training transformed women into assembly-line perfection, airlines claimed that grooming programs encouraged each stewardess to cultivate her own unique look.[64]

In this way, airlines marked stewardesses' bodies as distinctly American—after all, even their physical traits supposedly featured individuality—a trademark of the American way. Stewardess individuality was particularly important within the Cold War, when conformity was popularly considered the hallmark of Communism. While "conformity" was anti-American, "individuality" became a Cold War buzzword that distinguished American capitalism. American clichés about individuality gained currency as they came to define the "free world" against Communist Russia.[65] Airlines picked up on this larger dialogue and presented stewardesses as unique individuals with beauty regimens that expressed their individuality.

As airlines sought to create a standard glamour girl look, hiring procedures became more centered on beauty. Airlines had previously requested prospective stewardesses' photos and supervisors made cursory appearance evaluations during interviews (such as "teeth: good; and figure: check").[66] But by 1958, the rules had changed. When Pan Am quizzed supervisors in training on the most important qualification for stewardess applicants, the answer was appearance.[67] The supervisor handbook for American Airlines in 1963 articulated the new cardinal rule of stewardess hiring: "Attractive appearance will be foremost in importance." In fact, management considered this concept so fundamental that the statement was underlined. "The first fundamental is appearance," the handbook went on to say. "A stewardess must be attractive. We can sometimes pretend a person is attractive, if we admire them for some other reason. This should be avoided." Supervisors were instructed to "obtain girls who are above average in appearance, personality and intelligence. If a girl is beautiful, pretty, attractive, she has any woman's most effective attribute in dealing with the public, either men or women. That then, must be our first consideration in obtaining stewardesses."[68]

In elaborate, nearly scientific detail, the American Airlines supervisor handbook outlined physical characteristics for supervisors to consider when recruiting stewardesses. "Facial composition: first of all, the applicant should have a nice, pleasing, well proportioned face. Avoid round face applicants," the manual cautioned. "Watch for scars, moles, superfluous hair. Freckles are okay if becoming." Another no-no: "red rimmed or heavily circled eyes and extremely close set eyes."[69]

In 1960, Pan Am supervisors' written evaluations of interviewees unveiled their primary hiring concerns. They assessed aspiring stewardesses as follows:

Unattractive. 10 lbs overweight, but pretty.
Not attractive. Too thin—unattractive. Dull personality.
Unattractive—red hair. Nice figure, poor complexion.
Poor grooming. Hair unkempt. Heavy legs. Cute but overweight.
Needs to have teeth fixed. Model—cold, passive.
Pretty smile, no personality. Dumpy—head small for body.
Theatrical, too much eyebrow. Pretty eyes, no girdle.
Bleached blonde. Large nose.[70]

In the late 1950s, a Northwest Airlines interviewer deemed one stewardess applicant "very charming—good conversationalist," but noted a "small surface artery on [her] nose" and a burn mark on her lip, which disqualified her.[71]

Body shape was now critical for stewardess hopefuls as well. Supervisors were trained to ferret out whether applicants had pretty legs and were forbidden from hiring women with "large calves," "exceptionally thin calves," or "exceptionally large ankles."[72] During interviews, prospective stewardesses were asked to pull their skirts above their knees to display their legs, and to walk across the room. One prospective stewardess reported that her second interview for Western Airlines was conducted by three men—one of whom measured her head, neck, shoulder, upper arm, wrist, bodice, waist, hips, upper thigh, calf, and ankle.[73]

"A perfect figure is a bust and hip measurement of the same dimension and a waist 10 inches less," according to a stewardess supervisor manual of 1963. The manual, however, permitted a bust three inches smaller than the hips, with the caveat that this smaller bust allowance was for a "trial period" only. "Our applicants should have well-proportioned figures," Pan Am told stewardess supervisors. "Preferably with small hips as they are at eye-level when a passenger is seated."[74]

Although the official weight limits for stewardesses remained similar before and during the jet age, airlines began hiring thinner stewardesses as they sought to convey an image of upper-class feminine beauty. By 1958, slimmer was better. The height/weight ratios (calculated as body mass indexes—BMIs) for Pan Am stewardess hires had dropped substantially by the jet age. In the pre-jet years, only 59 percent of newly hired Pan Am stewardesses had BMIs between 18 and 20; by the jet age, 89 percent of new Pan Am stewardesses had BMIs that low. During the earlier era, more than 34 percent had BMIs over 21; by the jet age, only 5.4 percent had BMIs that high.[75]

Airlines hired thinner stewardesses during the late 1950s and the 1960s partly because slim bodies suggested a particular class identity. Trim figures were central to defining the aristocratic brand of American womanhood that was becoming popular in America. Slimmer stewardesses also reflected a broader cultural trend toward a thinner female figure ideal. A number of studies have documented a trend toward declining weights of fashion models, Miss America contestants, and *Playboy* centerfolds since the 1950s. While full-breasted, curvy female figures were popular in the 1950s, by the 1960s the ideal female body in America had become slimmer, with an androgynous and childlike figure.[76] Airlines hired thinner stewardesses to represent the ideal American woman and to embody the new upper-class model of American womanhood.

Airlines rarely accepted applicants who were a few pounds over airline weight restrictions and, when they did, their employment was conditional upon weight loss. "I positively starve to keep my weight down. . . . The secret is—just don't eat," declared Lucinda Lee Goodrich, a stewardess who represented Pan Am in the International Air Hostess Contest of 1966.[77] Her dieting advice was published in Pan Am's employee newsletter. Airlines even issued figure measurement reference charts, and stewardesses in training were expected to compare their bust, waist, hip, thigh, calf, and ankle measurements to these charts to determine whether they had "good proportions." Stewardesses were weighed weekly during training and faced suspension if they failed to keep their weight within the permitted range.

Beyond weekly weigh-ins, stewardess school had become a veritable beauty boot camp, complete with instructions on everything from body hair removal methods to which color panties to wear. In 1960, American Airlines' six-week stewardess training program totaled roughly 120 hours, with 20 hours dedicated exclusively to beauty. The same year, Pan Am's stewardess training devoted 27 hours to grooming and only 20 to first aid.[78]

Stewardess training featured posture instruction, stomach-slimming exercises, and skin care procedures as well as detailed lessons on rouge application and face cleansing. The Pan Am manual even included diagrams of various mouth shapes with coaching on how to apply lipstick to each mouth type and how to have a "more beautiful smile." Instructors warned trainees about the perils of "body odor" and "superfluous hair." Pan Am's manual now expressly regulated body hair: "Female attendants must remove hair from legs and underarms. Excessive hairs on face, forearms, or feet must be removed by depilatories or electrolysis."[79] Even though stewardesses' feet were always covered with shoes, foot hair was also listed as a no-no.

At United Airlines, supervisors educated fledgling stewardesses on how to "sit like a lady, stand like a model, walk like a queen." Turning out regal stewardesses required extensive training in the charm-school fundamental— "visual poise." Beyond learning to stand with a back foot at a 45-degree angle, these budding models of ladylike poise received comprehensive instruction on how to walk up stairs elegantly and how to "eradicate mannerisms." United even issued a handout on standing gracefully to outline the basics: "hands look graceful in profile only. The motion should fall naturally from the wrist into a graceful pose." And, of course, the fingers should always be curved. "When hands are empty, place one hand behind your hip so it is invisible from the front. Place other hand on thigh with forefinger resting on thigh." The "RULES OF NEVER!!!" cautioned: "Never sit in a position that causes your calves to bulge!"[80]

Grooming training still emphasized "the importance of the natural look," but stewardess school now featured even more detailed instruction on cultivating this look of sophistication sans sexual availability. Stewardesses were warned to "beware" of certain cosmetics (such as eye shadow and mascara) that could result in a "hard" or "jaded look," which suggested promiscuity; and, airlines issued particular instructions about eyebrows. By the 1950s, American women had adopted the trend (started by the Swedish-born film star Greta Garbo) of removing their eyebrows and penciling them in. But Garbo had originally been portrayed as a vamp in Hollywood films and airlines did not want stewardesses to be associated with this seductive, dangerous female archetype. They therefore taught stewardesses to pencil their eyebrows in a way that steered clear of that sexually threatening female archetype. American Airlines issued diagrams of prohibited eyebrow shapes that were "too sharp" or gave a "Halloween look."[81]

Cosmetic color choices conveyed meaning as well, so airlines carefully outlined permitted options. A memo for Pan Am stewardesses in 1959 provided a rationale for limiting make-up color choices based on a survey by a team of psychiatrists. Since "outlandish" make-up and nail polish shades usually indicated some "unsatisfied personality need" or "emotional disturbance," these colors were forbidden. Pan Am proclaimed: "Lipstick must be worn at all times while in uniform. Nail polish is optional. Lipstick and nail polish must be in basic shades—such as red, rose-red, or coral shades. Lavender, purple, orange, insipid pink, iridescent or flesh color lipsticks and nail polish are not permitted."[82]

Airlines also controlled stewardesses' hairstyles and colors to concoct the right image. While the perfect stewardess had previously been a brunette, by the jet age the ideal stewardess was a blonde. This shift reflected broader beauty trends. In the late 1950s and the early 1960s, dyed blonde hair had become widely acceptable in American culture and was no longer heavily associated with burlesque dancers. Blondes had replaced brunettes as the dominant beauty type in America by the late 1950s—after Marilyn Monroe had erupted onto the cultural scene. The Clairol company had also catalyzed this shift by improving artificial hair dye to give a more natural look and by launching a major ad campaign for blonde hair in 1956. But even though blonde dye had become mainstream by the late 1950s, airlines continued to forbid it. A guide for aspiring stewardesses written in 1966 by a former stewardess and stewardess school director warned: "More applicants are turned down because of bleached, tinted, dyed or artificially streaked hair than for any other single reason!"[83]

The new blonde stewardess did not represent the iconic corn-fed wholesome midwestern girl, nor did she represent the brazen sexuality of Marilyn Monroe; rather, she was a cosmopolitan glamour girl who knew about style and traveled the world. She was still a "natural" blonde—and, thus, devoid of any implications of promiscuity—but now blonde hair marked her as international. Airlines even began recruiting Scandinavian stewardesses because they were often natural blondes. Airlines publicized blonde stewardesses, highlighting their European cachet. In 1963, for example, National Airlines started a stewardess exchange program with Scandinavian Airlines stewardesses and press releases touted the "pretty Swedish born stewardess," "blonde beauties," and the "blonde, statuesque Bjory Grosfield, who deserted the ranks of international fashion models" to become a stewardess. In 1958, a Pan Am promotional story about stewardesses contained a press release with blanks to be filled out in each local area. "Blond, blue-eyed ____ (stewardess name) has no intention of settling down but wants to go right on flying until she has seen all the countries that Pan American flies to, which includes most of the world."[84]

Stewardesses received mandatory haircuts in training and airlines prohibited seductive, "masculine," or "extreme" styles. While airlines had required hair above the collar, now manuals contained elaborate instructions on hairstyles permitted, featuring photographs of acceptable (and unacceptable) hairstyles. American Airlines mandated that hairstyles be both "feminine and business-like." Pan Am also emphasized a conservative, feminine look and the airline's list of banned styles reflected that image: "French twist, shaggy, masculine hair cuts, hair split on either side of exposed ear, theatrical or extreme styles, which includes frosting or streaking, bouffant or excessive hair back combing." Stewardesses had to request management's permission to change their hairstyle or color.[85]

"We had beehive hairdos with hats on top. We looked ridiculous, but it was the style then. We thought we were high fashion," said one former stewardess.[86] Stewardesses relished being part of beauty culture; they cherished being international fashion icons. One stewardess trainee for Pan Am brimmed with excitement about her new look in a letter home: "The first thing we had to do was to have our hair done by Mr. Leon. . . . They are very strict about the short hairdos. Absolutely no hair on the collar, no French rolls, pony tails, etc. I have large spit curls on the sides of my face. It's supposed to be very stylish."[87] Stylish uniforms, chic hair, and immaculate appearances bolstered these women's sense of professional prestige.

Airlines' high standards and rigorous training programs (including beauty school) contributed to building a sense of self-confidence, professional pride, and camaraderie among stewardesses. These young women created their professional identities around the difficult training program, their specialized knowledge, and their flawless physical appearances.

But while stewardesses savored their stylishness, at times they also found airline beauty policies restrictive and demeaning. One former Eastern Airlines stewardess remembered removing her hat while dining with the crew. Later she was called into her supervisor's office and reprimanded. "The supervisor circled me like I was her prey and I was told to never remove my hat again," she recalled.[88]

"Even our underwear was an issue," said one former Pan Am stewardess. "The word was that a pat on the fanny to verify the wearing of a girdle was part of the checklist." Even though stewardess work involved a substantial amount of bending for many hours, girdles were required. "Girdles, white bras and white full-length slips must be worn at all times when in uniform, regardless of physical build or climatic conditions," decreed the Pan Am manual.[89]

By regulating the stewardess look down to underwear, airlines extended authority over women's whole bodies. In addition to cultivating the precise look they wanted in order to sell air travel, airlines used strict grooming training to indoctrinate stewardesses into corporate ideals and behaviors. In this way, airlines built a corps of proud customer-service perfectionists with high standards and company loyalty.

Stewardesses were routinely examined by "grooming monitors," who conducted meticulous inspections to ensure slim figures and company-approved nail polish colors. Jet-age grooming monitors became even more detail-oriented in their appearance checks and began issuing more beauty violations. Earlier stewardess evaluations had concentrated primarily on performance and only briefly mentioned "appearance." For example, TWA's 1942 "hostess personal check report" included several categories about general appearance ("cosmetics, uniform cleanliness"), but this section comprised less than one-eighth of the entire evaluation form. Most of the form concerned stewardess duties, such as whether stewardesses checked seat belts. Similarly, Pan Am stewardess checks in the mid-1940s were completed by male captains and focused primarily on "efficiency," duties performed, and personality. Reports included such remarks as "intelligent and a good worker" with only a cursory mention of appearance (such as "neat" or "very neat").[90]

By the late 1950s and the 1960s, airlines had introduced new steward-ess evaluation forms that focused more on appearance. In 1962, United's new in-flight report form for stewardesses was divided into three sections: grooming, manner, and procedures. The grooming section contained a detailed list, including "uniform, shoes, purse, suitcase, make-up, hair style/color, nails manicured." Moreover, supervisors no longer simply checked off every item; now, they commented on each category.[91]

It was common for stewardesses to get reprimanded (and punished) for beauty infractions. For example, in 1961, a grooming monitor reported one stewardess because her hair was "a little too long and is not of natural color." In 1964, another evaluation determined that the hair of this same stewardess was "thin on sides—ears protrude—hair style is flat and not attractive." She was then required to show her hairstyle to management for approval before flights. Stewardesses were often put on probation, grounded, or fired for beauty infractions.[92] Ultimately, beauty would become the central battleground in stewardesses' fight to keep their jobs.

Beacons of Beauty, Consumerism, and Technology to the Globe

The pretty American stewardess was not simply an innocuous, apolitical symbol designed to sell travel domestically. She was also an international icon who sold America to the world. Beauty was a powerful political weapon. On the Cold War propaganda stage, beauty played a potent role in asserting each nation's superiority abroad and selling each nation's political and economic system to the world. In the midst of this global contest, the American jet stewardess represented a particular vision of the nation itself—an embodi-ment of abundance, freedom, consumerism, and glamour. As a cultural ambassador, the American jet stewardess would assume an important post at international cultural exchanges during the Cold War.

The jet age overlapped with a period of increased cultural contact between the Soviet Union and the West, which American politicians and corporations used to promote the American way. The 1958 Brussels World's Fair, for example, served as a forum for the United States and Europe to garner popular support for the crusade against Communism and to glorify the globalization of corporate capitalism. Drawing on this larger ideology, Pan Am's exhibit at the fair, titled "Pan American World," envisioned the airline's global expansion as a benevolent project that spread America's technologically based consumer paradise. The display featured an enormous inflatable globe (fifty-two feet in diameter) that seated 160 people and was complete with "astral effects including twilight, moving clouds and a star-filled sky which serve[d] as the background for a short film dramatizing the shrink-

The Pan Am exhibit at the 1958 Brussels World's Fair.
Courtesy Smithsonian National Air and Space Museum.

ing time and space from Magellan's cruise 400 years ago to the Jet Clippers of today" and a "simulated light of a U.S. satellite missile across space."[93] The crowning glory of the airline's international conquest: the corps of smiling, stylish Pan Am stewardesses who stood, hand-in-hand, circling this gigantic globe.

The exhibit exemplified Pan Am's larger jet age advertising strategy, which exploited larger Cold War narratives to sell tickets. As the number of Americans traveling overseas ballooned with jets, U.S. policymakers and airline executives promoted American tourists as ambassadors. Aligning consumption (through tourism) with diplomacy, the U.S. government promoted tourism as a way for American citizens to sell U.S. foreign policy overseas and to win the Cold War. In the late 1950s, President Eisenhower founded People to People, which promoted overseas tourism for American citizens as an important component of U.S. foreign policy during the Cold War.[94]

In America, one popular way of thinking about U.S. involvement around the globe was to see it as a benevolent enterprise—a consumer-friendly form of imperialism—that facilitated world peace through cross-cultural "friendship" and "understanding." This narrative configured America as a "friendly" nation that promoted benevolent, universal interests (such as peace)—and, thus, legitimized the globalization of corporate capitalism.[95]

Even the U.S. government considered projecting an image of American women as glamorous consumer-oriented style icons to be central to international politics. For example, as part of its campaign to shape global public opinion during the ideological war between the Soviets and the Americans, the United States Information Agency (USIA) capitalized on, and amplified, Jackie Kennedy's growing currency as a style icon. The USIA funded documentaries about her that were circulated widely overseas, catapulting her to international fame as a cultural diplomat with potent political clout. One presidential historian described her as a public relations asset both at home and abroad who forged "inroads against communism by wearing a pillbox hat and redecorating her home."[96] Kennedy aimed to use her style to promote a vision of America itself as glamorous overseas. Her fashion designer, Oleg Cassini, noted, "Jackie and I wanted to create an American-International fashion look, and at the same time give a boost to the American fashion industry. . . . At that time, people were looking to Europe for trends, and American fashion was not even considered . . . the 'Jackie Kennedy look' became a worldwide trendsetter."[97]

Similarly, airline executives used stewardesses as representatives of the glorious American way. In a speech about the federal program People to People, Pan Am president Juan Trippe called international air travel "an important contribution to [the American] economy" and a "strategy in selling the U.S. and [its] 'way-of-life' to people of other nations." Pan Am's jet-age ad team aimed to depict a "friendly company of patriotic human beings" and to "demonstrate the contribution that Pan Am is making to the U.S. and the free world as a whole" by promoting the airline as a "human link between the peoples of the world—and particularly between Americans and citizens of overseas lands." The core of the campaign was, of course, the stewardess. A beacon of the American way, she represented "national friendliness" and paraded the "friendliness" of each aviation corporation (and, of America itself) to the world.[98] Friendliness would later become the cornerstone of airline ad campaigns.

At the forefront of jet age advertising campaigns, these cosmopolitan, glamorous stewardesses represented American identity around the world. As foreign travel flourished, international airlines competed to win overseas-bound American travelers through stewardesses. Each airline depicted its stewardesses as an idealized vision of its nation's women. The cover of *Esquire* magazine for February 1964 featured a photograph of forty international airline stewardesses displaying a range of uniforms from saris to pillbox hats (see the illustration on page 92). Exploring the national characteristics of stewardesses from around the world, the cover story called these women the decisive factor in choosing an airline.

As each international airline claimed to have the world's finest women, U.S. airlines portrayed American stewardesses as the most modern, most glamorous, and most feminine women in the world. The American stewardess, who civilized the "uncivilized" women of the world by teaching American beauty secrets or delivering American beauty products, became an increasingly dominant trope in U.S. airline publicity during the post-Sputnik jet era through the late 1960s. American stewardesses often appeared teaching less feminine women of implicitly inferior Third World or Communist nations how to "become women"—particularly through cosmetics, grooming, and fashion. In this way, American stewardesses sold America abroad. Also, by "civilizing" or teaching foreign women how to be more feminine, according to American notions about womanhood, American stewardesses were positioning a particularly American model of femininity as the universal standard.

American stewardesses who volunteered overseas in the early 1960s, for example, were depicted as ambassadors who spread the American way abroad. Beginning in 1961, stewardesses from various U.S. airlines took leaves of absences to volunteer abroad with the Thomas A. Dooley Foundation, which promoted international health and education to help "people to understand people." During the 1960s, the Dooley Foundation Stewardess Program hosted more than 190 stewardesses from 26 airlines; the stewardesses volunteered in India, Laos, or Nepal for a minimum of three months at a time. Airlines considered these "Dooley girls" PR gold. "When girls like the Pan Am stewardesses go to help, they sell America by their own actions. [The Dooley foundation director] believes that free peoples should have the choice between the two systems of freedom and communism, but they can't make a good choice unless they know the free side," according to one Pan Am press release.[99] Stewardesses sold not only the corporation, but also America through their image and actions overseas—particularly, by teaching American grooming and consumption habits to female foreigners.

One "Dooley girl"—a blonde Pan Am stewardess dubbed "Angel Goddess" in the media—was featured in dozens of U.S. newspapers for her work with Tibetan orphans in northern India.[100] Pan Am issued numerous press releases on this stewardess-volunteer's exploits. In articles such as "Angel Teacher Brings America to Refugee Tots," the media heralded "the pretty blonde lady" for her ambassadorship overseas.[101] Mentioning that she was blonde several times, Pan Am's employee magazine boasted that this stewardess was the "first white woman" the children ever had contact with. When reflecting on working with Tibetan refugee orphans whose parents had fled Tibet or been killed during the Communist takeover, the stewardess's press comments focused on the orphan girls' hairstyles: "None of the poor little girls had combs. Their hair was pretty unkempt and ragged. But soon we got combs for them and they spent a lot of time combing their hair.

Combs were a priceless possession." She went on to say, "The general hair style was bangs, it was the only one I knew how to do . . . but I must say, I got better as I went along."[102] It was as if bad hair (and the absence of combs) was the real international tragedy—and style was America's humanitarian aid contribution.

Stewardess colleges in the United States even trained foreign women to become "modern" through American cosmetics and grooming practices. When Pan Am's stewardess college opened an "image improvement" course to teach beauty secrets to women employed in other departments, the airline's employee magazine commended the course for training a "girl who had ridden elephants, hobnobbed with maharajas and speaks fluent Hindu."[103] Another article in the *Clipper* titled "Girl on a Frontier" applauded an American-born Pan Am stewardess, who served as a chief hostess advisor for Pakistan International Airlines (PIA), for helping to "unveil the modern world of jet travel for a young and growing Eastern nation." This American stewardess reported, "Only a generation ago Pakistani women were not permitted to appear in public without a veil or to work outside their own homes" and she was proud to announce that under her supervision Pakistani girls had "changed their long veils for the native uniform of PIA."[104]

U.S. airlines positioned stewardesses as the world's prettiest, most glamorous women. Within the Cold War context, beauty became an even more important symbolic marker of American identity and an international assertion of America's political and economic dominance. At a time when few Americans traveled behind the Iron Curtain, American stewardesses represented the American way on the front line of the Cold War. These U.S. ambassadors would don glamorous garb and flawless lipstick to face America's rival empire.

5

Vodka, Tea, or Me?

IT WAS a glorious, clear day in New York. A cheering crowd gathered on the tarmac to watch as the behemoth blue and silver jet screeched to a halt at the John F. Kennedy International Airport. Stewardesses from America's enemy empire stepped off the plane, pausing in the aircraft doorway to wave and smile as reporters snapped photos.[1] Pan Am's chairman welcomed the Russians with open arms.

The cause for celebration was the inauguration of direct commercial air service between the Soviet Union and the United States. Throughout the bitter Cold War, there had been no direct air service between the rival nations, but after ten years of fitful negotiations that stalled and progressed in response to fluctuating Soviet-American political tensions, this all changed. On July 15, 1968, the first regularly scheduled Moscow–New York flights began under a joint agreement between Pan Am and Aeroflot.

Even though the flights between New York and Moscow would not be financially profitable, numerous U.S. airlines had lobbied hard for that prestigious route since winning it was considered a high-profile PR coup for an airline.[2] Pan Am was awarded the route and assumed its position as America's flagship carrier, and by extension Pan Am stewardesses would represent the United States on this historic voyage into enemy territory.

Despite the paltry number of travelers on the route (fewer than thirty thousand Americans visited the Soviet Union in 1966), politicians, airline executives, and reporters heralded the new flights as a momentous mile-

Life magazine, July 26, 1968.
Courtesy Time and Life Pictures/Getty Images.

stone in international relations and a barometer of Cold War thaw. Eugene Rostow, the U.S. undersecretary for political affairs, called the first flight "a new forum in the peaceful dialogue among our peoples," and in a welcome speech to the Soviets, Pan Am chairman Harold Gray heralded the flight as an opportunity "to bridge the gap of distance with friendship." A former diplomat in Moscow said the air service would "result in an improvement in relations between our countries and contribute to peace and stability in the world." One reporter called it "more symbolic than whole coveys of heavenly doves" and a greater move toward "world peace and understanding . . . than all the summit conferences and disarmament treaties." *Newsweek* proclaimed: "Blue Skies, Champagne and Caviar Make Cold War Seem Lost to Oblivion." *Air Travel*, the official airline guide, reported that the passenger volume was less important than the "symbolic air bridge linking the two nations."[3]

But for all the talk of bridges and doves, at its core the route was a flashpoint in the propaganda war—a global stage on which national ideals could be paraded. As Aeroflot and Pan Am faced off, the jet-setting women aboard were symbols of their nations' ideals. Deployed to glamorize technological achievements and to represent national identity overseas, stewardesses served as cultural ambassadors of rival empires—they became front-line icons in the global culture war and represented competing visions of ideal womanhood on the world stage.

American media coverage of the flight focused on technology, interior design, meal service, and, of course, stewardesses. Each element formed a critical component of national prestige—especially, the uniformed women. The American press covered the event with gusto—and nearly every article on the flight featured an evaluation of stewardesses and paid a substantial amount of attention to their physical appearances. The American stewardess appeared consistently as a specifically American brand of womanhood—she was a stylish, pretty, heterosexual, middle-class, consumer-oriented wife to be. At the same time, American reporters portrayed Aeroflot stewardesses as "plump and plain" and "a little chunkier than their American sisters." The *Journal of Commerce* reported: "The [Aeroflot] stewardesses will not be the usual slim, shiekly [*sic*] dressed girl. The Russians like their girls more on the dumpy side and the uniforms run to bulk, rather than trim lines." American media often assumed that modern design, friendly service, and pretty women were exclusive achievements of American capitalism—and that Communism bred dour, chubby stewardesses who were, according to the *San Francisco Chronicle*, "less inclined to pamper the clientele."[4]

This showdown between Soviet and American stewardesses reflected the broader ideological war between the Soviets and the Americans. The question of which nation's women had better lives was a recurring theme in the Soviet-American spin campaigns and beauty became central terrain in the battle for global prestige.[5]

In all the transatlantic Cold War mudslinging, the mainstream American media painted a decidedly unflattering portrait of Soviet women as frumpy, mannish, exploited workers set in stark contrast to stylish American women who applied lipstick and enjoyed shiny new toasters in their suburban dream homes. American policymakers (and journalists) touted pretty American women as a testament to the success of capitalism and democracy. Meanwhile, the Aeroflot stewardess embodied a distinctly Soviet vision of womanhood— she was a worker and loyal Communist Party member, rather than a pretty wife in training. Soviet propaganda flaunted Soviet women's workforce participation as evidence of gender equality and proof of Communism's superiority. American housewives were portrayed as oppressed victims of capitalist patriarchy, which limited women to unpaid household duties and granted men the bulk of power. These competing visions of femininity were deeply intertwined with larger Cold War debates about the merits of Communism and capitalism.[6] This ideological clash, however, also had unintended consequences as ideas about gender crept across international borders and ultimately transformed both nations.

Communist Butches, Pneumatic Drills, Prudes, and Lipstick

In 1956, the famed American Airline stewardess Mildred Jackson won another award for her remarkable record selling airline tickets. The prize was a trip around the world, including a stop in the Soviet Union, which seldom approved visas for American visitors. When Jackson won the trip, the two nations were deeply embroiled in the Cold War and there was no direct air service between them. Few Americans had the opportunity to travel to the Soviet Union and the American press had limited access to life behind the Iron Curtain; the Soviets were largely an enigma.

During Mildred Jackson's expedition into this mysterious empire, she wrote a series of tell-all articles for the *Chicago Daily Tribune* on her impressions of Soviet women. As an example of glamorous womanhood, the

American stewardess took it upon herself to teach a Soviet woman how to be more feminine. In "American Introduces Russian Girl to Lipstick," Jackson wrote: "I was putting on lipstick. Suddenly, I realized [the Russian woman] was standing at my shoulder, intrigued." When Jackson showed the Russian woman how to apply lipstick, "she was delighted and went running to the mirror with it. . . . It created an immediate bond—we were females collaborating in a masculine world to acquire adornment and glamour. Somehow it seemed sad to me. Here was a grown woman who had never before had lipstick."[7]

Jackson's take on Soviet women betrayed her own—very American— concepts about womanhood, consumerism, beauty, technology, and democracy. From Jackson's perspective, women needed consumer goods such as girdles, lipstick, and fashionable dresses to be pretty and feminine. Consumption was not only a way to express her true feminine identity, but it was also critical to her American identity. By yoking consumer choice to political freedom, Jackson disclosed a larger trend in American attitudes about consumption in the postwar era: mass consumption was now conflated with democratic political freedom.[8] Pretty, stylish women had become the hallmark of the American way.

Across the Atlantic, however, Soviet politicians claimed that women were better off red. Soviet notions about womanhood were fundamentally different from American conceptions. While the model American woman was a pretty, dependent, homemaker and consumer, the ideal Soviet woman was a worker, equal citizen, and loyal political participant. Soviet magazines imagined the perfect woman as confident, modest, ambitious, self-sacrificial, heroic, and strong.[9] Most importantly, the Soviet regime espoused a model of womanhood that hinged on women's status as workforce producers (rather than consumers—the heralded role for American women at the time). Women's role in the workforce was fundamental to Communist ideology—dating back to *The Origin of the Family, Private Property and the State*, written by Frederick Engels in 1884. In foundational Communist texts, women's social and economic inequality was seen as a capitalist byproduct and limiting women to unpaid household labor represented the apex of capitalist exploitation. After the Russian Revolution of 1917, the Soviet state removed legal restrictions on women's equal employment and attempted to alter the traditional family by shifting domestic responsibilities to public institutions, such as state-run childcare facilities. The Soviet Constitution of 1936 laid out women's role: "Women in the USSR are accorded equal rights with men, in all spheres of economic, government, cultural, political and other public activities."[10]

Beyond the ideological foundations of women's workforce participation, World War II radically altered the Soviet Union's demographics and made women even more integral to the Soviet labor force. The Soviets had lost approximately 20 million people (14 percent of the nation's population) during the war, and in 1946 women outnumbered men by 26 million in the Soviet Union. In 1946, among those aged thirty-five to fifty-nine, there were only 59.1 males for every 100 females. In 1945, women composed more than half of the Soviet workforce. Between 1922 and 1974, the total number of women workers in the Soviet Union rose from 1.5 million to over 51 million.

Soviet politicians used working women to bolster the nation's esteem in the global culture clash. Hyping up female politicians, astronauts, doctors, and pilots, Soviet propaganda touted women's workforce participation as evidence of Soviet gender equality and Communist superiority. The Soviets would even be the first to send a woman into space in 1963 (a full twenty years before Americans would follow suit), which they flaunted internationally to score points on gender equality.[11]

In 1956, the Soviet Union hosted an international seminar for the UN Commission on the Status of Women, with the professed purpose of teaching other nations about the "Soviet experience in establishing real equality for women." Ninety-eight women representing thirty-nine countries attended such lectures as "Soviet Women Have Equal Political Rights with Men and Take an Active Part in Government," "Soviet Women Enjoy Equal Civil Rights with Men," and "Equality of Soviet Women in the Economic Sphere." The upshot: the so-called free world oppressed women by confining them to domesticity and granting husbands greater legal control over family resources. Nina Popova, a member of the U.S.S.R. Central Council of Trade Unions, summed up Soviet notions about working women in her lecture: "The petty, dull and stupefying work in the kitchen and the home fettered woman and prevented her from displaying her intellectual abilities. For centuries it was considered that the housewife . . . was the personification of womanly virtues. . . . It is well known that in some countries married women are either dismissed from work or not engaged. . . . I cannot imagine myself shut off even for a short period from the common work, which has united our whole people into one family."[12]

Seminar speakers condemned capitalist countries for failing women by not ensuring equal pay for equal work: "Remuneration of feminine work by comparison with equal work done by men represents one of the most subtle and criminal forms of exploitation." The seminar praised Communism for providing women with "equal pay for equal work"—a slogan and demand that would later become a hallmark of the American women's movement in the late 1960s.[13]

But in the late 1940s throughout the 1950s, when feminism was virtually dormant in the United States and women were expected to become full-time homemakers, the Soviet women-in-the-workforce ethic did not sit well with the American public. Americans found Soviet women unsettling—to say the least. Soviet women exacerbated broader cultural anxieties about women's roles in midcentury America. During the postwar years, more women in America were, in fact, entering the workforce in spite of dominant media messages that portrayed homemaking as the *sin qua non* of womanhood. The disjuncture between the American feminine ideal and the reality of more women in the workforce stirred up deep cultural tensions about gender roles. Working women in America dodged criticism by casting their work as "feminine" and by promising to fulfill their true feminine destinies as full-time homemakers upon receiving a marriage proposal (a la the mythical American stewardess).[14] The Soviet woman, however, was a loud and proud worker who made no promise to abandon wage work for full-time domesticity; and this type of woman ran directly counter to mainstream feminine ideals in America, which hinged on dependence, domesticity, and consumerism.

This Soviet-American ideological contest between models of womanhood also played out vividly during Cold War cultural exchanges, which became more common during the post-Stalin era known as the Thaw, when the Soviet Union partially reversed repression and allowed more cultural contact with the West through art shows, international festivals, and other cultural events. American politicians considered these affairs important opportunities for "cultural diplomacy" by boosting America's image overseas to gain allies around the world.[15]

The 1959 American national exhibition in Moscow offered one such opportunity. Although the exhibition was couched as an attempt to forge mutual understanding between the two nations, U.S. politicians considered it a platform for selling the American way of life. The national exhibition, which was sponsored by the U.S. government, displayed America as a dazzling, technologically advanced consumer paradise. Eight hundred U.S. manufacturers paraded the latest gadgets—all purportedly priced to sell to an "average" American family. The centerpiece of this technological pageant was a model suburban home (cut in half so it could be viewed easily), brimming with consumer devices that demonstrated the glories of American capitalism.

The opening of the exhibition featured the "kitchen debate"—an infamous impromptu tête-à-tête between Premier Khrushchev of the Soviet Union and Vice President Nixon of the United States, which took place in the symbolic heart of 1950s America—the kitchen. As Khrushchev toured the model American kitchen, Nixon launched into a scathing critique of the Communist economy and claimed America's technological preeminence based on the modern consumer amenities available to American housewives—such as dishwashers, lipstick, and TV dinners. Nixon evoked the image of a homely Soviet woman suffering from a dearth of modern appliances pitted against the pretty American homemaker, who epitomized Western freedom, prosperity, and glamour. The Soviet magazine *Izvestia*, however, slammed the display: "What is this? A national exhibit of a great country, or a branch department store?"[16] Khrushchev staked claims of Communist superiority on Soviet technology and women's participation in the labor force. "We think highly of our women . . . we never put them in the same class as capitalists," Khrushchev retorted. "Our women work."[17]

This standoff represented the core of the Soviet-American war of ideas. The debate between two fundamentally opposed ways of life shows how America's identity and image centered on the critical trifecta: technology, consumerism, and gender. Nixon sold America as a technologically based consumer wonderland where women could be real women by consuming (rather than producing), beautifying, and being domestic. In America, technology had paved the way for consumerism—now the central feature of democracy. Meanwhile, Khrushchev represented the Soviet Union as a nation with powerful industrial and space technology (such as Sputnik), where women were treated as equal workers/producers and political participants.

And, in the global image war, U.S. politicians used the flourishing mass consumption economy to represent the nation's political superiority over the Soviet Union. Consumerism had become central to American identity and image during the Cold War—and it was fundamental to America's political strategy. Instead of relying exclusively on an arms race, U.S. politicians embraced a Cold War strategy dubbed the "Nylon War"—whereby they displayed American consumer goods in attempts to dazzle Soviets so much that they would revolt against the Communist regime.[18]

Politicians were not the only ones spouting this techno-consumerist vision of national identity. The deeply embedded notion that technologically advanced consumerism was essential to expressing identity made the Soviet way of life utterly perplexing. Soviet women's bizarre, seemingly unfeminine behavior and appearance served as a lightning rod for this larger Cold War culture clash. This very American consumer ideal bled into mainstream American discourse as well as airline stewardess travelogues.

While Mildred Jackson reveled in the technologically advanced consumer splendor available to American women, the mainstream American press disparaged Soviet homes and kitchens as "old fashioned" and generally "backward" because they lacked "luxuries" and "labor-saving devices."[19] The *Saturday Evening Post*, in "The Sorry Life of Soviet Women," presented a dismal view of Soviet domesticity: "Has the Soviet female also been freed from homemaking? To a large extent, yes. Not as her American counterpart has, through the development of labor-saving devices and services, but because in Russia there is very little home to make."[20] Denouncing Soviet domestic life constituted a weighty criticism in an era when Americans considered the suburban dream house—and its attendant consumer appliances—central to the good life. The dearth of domestic consumer goods implied not only that the Soviets mistreated their women, but also that Communism itself was floundering.

During the early Cold War years, as the Red Scare in America swelled, American travel writers and journalists (often women writers who traveled to the Soviet Union with their reporter husbands) painted bleak portraits of Soviet women, casting them primarily as ugly, unfeminine, exploited workers—deprived of the domestic bliss and consumer wonders available to American women. Throughout the Cold War, American media portrayals of Soviet women focused on their frumpy looks, chubby physiques, shoddy cosmetics, unfashionable clothing, back-breaking work, and generally "mannish" appearances. American writers characterized Soviet women as "plump," "plain," "dowdy," "stocky," "husky," "robust," "chunky," and "mannish." An American journalist summed up this take on Soviet women: "On the whole Russian women are not pretty. They tend toward the heavy or chunky side."[21] For Americans, looking ugly had important international consequences. It suggested a faulty political and economic system and national inferiority.

From the American perspective, Soviet women were, in essence, not real women—they were gender-bending curiosities that presented a host of confusing and troubling questions for the American public. In the era when June Cleaver homemakers pervaded the American cultural landscape, Soviet women's wage-work rendered their femininity suspect and generated substantial debate in the American press during the Cold War. Although American journalists came to different conclusions about whether Soviet women managed to retain their "femininity" in spite of their "hard work," the issue itself was central to American narratives about Soviet women. At the heart of these discussions was the question: could women be workers who performed "men's jobs" and still be *women*? The question itself reveals an undercurrent of concerns about what it meant to be an American woman at the time and suggests the extent to which domestic roles, heterosexual marriage, beauty, and consumerism defined womanhood in Cold War America.

While Soviet politicians used working women to profess Soviet women's equality in the global propaganda war, the American press pitied Soviet women as "exploited toilers" who performed "men's work."[22] American journalists were preoccupied with the fact that Soviet women worked in fields that Americans deemed masculine—such as manual labor (that is, digging ditches), science, technology, or politics.

Eclipsing the possibility that women might *want* to work, the American media cast Soviet women as victims of an unfair, inferior political system and unfortunate social reality that forced them to abandon their feminine essences for—horror of all horrors— "men's jobs." The reasons cited for Soviet women's work: Communist indoctrination, the manpower shortage from World War II, and low wages that made it impossible for Soviet men to support their families. By describing Soviet women's workforce participation as economic necessity or Communist brainwashing, American writers delegitimized and circumvented Communist critiques of gender inequality in America.[23]

In 1958, the *New York Times Magazine* openly mocked Soviet women's "equal rights": "Clearly, these include the 'equal right' to be hired for jobs that women in more socially developed countries would recoil from. Like the men, the women work a forty-six hour week."[24]

This hard work also made Soviet women ugly. *Look* magazine's "Women: Russia's Second-Class Citizens" featured a photograph of a Soviet woman construction worker with the tagline: "Femininity gets short shrift in Russia, where women wield pneumatic drills, not lipsticks." Another American writer claimed that he had walked the streets of Moscow for hours without seeing one "really beautiful woman"; he attributed "the poor appearance of the Russian women" to their "heavy work."[25]

Soviet women's office garb was considered mannish at a time when deviating from established gender roles had menacing consequences. At the time, prominent sexologists considered straying from prescribed gender norms an indication of homosexuality and the mannish woman was a popular symbol of lesbianism. As cross-dressers clad in mannish work garb, Soviet women were suspected of deviant sexual behavior. Even though the popular media did not explicitly label Soviet women lesbian, the press hinted at lesbianism by calling them "mannish" in style and behavior. As anxiety about the sexual order reached a fever pitch in American culture, lesbianism was an especially vexing threat and homosexuality was tied to Communist conspiracy. To ferret out the "lavender menace" in Washington, the red-hunter Joseph McCarthy and his allies classified homosexuals as a risk to national security and systematically purged suspected homosexuals from federal jobs.[26]

Soviet women were also homely and mannish because their clothing was "hideous," "unbecoming," "truly pathetic," and in "shockingly bad condition." In 1956, the *New York Times Magazine* declared that the typical Soviet woman made "little effort at beautifying herself" and never wore make-up. Another *New York Times Magazine* article blamed the Communist government for Soviet women's frumpiness—particularly, the "miserable soviet garment industry, inadequate cosmetics trade, and the absence of really good hairdressers."[27]

In the *Saturday Evening Post* in 1959, the American journalist Toni Howard waxed poetic on Soviet women's quashed consumer desires: "For [Soviet woman] is, after all, a woman. She would like to be pretty and have men pay her compliments. . . . She would like some furniture and a few household gadgets and a small apartment to put them in, with a kitchen of her own. She would love to have a few beauty aids other than rice powder and waxy lip pomade, and perhaps even a hairdressing shop. . . . Above all, she would love to have a girdle and bra."[28] The American press positioned capitalism as the optimal economic system for women—because it allowed women to be real women by consuming beauty products and performing their appropriate domestic roles. These American narratives about Soviet women articulated American identity and justified America's expanding role as a global superpower during the Cold War.[29] Consumption had become so fundamental to feminine identity in America—and to the nation's identity in general—that American journalists could not even imagine a person (especially a woman) not needing consumer goods to express herself.

While consumption was key to American gender identity, the official Soviet take on consumerism and fashion was different. Official Soviet policy in the late 1920s deemed provocative short skirts (which originated in "capitalist Paris") appropriate for women who needed to attract a man in order to survive; however, Soviet women were independent wage earners and thus did not need to seduce men with fashionable clothing.[30] During the postwar years, official fashion sources began propounding looking good as a vehicle for Soviet society's improvement, without specifying gender. For example, one official booklet on the matter professed that "the development of taste is one of the most important forms of struggle for the raising of Soviet socialist culture, for the cultural growth of all Soviet people."

By the 1950s, Soviet fashion magazines and official booklets on the art of looking good proliferated. Fashion also became an integral component of *Rabotnitsa*, the popular Soviet magazine for working women: "The Soviet person has become more beautiful, both in mind and soul. His clothes must also be beautiful!"[31]

But Soviets were expected to consume products that appropriately represented Communist ideology. Consumer choices carried weighty political meaning. While Stalin-era homes were ornately decorated, by the late 1950s, when Khrushchev took power, officially endorsed notions about taste had changed. The new regime denounced the previous style as wasteful and, instead, promoted simple, functional design both in home décor and fashion. Khrushchev's regime promulgated a certain vision of Soviet taste and consumption through magazines, which identified "good taste" as simplicity, modesty, and moderation. Verboten styles were those that reeked of capitalist consumer excess. "Bad taste" was Western-style fashion—specifically, trendy, tight, brightly colored clothing designed for "inactive" women. Bright colors—a mark of flamboyance, vulgarity, and elitist frivolity—were particularly dubious. More respectable neutral shades symbolized simplicity, purity, and loyalty to the collective.[32] Soviet women were expected to adhere to this fashion ethos at work.

Across the Atlantic, the American press labeled Soviet fashion choices "puritanical" and likened "Communist Puritanism" to Victorian England, claiming that the Communist regime believed that sex took time away from productivity. One reporter even wrongly asserted that Russians did not even have a word for "sexy." In 1956, the *Ladies' Home Journal* called Russia's "prevailing atmosphere . . . icily puritanical."[33]

This was a sharp criticism considering the new sexual attitudes emerging in America. With the advent of *Playboy* magazine in 1953, Hugh Hefner, the magazine's creator, regularly condemned "puritanical" morality and linked sexual expression to the principles of democracy. This sentiment was not limited to the pages of *Playboy*. By the early 1960s, the American sexual revolution was under way and public displays of scantily clad women were increasingly common in advertising and beyond. The new sexual mores sweeping across America were considered a hallmark of female liberation, and youth culture celebrated sexual freedom as a revolutionary break from tradition. Showing some leg was now popularly endorsed as the modern, glamorous, American way—and Soviet sexual mores and style were cast as a throwback to a more repressive, backward era.[34]

The Aeroflot Stewardess Shines Soviet Pride

On the other side of the Iron Curtain, Soviet stewardesses represented a uniquely Soviet womanhood. Since women's employment was deeply ingrained in Soviet ideology, female cabin crews did not threaten the gender order in Soviet culture. Aeroflot stewardesses embodied a typical vision of Soviet womanhood that was vastly different from American models of working womanhood. Aeroflot stewardesses were expected to be workers first and foremost—this was a respected identity for women in Soviet culture. Thus, they were not required to meet stringent beauty regulations or to cultivate a particularly feminine professional identity. The Soviet stewardess was a gracious hostesses who was "enthusiastic about her job" and a loyal member of the Communist Party, rather than a wife in training.[35] From the American vantage point, the Soviet stewardess appeared brusque and masculine, but she epitomized the ideal proud Soviet working woman—an equal part of the workforce who was not trained to smile or to cultivate American-style feminine charm.

Workplace smiles showcased these competing models of womanhood. Working women in the United States were often expected to display feminine charm (particularly, smiling and nurturing behaviors) as part of their job descriptions. While American stewardesses were instructed to display feminine emotions to passengers, Aeroflot stewardesses could feel the pride of being Soviet workers and, therefore, did not need to smile on command. The Aeroflot stewardess only smiled if "she had a smile in her soul, not out of obligation like American stewardesses," said one former Aeroflot stewardess.[36]

Aeroflot's policies on marriage reflected the Soviet female ideal, which heralded women as workers, mothers, and citizens. While American stewardesses were required to resign upon marriage or pregnancy, Soviet stewardesses received paid maternity leave and were fired only upon divorce, which was taken as a sign of disloyalty to the family and potentially the state. In addition to promoting a vision of Soviet women as workers, the Soviet system also promoted motherhood, treating it as a "sacred duty" to the state, rather than a private matter. State policies encouraged reproduction (by outlawing abortion in 1936) and granting mothers (regardless of marital status) substantial financial assistance and awards.[37] Reflecting this model of Soviet womanhood, the Aeroflot stewardess was portrayed as a serious worker, a hostess, and a loyal Communist.

While U.S. airlines beefed up stewardess training and used stewardesses as the centerpieces of postwar advertising campaigns, the state-run Aeroflot was the only airline operating in the Soviet Union so stewardesses were not necessary to lure passengers. The Soviet stewardess was designed to exhibit flawless Soviet citizenship. While Aeroflot spent twenty-five hours training its stewardesses in 1945, it dedicated a mere two hours to customer service.[38] An Aeroflot training manual of 1955 instructed stewardesses to be "attentive, polite, courteous, discreet, sociable but not annoying, friendly, proper and dignified." They were directed not to "speak and behave forwardly, or speak too loudly, using imperative intonation and phrases," and to always say "please." Beyond basic etiquette, Aeroflot stewardesses were expected to bolster Soviet pride by organizing chess tournaments and by leading "collective singing" in-flight.[39]

Aeroflot stewardesses were also trained to represent official Soviet ideology aloft. They were expected to be well versed in art, politics, culture, and geography, but their conversations were required to conform to political regulations. They were instructed to speak to passengers using "only officially published sources." The Aeroflot training manual stated: "If a flight attendant notices that the topic of the conversation differs from the described she should change it unnoticeably. During all such conversations and while providing general information to the passengers, flight attendants should show high political awareness, answer the questions clearly and shortly, thinking through the phrases and selecting appropriate vocabulary." Stewardesses were trained by the head of the political department of the territory divisions and the deputy commanders of the aviation groups responsible for political training.[40]

Aeroflot also taught stewardesses to be neat, clean, and "modest," but there were none of the beauty lessons central to American stewardess training. Appearance rules were simple: the 1955 Aeroflot manual instructed stewardesses to wear "modest hairstyles" and banned "excessive make-up (including bright lipstick, red fingernails, and bright blush)."[41] In 1953 the Aeroflot stewardess uniform was a dark blue, single-breasted suit in "Boston" fabric, a white blouse, a cap, and black pumps.[42] Aeroflot uniforms maintained a military look throughout the 1950s and early 1960s, while American stewardess uniforms ventured toward designer styles to elicit American travelers' consumer dreams. The Aeroflot stewardess look, however, would soon change.

The look of Aeroflot stewardesses reflected the broader Soviet ethos regarding fashion and beauty. The meanings of Soviet clothing were derived largely from their use and context. Soviets were expected to dress differently for three contexts: home, work, and theater. Officially, the appropriate style for women in the workplace was a white top with a dark bottom; fancy dresses, jewelry, and fashionable clothing were taboo at the office. Aeroflot

Grazhdanskoi Aviatsii, "One of the Best Stewardesses,"
December 1958. Courtesy Library of Congress.

stewardesses were uniformed in professional suits with buttoned-up blouses, which conformed to standard Soviet workplace style. Aeroflot officials defined the airplane as a workplace and, therefore, not an appropriate venue for fashion.[43] From the American perspective, Soviet working women (including Aeroflot stewardesses) looked disastrously "drab" and "mannish." But Aeroflot uniforms conformed to the Soviet fashion philosophy of "good taste"—featuring simplicity, neutral colors, and modesty.

By the late 1950s, however, major changes were afoot in the Soviet government that would ultimately influence Soviet stewardess uniforms (and Soviet style in general). During the Thaw, the period of heightened cultural contact between the Soviet Union and the "free world," the Soviet public became more exposed to Western fashions as the Soviet regime allowed foreign fashion designers to show their collections in Moscow. When Christian Dior brought the same extravagant collection he had shown in Paris to Moscow in 1959, American reporters assumed that while Soviet women were shocked, they secretly yearned to wear Dior-type fashions. But in fact, Dior was not universally embraced in Europe—the Germans, for example, reviled Dior's extravagant "New Look." Soviet women too might have recoiled from such displays of extravagance.[44] But regardless of Soviet women's response to Dior in the late 1950s, Western fashions would influence Soviet style. Soviet officials would incorporate foreign styles as they reinvented the Aeroflot stewardess for international audiences.

At the same time, as Soviet contact with the "free world" increased during the Thaw, Soviet authorities became increasingly interested in attracting foreign currency through international tourism.[45] As part of this foreign travel initiative, the Soviet government opened a new organization to promote tourism to the Soviet Union and Aeroflot markedly expanded its international routes. The push to lure foreign travelers also had a major impact on Aeroflot's passenger service. While the Soviet government did not even consider improving Aeroflot's domestic service, it invested heavily in revamping stewardess service for international flights. By 1957, Aeroflot's ninety-five-hour standard stewardess training included topics such as geography and safety (for which two hours were allotted). Passenger service now received thirty-three hours of training time—up from a mere two hours devoted to the topic in 1945. Noting that stewardesses were removing

An Aeroflot brochure circa 1958. Courtesy Special Collections,
University of Miami Libraries, Coral Gables, Florida.

trays before passengers had finished eating, in 1958 the Ministry of Civil
Aviation called for better service aloft and instituted additional training for
stewardesses. In 1961 Eugeny Loginov, the chief of Aeroflot, told the international press that Aeroflot planned to refurbish "the culture of services to
passengers," along with stewardesses' "neat appearances."[46]

The effort to improve the Aeroflot stewardess look and service style was
not just about wooing passenger traffic away from international airlines—it
was about portraying a compelling image of Soviet women and the nation
itself overseas. With Aeroflot's numerous new routes extending beyond the
Communist bloc into Western Europe, Aeroflot officials and Soviet authorities recognized the stewardess's significance in representing both the airline
and the nation overseas. Soviet officials aimed to craft a stewardess image
that would convey Soviet superiority in the global propaganda war. "The
Aeroflot stewardess should be an example to the world in morals, behavior,
and self-expression," Aeroflot instructors told stewardesses. Aeroflot stewardesses were taught: "You are the face of the country."[47]

The Soviet stewardess image became even more important when Soviet officials began toying with the prospect of opening commercial flights to the United States as part of its sprawling global expansion plan in the late 1950s. As Soviet and American officials began long-term negotiations about beginning flights between the Soviet Union and the United States, Aeroflot's international route system continued to extend farther into Western Europe. Meanwhile, Aeroflot scrambled to refurbish its stewardess service and image.

Grazhdanskoi Aviatsii, cover, March 1968. Courtesy Library of Congress, Russian division.

In efforts to ensure that stewardesses would represent the ideal Soviet woman (who was especially a loyal Communist Party member), Aeroflot went to great lengths in hiring its in-flight staff for international routes. The international stewardess position was highly coveted because such stewardesses were permitted to travel abroad (a rare privilege considering tight Soviet regulations limiting travel outside the Soviet bloc), plus they earned a decent salary with a travel allowance, which allowed them to buy products abroad. Aeroflot also sought women who would not defect on overseas trips so it accepted only stewardesses recommended by the Komsomol, the youth wing of the Communist Party.[48] International stewardesses also had to pass KGB psychology examinations, received special KGB training, and were plucked from education and foreign language departments of Soviet universities. To ensure loyalty, Aeroflot stewardesses were also required to remain in groups of three at all times during trips abroad and were forbidden from communicating with foreign crews.[49]

Meanwhile, the Soviet Union and America were still embroiled in negotiations over opening commercial air service between Moscow and New York. Preparing to square off against U.S. airlines, Aeroflot officials schemed to serve the finest caviar and top-shelf vodka, and to unveil an improved Aeroflot stewardess as the face of the Soviet Union on American soil.

Open Skies and Caviar, 1968

The opening of commercial air service between the Soviet Union and the United States in 1968 was memorialized on the cover of *Life* magazine with a photograph of Aeroflot stewardess Natasha Arutyunova and Pan Am stewardess Susan Sicari hugging. In spite of this public snuggle, Soviet and American stewardesses did not consider themselves "sisters of the sky"—instead, these women viewed themselves as ambassadors of their respective nations. Soviet stewardesses remarked on American stewardesses' phony smiles and American stewardesses criticized Soviet stewardesses' physiques and brusque service style.[50] The epic embrace represented yet another forum for parading competing gender ideals in the global culture clash, but it also symbolized the transnational transfer of ideas in the globalizing world. These hugging ambassadors raise intriguing questions about how these competing

The Cold War hug between a Pan Am stewardess and an Aeroflot stewardess, 1968. Courtesy Special Collections, University of Miami Libraries, Coral Gables, Florida.

models of womanhood cross-pollinated each other during the Cold War. As cultural contact between the rival nations increased during the Thaw, ideas about gender filtered across international borders in fluid, porous ways and ultimately influenced gender ideals in each nation.[51]

While the American media had painted a dismal portrait of Soviet women for decades and much coverage of the 1968 flight continued this trend, there was also a new, less-damning portrait of Soviet women appearing in mainstream American culture. Aeroflot stewardesses even won some gold stars. *Newsday*, for example, praised Aeroflot stewardesses as "pretty and gracious."[52] The ugly Russian working woman stereotype was so ingrained, however, that the question of whether Aeroflot stewardesses were pretty was considered newsworthy, and those who deemed Aeroflot stewardesses attractive found it surprising enough to warrant significant commentary.

Some American reporters noted that Aeroflot stewardesses were once known for their "heftiness" but were now "slimmed down, girdled and smartly coifed [sic]." A writer for *Aviation Week and Space Technology* reported that when he first flew Aeroflot in 1956, the Aeroflot stewardess was a "muscular 200-pounder who wore a baggy red sweater as the only semblance of a uniform" and ignored passengers. But on the 1968 flight he found "10 petite and pretty stewardii . . . clad in pert blue and white uniforms with gold embroidered wings and wearing white gloves." A *Wall Street Journal* reporter noted that when he traveled on Aeroflot in 1959, the hostesses were "beefy and middle-aged with personalities that matched the drab décor of the passenger cabins," but the "new breed of Aeroflot hostesses with their upswept coiffures and youthful good looks, display both courtesy and charm." The *New York Times* called Russian stewardesses "young" and "attractive": "Watching them walk up and down the aisles, one would know they are airline stewardesses, but one would guess they were from this side, not the other side of the iron curtain."[53]

The look of the Aeroflot stewardess, in fact, had changed dramatically. When Aeroflot extended its international routes in the mid-1960s and the airline was gearing up for service to America, the Soviet government had mandated service improvements on flights abroad. The service facelift—exclusively for first-class international service—was designed to impress foreign dignitaries, journalists, and political bigwigs. Following a state inspection that rated Aeroflot's customer service inadequate in 1965, the Ministry of Civil Aviation instituted new service for first-class passengers "according to the best international standards for air service" and ordered a new stewardess corps specifically trained and assigned to first-class passengers on international flights. The directive also called for a stewardess makeover—including new uniforms of "higher quality fabrics from first-class shops" for stewardesses on international flights.[54]

In 1967, influenced by foreign airlines, Aeroflot also introduced an age maximum of twenty-seven years for newly hired stewardesses, and began requiring all its stewardesses to be between the ages of nineteen and thirty-

Aeroflot stewardesses, 1968. Author's collection.

five—"the same age bracket for ballerinas," said a former Aeroflot stewardess. American carriers had imposed stewardess age limits decades earlier and by the late 1960s many U.S. airlines were rescinding them. Aeroflot stewardesses working international flights were also required to speak English and French, and they had to be knowledgeable about sociopolitical issues. Although Aeroflot stewardesses still had no precise weight requirements, they were now required to be size 44 or 46 (the equivalent of the contemporary American sizes 10 and 12).[55]

Aeroflot's new stewardess look was beginning to display an American brand of "feminine charm" and glamour. As American-style femininity was increasingly defined by consumerism and glamour, the Soviet Union began gussying up its stewardesses. The Soviet Union had been increasingly exposed to Western-style fashions since the thaw of the late 1950s, and by the time Aeroflot started flying to the United States the airline had reinvented its stewardesses with American flair. Aeroflot's new uniforms would fly in the face of traditional Soviet workplace style. In 1968, Aeroflot stewardesses were dolled up in a new uniform that was a near replica of Pan Am stewardess uniforms—a tailored blue uniform (now made from expensive fabrics), with a blue pillbox hat, white gloves, and pumps.[56]

Just after the flights between Moscow and New York began, the Soviet Union's Ministry of Civil Aviation issued yet another order to spruce up Aeroflot's stewardesses for international flights to project a more fashionable vision of the Soviet Union to the world. The higher-ups at Aeroflot still accused the airline's stewardesses of "rudeness," "indifference," and "overuse of make-up and violations of uniform rules" so they established a merit system to encourage stewardesses to provide better service. They constructed new stewardess dressing rooms devoted to preflight primping, more stringent higher education and experience requirements for chief stewardesses, and a new three-month stewardess training program.[57]

But the favorable American reviews of Soviet stewardesses were not just reflecting Aeroflot's new Western-style panache. These flattering portraits of Soviet women appeared in the American press at the same time that feminism was dawning in mainstream America and a new take on working women was developing. Working women were becoming less threatening to the American public. Wage work now offered women an opportunity for equality and personal fulfillment. Positive press on Soviet stewardesses (and working women in general) reflected these burgeoning attitudes about women and work in American culture.

By the mid- to late 1960s, the *New York Times* and other mainstream media had started to reframe Soviet women's work as "fulfilling," rather than demeaning. In 1965 the *New York Times Magazine* declared that Soviet women found the life of a housewife "appalling" and quoted a Soviet woman expressing disgust at the prospect of becoming one: "I'd prefer almost anything to that. . . . Because being a housewife is, well, degrading. . . . A job's a person's contact with the world, it's her chance to develop as a full person." Another story in the *New York Times Magazine* reflected this new take on Soviet women as well: "They considered themselves free from the bondage of housewifery. . . . For them, work was an exciting challenge, taxing their best talents and keeping them alert."[58]

The mainstream American press also began to suggest that Soviet women were both feminine and workers—a substantial turn from the previous

Pan Am stewardesses, 1968. World Wings International calendar, 2000.

representations of Soviet working women. In 1965 the *Saturday Evening Post* compared Russia's *Working Woman* magazine to American women's magazines, concluding that the Russian publication focused on work, unlike American women's magazines, which centered on "looking attractive for men." The *Saturday Evening Post* declared that the Russian woman has "a buoyant, vital, feminine charm peculiarly her own. She has a pride and an energy peculiarly her own and, whatever husbands may prefer, she is not likely to return to a life of domesticity, or to abandon the challenges which have given her a unique fulfillment."[59]

This laudatory vision of working women did not sprout out of the clear blue. Even though dominant popular culture in America had painted dreary portraits of working Soviet women from the late 1940s to the early 1960s, these media conversations still raised important questions about the role of women in society. The Soviet take on women's roles seeped into American consciousness and offered a subversive fissure in dominant media messages that heralded homemaking as women's primary role in America. Soviet ideas about gender trickled onto American soil and generated new possibilities for women's roles in America.

The American journalist Betty Friedan, for example, had established strong ties with Communist organizations during the 1940s and 1950s. She had spent a year studying at Berkeley in 1943, where she cavorted with Marxists and fomented leftist political activism; and she subsequently worked as a journalist for leftist and union publications. Friedan had been exposed to Soviet gender ideals through her affiliation with Communist organizations—and the Soviets had inspired and informed her radical vision for American women. Friedan's association with radical Communist organizations that espoused women's equality through wage work would shape the language and concepts that she would later use in her feminist manifesto, the bestselling *The Feminine Mystique* of 1963, which would both revolutionize women's roles and catalyze second-wave feminism in the United States.[60] Her popular book for the American public called for a combination of careers and domesticity for women—something the Soviets had been expounding for decades.

Friedan was not the only American who had picked up on Soviet notions about women's equality in the workforce. In fact, for a brief period in the mid-1940s, just after Rosie-the-Riveters had been encouraged to work men's jobs during World War II and before the happy homemaker ideal had permeated American culture, some mainstream American women journalists had written glowingly of Soviet women's role in the workforce. Their articles supported the idea that women should be equal participants in it. In 1946, for example, the American journalist Oriana Atkinson went to the Soviet Union with her husband, who was a *New York Times* correspondent on assignment there. She heralded the Soviet Union's treatment of women in mainstream American magazines: "If, as somebody once said, any civilization is to be judged according to the status of women therein, the Soviet Union is in the top drawer so far as civilization goes. According to my own observations, Moscow women have a far greater place in the daily business of life than the women of, say, New York."[61] Atkinson, who wrote several articles on Soviet women for the *New York Times*, was particularly awed by Soviet women's participation in the workforce: "I was impressed by the opportunities for women. There is far greater freedom for women to earn a living and take part in national life in Russia than there is in America. Every field of endeavor is open. Not only are there women teachers, nurses, lawyers, judges, doctors and government officials; there are women engineers on subway trains, women electricians, women watchmakers."[62]

During this brief period in the mid-1940s, prior to the swell of McCarthyism in the United States, progressive women in America found feminist inspiration in Soviet women.[63] They painted unabashedly laudatory depictions of Soviet women as domestic, feminine, pretty, and wage earning.

These celebratory perspectives on Soviet working women had vanished from the mainstream American press by 1947 as anticommunism spread across the nation and feminism was driven underground for more than a decade.[64] However, these positive portraits of working women sowed seeds of feminist consciousness in American culture that would sprout years later. By the time air service began between Moscow and New York, feminism had grown into a definable movement in the United States and women's workforce equality had become part of the mainstream American lexicon.

In a world where most legitimate travelers through the Iron Curtain were men, stewardesses were not just representatives of their airlines, they were representatives of their nation's feminine ideals, and the airplane cabin became an ideological theater for Cold War operations. This competition between each nation's female ambassadors underscores the important roles of beauty, gender, technology, and consumption in the international contest for prestige and power. During the Cold War, gender and sexuality figured prominently into larger cultural conversations about national identity and international image. The glamorous American stewardess symbolically justified global hierarchies, legitimized the spread of capitalism, and sold the American way abroad. Meanwhile, the Aeroflot stewardess represented Soviet working women as beacons of equality for women and proof of Soviet superiority in the international propaganda war.

More broadly, the Soviet-American stewardess showdown raises larger questions about the relationship between gender and world politics.[65] In order to understand the transformation of mid-century American gender roles, we need to recognize that American social change did not happen in a vacuum. Ideas about gender and sexuality circulated across international borders. In the globalizing world, foreign ideas about gender deeply influenced both the United States and the Soviet Union. As America increasingly defined glamour as essential to womanhood, this vision of femininity was exported around the world and Aeroflot restyled its stewardesses to mirror American-style feminine glamour. At the same time, Soviet ideas about working women penetrated American culture. The American media dialogue about Soviet women in the workforce sparked feminist arguments for women's workforce equality during the 1960s. By the late 1960s, American women were claiming the right to work outside the home—an assertion that had been central to Soviet propaganda for decades. Thus, the Cold War offers a critical new piece of the puzzle for understanding how American gender norms went from the conservativeness of the 1950s to second-wave feminism in the late 1960s and the 1970s.

While Pan Am's prim stewardesses epitomized grace and class in the global culture clash, U.S. airlines were strategizing to radically revamp the American stewardess image, and this new stewardess incarnation would threaten to sully America's global reputation.

6

From Warm-Hearted Hostesses
to In-Flight Strippers

WILLIAM PATTERSON, the president of United Airlines, had built the airline from its beginnings in 1934 and he believed in loyalty. However, after twenty-seven years with the well-established, Philadelphia-based N. W. Ayer & Son (founded in 1869), Patterson decided to call it quits. United's image needed a fresh perspective. At the time, United was head-quartered in Chicago, so Patterson invited the Leo Burnett Advertising Agency, a newer Chicago-based boutique firm, to bid for the prestigious airline account.

Leo Burnett, the acclaimed ad man behind the small Chicago ad agency, corralled his top creative team. They poured themselves into brainstorm-ing sessions—analyzing United's image, strategizing the pitch, and waxing philosophical about the future of air travel. In 1963, a cadre of United executives in pinstriped suits convened in a smoky boardroom to hear the ad men's pitch. The Burnett team laid it out: United was the General Motors of air travel— "professional, official-looking" and "a little stuffy and cold—coldly efficient, with a production-line attitude." Then came the real blow: the ad team called United "stodgy" and "dull."[1] Patterson prided himself on the airline's hard-won reputation for reliability, but he knew that United desperately needed to sell more seats.

Pacific Southwest Airlines publicity photos, early 1970s. Courtesy San
Diego Air and Space Museum.

He also knew that a stodgy image was a death knell for a corporation—
after all, this was the 1960s, when youth culture ruled the American cultural
landscape. The trouble with United's image, according to Burnett's team,
was its lack of "friendliness, warmth and humanness and . . . fun." Burnett's
team summed it up by quoting a male passenger, "'United has a reputation
for great dependability, reliability and soundness . . . all the wonderful scientific advances known to the field of electronics and computers. However,
they ain't got no sex appeal.'"[2] In 1965, United hired the Burnett agency to
develop a new image for the airline, but their relationship would be fraught

with tension as United's executives and Burnett's ad men clashed over how to sex up the airline's stuffy image.

Internal corporate records from the Burnett advertising agency and United Airlines show precisely how and why airlines began radically altering their depictions of stewardesses in advertising during the mid-1960s. While earlier ads featured all-American girl-next-door stewardesses feeding bottles to babies and serving dinner to businessmen, by the mid-1960s, ads were introducing a beguiling new stewardess who performed in-flight stripteases. This bombshell stewardess in short shorts, fishnets, and go-go boots rapidly ascended to fame as a mythical American sex icon.

This shift to a sexier stewardess image occurred in tandem with the broader cultural trend of increasingly sexualized female bodies in American advertising. Over the course of the twentieth century, images of semi-nude women that had once been considered tawdry became common on billboards, television, and mainstream magazines. By the 1950s, mainstream magazines had begun to feature blouseless women in bra ads and titillating romantic encounters in perfume ads.[3] Sexual content in ads proliferated during the 1960s, when the sexual revolution unfurled across America and liberalized sexual mores spread. As advertisers attempted to connect with consumers during these turbulent cultural changes, sexual images became more prominent and more palatable to the American public. Airline advertising epitomized the commercialization of the sexual revolution. Thus, the story behind the sultry stewardess offers an invaluable case study of this pivotal development in twentieth-century American gender history.

The Burnett Agency, the "Creative Revolution," and the Invention of Hip

By the time Leo Burnett won the United account in 1965, he was in his seventies and he had already made a name for himself in the world of advertising. Burnett had grown up in small-town Michigan and did not exactly have the look of a savvy Madison Avenue ad man—he wore a crumpled suit and heavy glasses with a dark frame. A former accountant, Burnett was a quiet man and an awkward public speaker known for mumbling. He worked contentedly for several small midwestern ad agencies and was reluctant to take the risks necessary to start his own agency. Finally, unable to stand the onslaught of "dull advertising," he struck out on his own. In 1936, at the age of forty-four, Burnett sold his house and borrowed on his insurance to start his own agency in Chicago. His plan for the new agency emphasized the importance of risk-taking creativity. Burnett's approach: focus on style and creating an image around the product. He would go on to develop major icons such as the Marlboro Man, Morris the Cat, and the Pillsbury Doughboy.[4] For Burnett, creativity was king. His advertising philosophy prefigured the revolution that would hit Madison Avenue years later.

Meanwhile, during the 1950s, the large, old-school ad agencies on Madison Avenue had started focusing on research. In the postwar consumer boom, advertising had become big business and agencies began concentrating on studying "unique selling propositions" instead of creating interesting copy or artwork. This method aggravated those who considered advertising an art, such as Leo Burnett. Burnett was not alone. The New York copywriter Bill Bernbach declared that the big ad agencies had it all wrong: "Advertising is not a science, it is persuasion, and persuasion is an art."[5] Bemoaning that ad agencies were turning creative people into "mimeograph machines," Bernbach founded a new agency (called Doyle Dane Bernbach [DDB]) to buck this trend. His agency quickly became the place to be on Madison Avenue. The battle lines were clearly drawn between the "creatives," who believed art inspired buyers, and those who believed that research and facts sold products. This tug of war would become a central feature in the history of advertising.

By the 1960s, Burnett in Chicago and Bernbach in New York were at the vanguard of major changes sweeping the advertising industry. Among these was the advent of the "creative revolution," which gave "creatives" (art directors and copywriters) more influence in the management of ad agencies, and the look and feel of ads. The emphasis shifted from science and research to art. Unconstrained by established bureaucracy and conventional attitudes, Bernbach and Burnett hired stables of young creatives eager to have an impact on the advertising world with imaginative ads. One of the young creatives under Bernbach's tutelage, Mary Wells, would go on to become one of the most influential creative revolutionaries in the ad industry who would radically redirect the trajectory of airline advertising.

The creative revolution in advertising occurred in tandem with major social and cultural changes sweeping across America during the 1960s. A cultural revolution of sorts was taking place and ads would have to incorporate this emerging cultural milieu. While ads in the 1950s promised a chicken in every pot, smiling white families, and suburban conformity, this imagery began losing cultural currency as a new consumer mood arose. By the mid-1950s, mainstream America was awash in criticism of this blossoming culture of abundance as sociologists, novelists, and public intellectuals bemoaned increasingly bureaucratic corporate environments, conformity, and empty consumerism in popular books such as John Keat's *The Crack in the Picture Window* (1957), Vance Packard's *The Hidden Persuaders* (1957), William H. Whyte's *The Organization Man* (1956), and Sloan Wilson's *The Man in the Grey Flannel Suit* (1955). Jack Kerouac and other "beat poets," who rebelled against what they considered soulless middle-class consumerism and conformity, also popularized critiques of mass consumption. The term "hip" was derived from "hipster," a term Jack Kerouac had used in 1958 to describe the Beat Generation, which meant an alternative to middle-class style and values.[6]

By the 1960s, young people with similar attitudes were taking the helm of American culture.[7] This new youth counterculture also brewed critiques of the mainstream culture of the 1950s; young people challenged the impersonality, emptiness, and overall conformity of middle-class consumer culture.[8] The youth counterculture heralded antimaterialism and antiestablishment values—eschewing elitism and big business. Corporations were vilified as purveyors of rampant, vapid consumerism. The antiestablishment mood became a cause célèbre as rebellion spread across colleges. By the late 1960s, this countercultural current had spilled into mainstream American culture and had begun to be used to sell products, especially by advertising teams who saw it as a way to add an aura of youth to ads.

While advertising agencies had not considered teenagers a valuable demographic before World War II, by the 1960s advertising agencies were considering young people to be economically vital to business revenue in general. Young people, between the ages of thirteen and twenty-two, had control of some $25 billion in discretionary spending.[9] The actual "youth market," defined as consumers under thirty, or twenty-five, or twenty-one, or nineteen (depending on the context), was clearly important to ad agencies in the 1960s. But youth had an appeal that extended far beyond the youth market proper.

"You had the feeling youth was taking over the world . . . and the advertising industry was part of the total change going on in culture," Mary Wells, one of Bernbach's protégés who became an influential advertising executive, recalled.[10] "In 1967, so many people wanted to look and feel totally hip."[11]

Youth had become the decade's arbiters of style. The look and mood of youth counterculture took over mainstream culture. Young people influenced everything from fashion to music to sexual mores. Everyone wanted to look and feel young. The advertising industry considered youth an enticing consumer fantasy they could offer to older Americans. In 1967, *Madison Avenue Magazine* quoted an adman: "the youth market has become the American market. It now includes not only everyone under 35, but most people over 35."[12] As youth culture spread across mainstream America in the 1960s, advertising agencies focused on ways to target the "now generation" and to tap youth-derived trends to lure older consumers who wanted to feel young and hip.[13]

Youth culture also advocated sexual liberalization. College students across the nation began rebelling against traditional sexual taboos such as premarital sex and homosexuality. Single, young women challenged conservative sexual mores by living openly with men and by espousing premarital sex as an equal right. These new sexual attitudes swept across the nation with the advent of the birth control pill in 1960, the opening of Playboy clubs, and increasingly sexualized advertising campaigns. This vision of equality and freedom for both sexes was one aspect of the sexual revolution, but savvy advertisers would find ways to co-opt freer sexuality to market products.[14]

Ads needed new strategies to meet this shifting cultural climate. The youth-fueled cultural revolution became integral to advertising copy as ads began to focus on whatever was cool, young, sexually liberated, and rebellious. Ironically, ads picked up the slogans, symbols, icons, and themes of the youth revolution that reviled conformity and consumerism. They often focused on cultivating an "honest," less "snobby," and "informal" tone, which reflected the youth rebellion against the establishment and elitism. This new tone became the hallmark of the creative revolution. Even the middle-American stalwart Dodge created the "Dodge Rebellion" in the 1960s.[15]

Many creatives at the newer ad agencies considered the counterculture not an enemy that potentially undermined consumer culture, but rather a kindred ally in their struggles against creativity-quashing aspects of old business culture such as hierarchy, procedure, and overblown organization. The youth counterculture philosophy seemed to reflect the newer ad agencies' impulse for creativity.[16]

The ads of the 1960s also adopted a different visual style. While previous advertising had centered on the "hard sell" with long text descriptions of the product, focusing on differentiating the product from its competitors, the new style was minimalist with simple copy and unassuming humor. For example, the most influential ad campaign of the 1960s was an ad for the Volkswagen Beetle with plain, serif-free headlines and concise copy. The campaign picked up on youth counterculture by selling the car as a way to eschew conformity.

A pioneer in the creative revolution, Leo Burnett wanted to bring that level of innovation to United's image. In confidential internal corporate memos, Burnett set his creative sights high for the United campaign: he wanted to "change the battleground" of airline advertising with ads as innovative as the Volkswagen campaign. Burnett praised the Volkswagen campaign for its simplicity, "personal tone," and "honesty," qualities that Burnett's own advertising style embodied. In an internal memo to his creative team, he suggested they take a similar tack in shifting United's image from its "official" and "stuffy" image to a more "personal, human" image.[17]

Burnett was eager to overhaul United's image and his creative team rolled into United's headquarters with a bang—bursting with shocking marketing ideas for the airline. "We looked around the table and saw the senior people at United with their mouths screwed up like pickles. And, I thought, 'Oh, this one is going to be tough,'" said Dick Stanwood, Burnett's creative director for the United campaign.[18] Stanwood realized his creative team did not have free reign with the campaign. They needed to win approval from the pinstriped suits at United, which, it turned out, would be a daunting task. The men at United were largely older, conservative executives who had their own trenchant notions about the airline's image and advertising in general.

They were put off by the ad team's presentation. United's executives were reluctant to change and the bright-eyed, bushy-tailed creatives at Burnett would have to find a way to diplomatically sweet-talk them into radically reinventing United's image.

Plus, Leo Burnett wanted to please United's president, William Patterson. A veteran in the airline industry, Patterson had been United's chief executive for more than thirty years and he was in his sixties when Burnett's agency took over the airline's ad campaign. Patterson had built United from the ground up and he was proud of United's dependability. He had a reputation as a "smart, savvy man who kn[ew] his business," according to Phil Schaff, a creative director at Burnett. Leo Burnett considered Patterson a "down-to-earth" man with "integrity." In an internal memo to his staff, Burnett mentioned that he did not want to upset Patterson by pitching a sleazy campaign.[19] So, Burnett advised his team to tread carefully.

Stanwood saw the conflict between Burnett's creative team and United executives as a generational divide: United executives had "grown up in a different time and were not ready for this new attack on the business," Stanwood said in an interview. The "desire for change," according to Stanwood, came very much from Burnett's team. This tension between United's conservative executives and Burnett's creative team would become a persistent, thorny thicket that would shape the outcome of United's ad campaign as well as the use of stewardesses in it. Burnett's team decided to back off and brainstorm a new tack. "We didn't want the United folks to be too badly jolted," said Stanwood.[20]

The first bone of contention: stewardesses. Stewardesses were critical to airline ticket sales and the Burnett team planned to use them as the linchpin of United's new image. But United's executives restricted the agency's creative freedom from the get-go. United's senior vice president of marketing, Bob Johnson, a bulwark of traditionalism, would become the Burnett team's nemesis throughout the campaign.

From the start, Johnson cautioned Leo Burnett to develop a respectable campaign—particularly, when it came to the use of stewardesses. In a briefing to Leo Burnett, Johnson laid down United's policy. He warned Burnett to be "very careful about the handling of stewardesses in advertising." Johnson explained that stewardesses were "sacred cows" and their special position had always been recognized in United's advertising. According to Johnson, "Until recently all girls in UAL advertising were, in fact, stewardesses and UAL tries to convey the impression in its stewardesses of 'the girl next door, your daughter.'"[21] Throughout the 1940s and 1950s, United ads had reflected that ethos: the United stewardess was portrayed as a wholesome "girl next door."

By instructing Burnett to treat stewardesses with caution, Johnson was partly the mouthpiece for United's president, William Patterson. Patterson felt a special responsibility to stewardesses, since he was credited with hiring the first female stewardesses in 1930. Moreover, Patterson's daughter, Patricia, had also worked briefly as a stewardess during the 1950s, so Patterson was personally invested in maintaining a wholesome stewardess image in United's advertising. "Dad was very conservative and he didn't want the girls bothered. He referred to them as his 'young ladies,'" said Patterson's daughter, Patricia. "And I became a stewardess, so he had to be protective! He was a gentleman and he was very protective of women. Girls in short skirts might have been harassed by smart-alecky men and he wouldn't have wanted that."[22]

Aware of Patterson's gentlemanly ways, Burnett promised not to resort to "slick, hip" images or to make stewardesses look smutty. In other words, the agency pledged to steer clear of youth-derived trends. In attempts to win United's executives over, Burnett assured them that the campaign would retain United's established character, which the agency described as "size, efficiency and trust-worthiness."[23]

But while United's big business image was an asset during the 1950s, it had, in fact, become a liability by the 1960s—and Leo Burnett knew it. He considered a big-business image a problem partly because of the widespread American cultural critique of large corporations and mass consumption during the 1960s. This broad anticorporate sentiment dovetailed with another critical issue in the airline industry: air travel was in the midst of a major transition from being an elite mode of travel to becoming transportation for the masses.

Airlines were expanding at record speed. In 1965, airlines began preparing for an influx of new wide-bodied Boeing 747s, which were known as jumbo jets. The new Boeing 747 would carry up to 490 passengers (more than twice the capacity of its predecessor, Boeing's 707 jet) and have a longer range of up to 8,300 miles. United's order for new jumbo jets in 1965 would double the airline's seat capacity by 1969. During a slide presentation to United, Leo Burnett pointed out that this represented an investment of $750 million—the biggest jet order ever placed.[24]

Everyone involved knew this meant that United desperately needed to fill seats. Anticipating that the doubled seating capacity of jumbo jets would result in huge financial losses if the number of air travelers remained stable, the Burnett team emphasized the importance of a long-range campaign that would rapidly expand the air travel market. Air travel had long been reserved for the wealthy and business travelers, but with the coming of jumbo jets, Burnett pushed for innovative ad strategies to transform air travel into just another consumer service available to the broad middle class. The air travel market would, in fact, expand enormously during the 1960s—more than tripling its passenger load over the course of the decade.[25]

Even though airline marketing teams wanted to expand the air travel market to fill the seats on their new bigger jets, Leo Burnett also worried that the desirable image of air travel would be reversed as airlines served a larger market with increasingly impersonal customer service. He feared that cheaper fares and making air travel accessible to the general public would mar the alluring image of air travel. But in Burnett's first pitch to United executives in 1963, he touted personal travelers as a vital future market.[26]

United needed a savvy advertising strategy to handle this complex transition to mass transportation.[27] Airlines had already won business travelers, but personal travelers often still traveled by car, bus, train, or ship. While airlines in the jet age had started directing more advertising dollars into attracting the personal travel market, most carriers were reluctant to invest heavily in it since businessmen constituted the majority of the domestic air travel market even until 1963. In 1964, however, the tide turned: marketing surveys reported that the personal travel market on domestic flights accounted for a higher proportion of passengers than business travelers. In 1964, marketing reports for American Airlines showed that personal travel accounted for over 69 percent of traffic on transcontinental routes, the backbone of its profits. The report concluded that the airline "should develop a policy and plans that will assure American of a fully competitive share of [the personal travel market]."[28] Now, for the first time, airline executives became interested in winning the mass market—predominantly personal travelers.

Occasional fliers, who constituted a large portion of the personal travel market, had substantially lower incomes and were less educated than frequent fliers. In 1963, 45 percent of personal travelers departing from New York City airports had annual incomes under $7,000. In 1960, approximately 70 percent of U.S. families had annual incomes under $7,000. Leo Burnett suggested that these personal travelers avoided flying because they felt that flying was for the wealthy; thus, he recommended "de-formalizing" United's image to appeal to this group.[29]

In the mid-1960s, for the first time, airlines became invested in selling tickets to middle-income personal travelers—including women and young people. Airlines began placing ads in magazines geared at young female audiences, such as *Seventeen* and *Cosmopolitan*. *Business Week* remarked on the trend in 1968: the "teen-ager is tomorrow's routine flyer, and airlines have been casting about for ways to reach him."[30]

However, not all ad agencies were tapped into the power of the youth culture and the trends of the creative revolution. For example, the behemoth J. Walter Thompson Agency (JWT), founded in 1864, which handled Pan Am's advertising campaign, was so steeped in hierarchy and procedures that it lagged behind. In spite of the widespread changes in American culture and in the advertising industry, JWT continued to generate ads touting traditional values and favoring research-oriented strategies over innovation. It was not until 1971 that the agency finally took note that other airlines had been targeting this critical youth demographic since 1965. At this point, the agency sketched the characteristics of the youth market, including countercultural ideas against large companies and antiestablishment values.[31]

Burnett's team, however, was already keenly aware that young people were becoming airlines' most crucial emerging market. In the first place, young people were traveling more. By the summer of 1960, more than 120,000 American students had stayed in European youth hostels and the junior year abroad had become a typical rite of passage. The youth market was especially important because, at the time, fliers were loyal to one airline, so luring the youth market could mean winning these new fliers for their whole lives.[32] Plus, since youth set the trends for the broad masses during the 1960s, the

Burnett team believed that poaching aspects of the youth culture could help market United to older Americans who still wanted to feel young and hip. But the vexing question remained: how could the agency develop a youth-oriented campaign without offending the old guard at United?

Turning Up the Chic Aloft

While Burnett's creative team struggled to develop a palatable, yet hip, campaign for United, Braniff Airlines hired a new advertising director—the über-stylish advertising upstart Mary Wells. A stylish blonde in her thirties, Wells had a background in theater and fashion. A voraciously ambitious rising star in the industry, Wells had been groomed by the advertising pioneer Bill Bernbach and went on to earn a reputation as an advertising trailblazer. Harding Lawrence, a former vice president of Continental Airlines, had just been recruited to lead Braniff and he was determined to give the obscure airline a snazzy, new, attention-getting image. Wells was just the woman for the job.

When Braniff hired her in 1965, Mary Wells was thirty-eight years old, notably young for her position. Plus, she was a hipster who was well versed in the youth culture scene. Known for her fashionable flair and glamorous jet-setting life, Wells tapped society decorators like Billy Baldwin to design her home and she created an extravagant lifestyle in homes in Cap Ferrat on the French Riviera, and Mustique—exclusive playgrounds for European aristocracy and international millionaires during the 1960s. She also cavorted with the likes of Frank Sinatra, Henry Ford II, Princess Grace of Monaco, and Hubert de Givenchy (a French aristocrat and fashion designer famous for creating wardrobes for celebrity clients such as Audrey Hepburn and Jacqueline Kennedy).

When Wells opened her own new ad agency (Wells Rich Greene) in 1966, she capitalized on her knowledge of the youth scene to create buzz about her agency. A savvy businesswoman, Wells knew how to appeal to prospective clients, who were often older corporate executives itching to tap the 1960s youth scene to sell products to the mainstream masses. She knew how to look the part. Under the age of forty when she started her own agency, Wells dressed like a high-fashion mannequin.[33] She charmed clients before she even spoke, then impressed them again with her articulate analysis of marketing problems.

In the 1960s, business executives hoped to find something really jaw dropping when they visited new, younger advertising agencies—and Wells delivered. More than anyone, Wells knew how to prove how au courant the agency was. She decorated the office with the look and symbols of youth counterculture—particularly, the music, fashion, sex, and drug scene. New clients were given tours of the agency's creative department to see mini-skirts and jeans; to lounge on psychedelic pillows; and to hear Mick Jagger blasting in the backrooms.[34] Beards, denim, and paisley were signs of the counterculture and considered proof of advertising genius. As Wells put it: "It helped paint us the way our clients wanted us to be. . . . We talked hip talk." She promised clients that her agency's creative talents were "harbingers of a world as hip and successful as the Beatles." To keep these older executives feeling they were in "the nest of flower power," she even alluded to "peyote problems" in her agency's backrooms.[35]

Wells also parlayed her knowledge of the language, imagery, and fashion of the youth scene and sexual revolution of the 1960s into smash hit ad campaigns. For example, she used the Beatles' "Love in the Open Air" to conceptualize a new line of make-up, called Love Cosmetics, which included a perfume (Eau De Love). She launched the line in the 1960s at a hip young hangout in Paris, the basement of Le Drugstore, where Donovan and Liza Minnelli performed for the glitterati of Paris, including the Duke and Duchess of Windsor. The perfume sold out overnight.[36]

In 1966, when Wells opened Wells Rich Greene (WRG), she became the first woman to own and operate an ad agency (and soon would be the first woman CEO of a company on the New York Stock Exchange). WRG became Madison Avenue's "hot shop" of the time. At the age of forty, Wells became the youngest person to be inducted into the Copywriters Hall of Fame. By 1968, WRG had annual billings over $90 million and boasted a heavy-hitting roster of clients such as Philip Morris, Proctor and Gamble, and General Motors. By the late 1960s, Wells would become one of the best-known, highest-paid executives in advertising.

When Braniff hired Wells, it expected her to furnish a striking makeover for the airline—which is exactly what it got. She hired the designer Alexander

Girard as the project designer and the artist Alexander Calder to develop aircraft paint schemes for the campaign. Under Wells's direction, Braniff would become the first airline to appeal directly to the new youth market and to use aspects of the hip, youth culture to attract the broad middle class. Wells found clever ways to import the language and symbols from youth culture and the sexual revolution into Braniff's new image.

Wells drew on her vast knowledge of fashion, design, and American cultural trends to develop the airline's new image. A jetsetter who partied with the hottest fashion designers, Wells was well aware that color was sweeping fashion during the 1960s. Bright color became a signature of 1960s style. Shirley Kennedy's book on the Italian designer Emilio Pucci summed it up: "Color—hot, bright, and clear . . . were key elements of 1960s furniture designs produced by Americans and Europeans . . . one could not help but notice color everywhere—in furniture, art, ads, movies, neon discothèque lights, black-light posters in teenagers' rooms, Day-Glo shades in boutiques. Color was a fact of life in the 1960s."[37]

Furthermore, hue was particularly potent in the context of the Cold War, when bright color became a hallmark of American capitalism and glamour. During the Cold War, the American press routinely described Soviet Russia as "drab," "gray," and colorless. Within this context, gray became a marker of the Communist system as old-fashioned and unglamorous. When Pucci visited the Soviet Union in 1957 to put on fifty public fashion shows, he remarked: "The impact of our designs on Russia was enormous. . . . This sudden explosion of color must have been quite overwhelming for a country still suffering from the upheaval of the war and very much in the rear of fashion development in the fifties." In the Soviet Union, during the 1950s and 1960s, however, bright colors were associated with Western style and deemed eccentric, flamboyant, déclassé, and "bad taste." During the "kitchen debate" between Nixon and Khrushchev, Nixon presented American democracy as the opportunity to choose from a limitless assortment of colors, features, and prices.[38] In addition to the lavish display of consumer appliances in a range of colors, the American Exhibition itself showed color videotape of life in America—a new technology pioneered in the United States. Nixon even pointed out that color video was one of America's many technological advances. Color had become glamorous because it signified not only modern trends, but also the consumer splendor of the "free world."

Wells recognized the potency of color in the 1960s and she realized that airlines had not yet adopted this trend. When she rolled out Braniff's new image in 1965, the airline was saturated with bold, bright color with which Braniff tapped a larger vision of America as a hip, modern, consumer wonderland within the global propaganda war. Braniff's 1965 "The End of the Plain Plane" campaign introduced airplanes in seven different colors from a wide palette of bright colors—beige, ochre, orange, shimmering turquoise, baby blue, medium blue, and lemon yellow. (They also initially introduced a lavender plane, but the airline dropped it within a month because the people of Mexico considered it bad luck.) Alexander Girard also outfitted plane interiors with fifty-seven different variations of Herman Miller fabrics, known for their geometric prints and wide array of colors.

On July 19, 1965, Braniff also became the first airline to introduce bright colors to stewardess uniforms. Stewardess uniforms had previously stayed within a muted range of military-style grays, blues, and tans. Wells completely reinvented sky style when she hired the red-hot Italian designer Emilio Pucci to design the uniforms. Pucci was obsessed with vivid hues and was known for popularizing the "it" colors of the 1960s. Pucci prints illustrated the colorful influence of psychedelic drugs from the counterculture scene. Braniff stewardesses were now clad in vibrantly colored, clingy mock turtlenecks and geometric print leotards with plastic, Space-Age bubble helmets. (The helmets were dropped after about a month because they proved to be too impractical). These stylish outfits barely resembled uniforms. Pucci even created "teeny-weeny bikinis" for stewardesses, which were worn only for magazine photo shoots.[39] Braniff stewardesses were now permitted to wear trendy make-up, including false eyelashes—a popular fashion in 1960s America, which other airlines still banned.

Wells also chose Pucci because he represented the glamorous 1960s jet set as well as the cultural shift toward the youth scene and freer sexual mores. Marilyn Bender, the author of *The Beautiful People* of 1967, which popularized the term referring to the jet-set elites such as the Kennedy family, cited Pucci's iconic role in this beauty culture. Bender wrote that the "Pucci dress was both symbol and passport of the new era. Fragile-looking but indestructible, chic and sexy, it was the capsule wardrobe for the mobile woman glorying the body beautiful."[40] Pucci represented a major departure from the stiffer fabrics and designs emerging from French couture, embodied by Dior. Pucci's designs were sportier with clingier fabrics that fit closer to the body, requiring women to remove their girdles. These form-fitting, girdle-free outfits suggested freer attitudes toward women's bodies and represented the new liberalized sexual attitudes spreading across the nation.

Braniff did not introduce the chic, seductive stewardess just to sell flights to wealthy, ogling businessmen (although it was likely an added bonus). Braniff invented the sexy stewardess to make air travel young and fashionable and appealing to the broad middle class—including women. Sexually provocative ads have, of course, presented women as sex objects to be relished by male audiences, but they also work by eliciting women's desires to be the women in the ad. Scholars have shown how advertisers have used erotic images of female bodies to appeal to heterosexual women consumers—using the logic that images of eroticized female bodies would encourage women to buy the attraction seen in the ad.[41] By using sexually appealing images of stylish stewardesses, Braniff employed a similar logic to sell air travel to women. The airline created the iconic sexy stewardess as a consumer dream for middle-class women—who fantasized about wearing trendy clothing, hobnobbing with beautiful people, and engaging in steamy erotic scenarios.

The new stewardess look appealed broadly to middle-class women. Young people were now, for the first time, the arbiters of style for mainstream consumers in America. At the time, the fashion system was changing in important ways—haute couture (by designers such as Yves St. Laurent), which had previously been restricted to select upper-class clients, was beginning to be mass marketed to middle-class American women in department stores.[42] Middle-class women were now purchasing upscale designer clothing produced for the mass market. Airlines capitalized on this trend by using high-fashion clothing to create a glamorous image of air travel for middle-class women, who now believed they could participate in this high style. The stylish stewardess of the 1960s operated as a fashion model designed to evoke these consumer fantasies.

The Braniff campaign's use of emerging liberal attitudes about sexuality in America also reverberated with larger Cold War rivalries. *Playboy*'s creator,

Hugh Hefner, conflated the playboy ethic of freer sexual mores with progress and democracy and this logic was especially potent within the context of the Soviet-American propaganda war. The mainstream American press portrayed Communist Russia as a bulwark of backward puritanism that shunned public display of female bodies, in contrast to America's forward-thinking sexual freedom. One *New York Times* journalist, for example, criticized the Soviet Union for banning the commercialization of sex and the female body because it deprived culture of one of its most "vital aspects," yielding a "dull" and "gray" Soviet culture.[43] Sex appeal—and the commercialization of women's bodies—became a trademark of American identity, democracy, and glamour.

In September 1965, Wells introduced an ad that tapped this vision of American sexual freedom and glamour: "The Air Strip" television ad, which featured a stewardess slowly removing pieces of her Pucci uniform as an airborne striptease. In the final frame, the stewardess made direct eye contact with the viewer while flipping her hair and casting a provocative glance. The ad, which ran during the Super Bowl, was a sensation. Drawing on freer sexual mores espoused by the youth scene and the counterculture movement, the ad blatantly commercialized the sexual revolution. The campaign was the most patently seductive representation of stewardesses in the his-

Braniff Airlines, "Air Strip" ad, 1965. Author's collection.

tory of airline advertising and it sparked the rapid transition of her image in advertising. Of course, the hit campaign had a dark side. The feminist spokesperson Gloria Steinem would later disparage Wells's advertising triumph: "Mary Wells uncle tommed it to the top." Wells unapologetically responded: "I worked as a man worked. I didn't preach it, I did it."

"Friendly Skies"

Braniff's striking, youth-oriented campaign made the Burnett team a bit edgy. When Braniff unveiled the campaign in July 1965, the Burnett team was still in the process of trying to convince United executives to take a radical new approach. They feared that United needed an image overhaul to win the crucial new youth market. The Burnett team worried that smaller airlines, such as Braniff, which took a more "relaxed attitude" in its advertising, would win these new young fliers.[44] The term "relaxed" was a code word for language and style derived from the youth counterculture scene. But United's executives were still reluctant to take an advertising approach derived too much from youth trends. So, the Burnett agency was still gingerly navigating ways to achieve a youth-oriented campaign without eliciting too much criticism from United's senior executives.

In keeping with creative revolution's impulse toward anti-elitism and "honesty" in ads, the Burnett team lambasted airline campaigns that centered on "glamour," a trend in airline advertising that had started in the late 1950s. United had never gone this route. They distinguished United's solid, reliable image from the now outdated glamour images sold by its competitors, such as Continental, which was, according to Burnett, "too Balaban and Katz" and "like a Miami beach hotel—too close to the beach." "Balaban and Katz" referred to the Chicago Movie Palace Company, famous for its elegant movie theaters in the 1920s and 1930s, which had architecture reminiscent of seventeenth-century European palaces. By the 1960s, movie palace audiences had declined substantially and many Balaban and Katz theaters had been demolished. TWA's image was also faltering. Owned by the infamous Howard Hughes, who had become an overglitzed marketing liability, TWA was popularly thought of as a Hollywood, international-set airline—an image that had become passé, according to the creatives at Burnett.[45]

Most airline ads blurred together, according to the Burnett agency, because they took the same tack—emphasizing "glamour and excitement." The agency criticized this strategy, noting that confidence was the basic underpinning necessary to sell an airline and that without it all the "fancy food, drinks and pretty stewardesses in the world" would not help. Burnett professed that the agency would not turn United's image into something it was not: "a glamorous airline for the jet set." Instead, Burnett proposed that United "take glamour by the tail and twist it."[46]

In November 1965, months after Braniff introduced Pucci uniforms, Burnett's team introduced United's new slogan: "Come fly the friendly skies of United." It was largely designed to appeal to the youth market, middle-class individuals, and women by assuming a friendlier image. For Dick Stanwood, who directed Burnett's forty-person team on the United campaign, the slogan represented a "drastic change, from an older airline to a younger, more with-it airline." In a confidential letter to his friend, the Chicago columnist Sydney Harris, on August 23, 1965, Leo Burnett wrote that "everyone involved seemed to like the phrase 'come fly the friendly skies of United,' which seems to have a nice invitational quality about it, which we could live with if we can make 'friendly skies' mean something beyond the weather." They did. The slogan was a success. The "friendly skies" campaign was not intended to carry sexual connotations, but it would later become a euphemism for stewardesses' sexual availability.[47]

The "friendly skies" campaign was designed to import "warmth," "softness," and "friendliness" into United's image. "At the creative table, the ad team aimed to show as much smiling humanness as chrome-steel efficiency.... Machines are cold. People are warm. Let us show the public our warm 'good-guy' genuine concern side, as well as the efficient side they already appreciate in us." The Burnett team aimed to convey that United was "cold-blooded about operating the ship and getting you there safely," but also interested in "comfort." The creative team brainstormed: "A 'down-to-earth' airline. Our pilots are cool-headed. Our stewardesses are warm-hearted. We think the balance is fine."[48]

The campaign used stewardesses to import missing qualities into United's image. The stewardess was the fulcrum of United's new "less formal" image and her inherently feminine qualities (such as "warmth" and "friendliness")

One of our gourmet meals

More babies fly United Air Lines than any other airline.

Is it because they like the food? We doubt it. Babies fly United because their parents do. Parents fly United for two reasons.

One, United serves more U.S. cities than any other airline.

Two, United gets you there with extra care.

Take our stewardesses. They can pamper you with vichyssoise, lobster tails and brut champagne.

For the littlest gourmets, they'll warm bottles. They were graduated from a stewardess college that has only two grades: 100% and failing.

Next time you fly United, talk to one of our stewardesses. Relax. Enjoy yourself. And watch her smile. When our gals smile, you can easily tell that they mean it.

We've got 2,769 of these bright-eyed young ladies. And not one of their smiles is pasted on.

"He looks just like his father."

fly the friendly skies of United.

United Airlines, "Gourmet Meals" ad, 1966. Author's collection.

became the centerpiece of the campaign. United exploited broader American gender stereotypes to project an image of personalized service and a caring corporation. The ads used gendered language to code technology, science, and pilots as "cold," "efficient," and masculine. Serving as a foil to masculine "efficiency," stewardesses imported "feminine" qualities into the corporate environment through "friendly" service; they "softened" technology and represented "warm-hearted concern."[49]

Burnett's team also suggested modifying both the stewardess image and service style. They advised United to give stewardesses permission to "talk about most anything they wanted with passengers" and to have a "much more relaxed air." Plus, under Burnett's direction, United began to hire younger stewardesses to lure younger passengers.[50]

Developing a "friendly" and "less formal" United was important in several ways. First, it transformed United's image from a reliable, big business into a caring corporation—a critical shift in the 1960s. This image of corporate caring promised to mediate the impact of serving a mass market with less personalized service as air travel transformed into mass transportation. Within the broader context of corporate expansion, the Burnett team became invested in selling an *image* of personalized service aloft.[51]

This strategy was part of a larger advertising trend that reflected the cultural milieu of the 1960s. As mass consumption was popularly vilified in American culture, ads were increasingly designed to assuage broad cultural anxieties about environments of impersonal mass consumption. In the 1960s, advertisements were transformed from formal, impersonal presentations of specific consumer goods into messages of corporations as caring.[52] Leo Burnett's close friend, Sydney Harris, who offered input on the United campaign, summed up this sentiment in a letter to Burnett on air travel: "What we most resent is being treated as an anonymous mass. . . . In this depersonalized, automatic age, the individual perpetually feels a threat to his identity and his integrity."[53]

The J. Walter Thompson Agency (JWT), Pan Am's ad agency, also fixated on shifting the airline's image from a large, efficient corporation to a caring company. The ad team at JWT forecast the coming of air travel as mass transportation with the advent of jets in the late 1950s. They worried that Pan Am's reputation for "experience" and "dependability" had made the airline look "cold, efficient and impersonal"—an image that "lack[ed] a warm personality." Studies showed that the public considered Pan Am "big, business like, efficient, safe, somewhat impersonal." Thus, Pan Am's jet age advertising objective was "to develop an image of the company as a warm[,] friendly, helpful organization, in addition to its accepted reputation for dependability and efficiency." Pan Am's advertising plan for 1964 also focused on creating a "relaxed, fresh, friendly, and unstuffy" new image.[54] But while Pan Am's advertising agency, JWT, identified the need for this new image, the agency would struggle to make the change while other airlines blazed ahead.

The Burnett team found innovative means to tap broader American cultural shifts in ways that met United's need for a caring corporate image. By shifting United's image from a big, impersonal corporation to a more informal, "friendly" organization, Burnett subtly adopted an advertising strategy that reverberated with larger American cultural trends in the 1960s—particularly, the critique of big business and mass consumer culture. "Friendliness" made the airline's corporate persona less big business, which resonated with the youth-derived mores of the era.

As anti-elitism swelled in American culture in the 1960s, Burnett's campaign carefully focused on constructing "down to earth," "friendly," and "informal" stewardesses. While this was designed to eschew snobbery in keeping with the 1960s cultural mores, it was also cleverly intended to lure middle-class fliers by giving them the impression that they would receive special, personalized attention. This reflected the broader theme of 1960s advertising by abandoning snobbishness and appealing to "the people."[55]

United's ads also capitalized on pride in the American military and technological strength by subtly linking United's aircraft to the nation's military power—an especially potent strategy given the Cold War technology showdown between the Soviets and the Americans.[56] Masculinized descriptions of aircraft (and pilots) connected commercial aviation to Cold War visions of virile masculinity as a way to link the airline to U.S. technological prowess. But United also played up "warmth" and "friendliness" in ways that transformed air travel into a consumer service that appealed broadly to its new target market of middle-income personal travelers, including women. Stewardess "friendliness" converted aviation technology from a masculine military product into a homey, consumer product. United relied on polarized descriptions of "cold" and "efficient" (read: masculine) aircraft technology versus "warm" and "friendly" (read: feminine) service in ways that tapped larger Cold War culture discourse about gender and technology.[57]

The Air Strip, Tousled Hair, and Bodies on Display

While most major airlines had begun to direct advertising to the youth market, to outfit stewardesses in youth-inspired uniforms, and to sexualize stewardesses in ads by the mid-1960s, United's executives were reluctant to follow suit. United's conservative executives and Burnett's creative team were still vying for control over the trajectory of the airline's ad campaign. By 1967, the standoff was reaching a climax. In light of other airlines' boldly youth-oriented campaigns, the younger creatives at Burnett began pushing aggressively for hipper ads at United. Bob Johnson, who was United's senior vice president, and other United executives had vehemently opposed several ad proposals, including a "Swingers" television commercial, because they were "too much for United."

One of the contested ads designed to appeal to youth was the "Take Me Along" campaign of 1967. In spite of opposition from some senior United executives (including Bob Johnson), Burnett's team went ahead with it. Leo Burnett approved the concept at a meeting of the Creative Review Committee. Ultimately, however, the campaign took a direction that angered Leo Burnett. The ad featured wives asking their husbands to let them accompany husbands on business trips, but the final product contained words that Burnett found "indistinguishable." In a confidential memo to the staff in August 1967, he wrote that it was the "first serious mistake on this account" and he questioned the "judgment applied to certain phrases of the execution of the 'take me along' promotion." He said the agency had developed some effective ads combining "youth-oriented appeals" with some "maturity and good taste," but the "Take Me Along" campaign was "pretty empty and childish stuff." Burnett believed that the ad would "turn the stomachs of a lot of people."[58] Leo Burnett was getting older and he found the youth-derived lingo appearing perplexing.

Burnett had always taken a hands-on approach at the agency—he would walk around late at night with a green felt tip pen and make notes on copy still stuck in typewriters. "We would find little green jottings on their work—it was like Santa Claus coming around late at night," said Jack Smith, who worked at Burnett's agency.[59] But by 1967, Leo Burnett was losing creative control of his agency.

Leo Burnett had forged a new direction for United by employing young creatives—this would be both his genius and, ultimately, his demise. Those younger creatives became so influential that they would ultimately edge Burnett out of his own company. That year, in his late seventies, Burnett stepped down as the agency's president. Phil Schaff, who was also working on the United campaign, became the agency's chairman and CEO. When Burnett resigned, he was asked to stop attending the meetings of the Creative Review Committee, the body that had the final say on creative work. Burnett conceded, but with a caveat. He agreed not to attend future meetings of the committee, but he felt a "special sense of responsibility on the [United] account" and he wanted to stay informed about it. In December 1967, at the agency's annual breakfast gathering, Burnett made a speech that would be considered his curtain call. It was a stirring evocation of the Burnett philosophy, in which he warned the staff of "spend[ing] more time trying to make money and less time making advertising."[60]

At the same time, the old guard at United was also losing its grip. United's president, William Patterson, had just retired in 1966. With Leo Burnett and William Patterson out of the way, the young creatives at the Burnett agency were poised to win the upper hand in the tug of war against the more conservative executives at United. Without these old-school, chivalrous gentlemen at the helm, United's wholesome stewardess was poised to morph into a salacious sex icon.

The final straw came when even United's senior vice president, Bob Johnson, confessed that he was baffled by the new trends in advertising. When the "Take Me Along" campaign, which Johnson had rejected, was a sensation, Johnson admitted that he "didn't trust his own judgment anymore" with regard to airline advertising. He then abdicated the decision making to the Burnett team.[61]

With that, in 1967, Burnett's younger creative team effectively won control of the United campaign. United's campaign would take a radical new direction: it targeted the youth market, used aspects of youth counterculture in ads, and depicted overtly sexualized stewardesses. In attempts to appeal to youth, Burnett's team changed the lyrics of a bestselling rock song, "Leaving on a Jet Plane," and used it in a commercial. It was a huge success. The campaign was pointedly aimed at trying to get the new group of younger people that were starting to fly.[62]

The same year, United hired the French-born designer Jean Louis to develop new stewardess uniforms that were patently youth-oriented. Barely resembling their military-derived predecessors, the new uniforms were brightly colored mini-dresses inspired by the trendy "Chelsea look" created by the hotshot British designer Mary Quant. In 1961, Quant had opened two boutiques in London, which were popular with the "Chelsea set" of "swinging London." Her brightly colored A-line dresses and miniskirts were controversial—especially among adults. Quant had launched her popular mass-marketed clothing line in 1965 with the intention of designing clothes

United stewardesses in their new uniforms, 1967. Image courtesy
Flight Path Learning Center, Los Angeles. Used by permission of
United Airlines.

for young people that broke the rules of conventional dress. Her styles began spreading to the United States in 1965, when the department store J. C. Penney hired Quant to design a clothing line for it. Quant is credited with popularizing the miniskirt, set six or seven inches above the knee, which became one of the defining fashion trends of the late 1960s. The Burnett team created a major ad campaign around the new uniforms, heralding "bright new uniforms" and "sleek new jets."[63] The same year, American Airlines spent nearly $2 million to design and advertise its new "American Beauty" stewardess wardrobe, brightly colored minidresses that mimicked the Chelsea look as well.

These new uniforms represented the explosion of "mod" in America—the Carnaby Street fashions worn by the Beatles, the Rolling Stones, and their young fans. By 1967, the brightly colored look of mod style, which came to represent the countercultural youth culture of the 1960s, had infiltrated mainstream America. The trend was so popular that *Life* magazine ran a cover story on it and Johnny Carson sported a mod-style Nehru jacket on *The Tonight Show*. Mainstream America rapidly consumed mod style and turned hip.[64] New stewardess uniforms reflected this broad mania for the style in American culture.

In 1967, United's ads began emphasizing stewardess sex appeal. A United ad of that year boasted: "We go all out to please you!" Another ad showed a smiling United stewardess walking at the airport with a tennis racket in hand. The text read: "In case you don't recognize her, she's a United stewardess. All dressed up in her new Jean Louis-designed outfit. . . . Plus a very attractive stewardess to serve you one of the Club's great meals. How's that for friendly?"[65]

By 1968, United stewardesses were patently provocative. That year, a United ad showed a close-up of a stewardess's face. Her head tilted forward, she looks up directly at the viewer with bedroom eyes, a parted mouth, and a knowing smile. The text read: "You won't see Little Girl Blue anymore. Our stewardesses have shaken their blues for a fashion show full of Jean Louis originals." United stewardesses had gone from "little girls" to "women."[66]

By 1968, most major airline ads had followed Braniff's lead—and the lusty bombshell stewardess was born. Now airlines only hired women with "good" figures and they weeded out undesirable body types before

We've improved everything on our Chicago nonstop except the stewardesses.
(We know when to leave well enough alone.)

You won't recognize our nonstop flight to Chicago anymore.

Now it leaves an hour and a half earlier. At 5:50 PM. This means you can make a fast getaway from the office. And get to Chicago almost before you know it.

The plane itself has been changed, too. Now it's a 737 jet. (We now have total jet service to Chicago.) Our 737 is the newest thing in short-hop jets. It's not only fast—it's comfortable. Inside, you get as much head, shoulder, and knee room as the biggest jet we fly.

And you'll need all that room. Because you'll be swiveling around a lot looking at the stewardesses.

One final thought: if our 5:50 PM flight isn't convenient for you, we have 3 other Chicago jets leaving morning, noon, and night. (Who could improve on that schedule?)

For reservations call your Travel Agent, or United at 746-0561.

fly the friendly skies of United.

United Airlines, "Improvements" ad, 1968. Author's collection.

allowing applicants to interview. Aspiring stewardesses now had to write their bust, waist, and hip measurements on their applications. In 1968 the stewardess application for Texas International Airways included a diagram of a female figure with blanks to be filled in for various measurements, including "shoulders, bust, waist, hip bone, hip (with and without girdle), thigh, calf, ankle."[67]

This new stewardess was dressed to seduce. Most major U.S.-based airlines shortened uniform hemlines to one to three inches above the knee and started allowing stewardesses to wear wigs, false eyelashes, and other beauty products previously banned for their promiscuous connotations. Airlines also revamped hairstyle requirements to conjure stewardess sex appeal. Stewardesses had previously been required to wear short, neatly trimmed hair tucked under hats and hair dye was verboten, but this all changed with the rise of the flying bombshell. While airlines still prohibited certain shades of blondeness considered too low class (platinum was forbidden), by the mid- to late 1960s airlines were beginning to allow bottle blonde hair "as long as it [was] not obviously bleached." The 1966 edition of one stewardess guide listed banned hairstyles: "beehives, bouffants, wind-blown Italian cuts, or severe upsweeps," but the updated 1970 edition dropped the list of banned styles, noting that airlines now allowed long hair.[68]

This playmate stewardess sprawled out shamelessly in ads. Stewardesses appeared in ads, for the first time, with long, tousled hair. Previously, stewardesses were not depicted making eye contact with the reader—now, most ads featured stewardesses gazing seductively (and directly) at the audience. Airline ads also featured more sexual innuendo and titillating images of stewardesses' bodies. Stewardesses now appeared in ads lying down, dancing, putting their hands on their hips, and assuming other informal—and sometimes patently provocative—poses. Stewardesses' tongues even appeared in ads.[69]

The ad campaign for TWA in 1968, for example, turned up stewardesses' erotic appeal. The airline's "foreign accent flight" ads featured stewardesses in their new theme "uniforms." Spread out on the floor, these women looked ready to go out on dates—or stay home in bed.[70] On these theme flights, stewardesses were outfitted in disposable paper uniforms (see illustration on page 181), which ripped easily.

TWA introduces "Foreign Accent" flights inside USA

Announcing the end of routine air travel : Now, when you fly non-stop from New York or Chicago to California (or back), you can fly one of our new "Foreign Accent" flights !

They come in four styles with hostesses to match : Italian (see toga), French (see gold mini), Olde English (see wench). And Manhattan Penthouse (see hostess pajamas—after all, hostesses should look like hostesses, right?)

You'll find a whole new atmosphere throughout the plane, first-class and coach. Foreign music. Foreign magazines and newspapers. Foreign touches all around. And the best in foreign cuisine. (Yes, you may still enjoy a steak cooked to order. That's a TWA specialty).

All in all, TWA's new "Foreign Accent" flights bring you the best the world has to offer. And if you're as bored with routine flying as we think you are, you're ready for it.

Call us, or Mr. Information (your travel agent). He knows all about it.

P.S. Get ready in Philadelphia, Washington, Baltimore and Boston. "Foreign Accent" flights coming soon.

up up and away TWA

TWA, "Foreign Accent" ad, 1968. Author's collection.

But while several airlines pioneered the risqué stewardess, Pan Am floundered in a slow, fitful transition to a sexier stewardess. This was partly based on Pan Am's international role and the company's desire to portray respectability abroad. Pan Am stewardesses shared this sentiment: "I certainly was not a prude and I wasn't an ardent women's libber. I wasn't insulted by [the sexier uniforms] and I understood the marketing, but it wasn't for Pan Am, it wasn't for us. We were a world airline and that kind of uniform wasn't appropriate in all the places we flew. It would have tarnished our airline's image," said one former Pan Am stewardess, who became a supervisor in 1969.[71] But Pan Am's stewardess uniforms were also more conservative because Pan Am's advertising agency, the old-school J. Walter Thompson Agency (JWT), was behind the curve in industry trends. JWT was a large corporation so weighed down by procedures and hierarchy that it could not easily adapt to changes in the ad industry. So, while JWT identified that Pan Am needed a "relaxed" and "unstuffy" image, JWT was not able to swiftly incorporate emerging trends in American culture and in the advertising industry to meet the problem head on. In spite of the creative revolution sweeping the ad industry, the agency continued to prioritize corporate procedure and scientific study over creativity. Big agencies, like JWT, discouraged anything too avant-garde and stifled creative concepts in the long, hierarchical approval process. Finally, JWT attempted to restructure its operations to be more conducive to creative output. In 1968, JWT defined the new operating standard for its employees as a "new tone of voice" that was "attuned to the idiom of today's affluent, hedonistic, youth-oriented society." The same year, JWT hired a thirty-two-year-old star copywriter from DDB, Bernbach's pioneer ad agency, as a vice president to give the agency a younger, more creative look.[72] Frustrated with the agency's inability to adapt, he resigned a year later.

The sluggish transformation of Pan Am's stewardess image and ad campaign reflected this stodgy business culture at JWT. Pan Am stewardesses maintained the Jackie Kennedy look with a pillbox hat into the late 1960s—long after it was fashionable. While Braniff stewardesses sported new brightly colored stewardess uniforms and cosmetics in 1965, Pan Am still clung to the "natural" look for stewardesses by requiring more conservative lipstick colors, banning false eyelashes, and emphasizing "naturalness" in the press.[73] In 1966, the airline's employee newsletter depicted a blonde Pan

Am stewardess crawling on all fours, wearing a skimpy leopard-print string bikini. The jarring text, however, betraying the airline's reluctance to fully embrace a racier stewardess image, called her a "typical all-American girl": "The blonde, blue-eyed stewardess roams the Pacific . . . with her interesting career, but her ambition is to marry, settle down, have four children, and live the life of an American housewife and mother."[74] In 1969, Pan Am finally introduced a more revealing, updated stewardess uniform, which raised the hemline two inches above the top of the kneecap.

By the early 1970s, the erotic stewardess had peaked in airline advertising. In 1970, Pacific Southwest Airlines ran an ad with eight smiling and laughing stewardesses sprawled on the seats, with their feet up. The ad text read: "Pssst, Stewardess Watchers: P.S.A.'s new Lockheed 1011 TriStar jetliners will each carry 8 lovely stewardesses (and up to 300 happy passengers)." The small text noted, "And 2 wide aisles for watching the most beautiful girls in the sky go by."[75]

In 1972, National Airlines rolled out: "I'm Cheryl. Fly Me." The ads featured close-up photographs of stewardesses' faces with this titillating tagline.[76] And, in 1974, Continental introduced: "We really move our tails for you."

The sultry stewardess stereotype also spread to popular culture. Porn flicks and urban legends cast her as a loose woman with men in every port, and she became a popular fetish for men fantasizing about the infamous mile high club (in which membership is granted by having sex onboard a flying plane).[77] The sexy stewardess appeared in the wildly popular sex-oriented "memoir" *Coffee, Tea or Me* (1967), which told the adventures of two stewardesses—including party scenes with potential lesbian sex encounters, and a stewardess who worked as a part-time prostitute. The introduction noted, "You had to be promiscuous to want to be a stewardess, was the consensus of family and friends. We would have to spend our days and nights warding off rape attempts of captains, passengers and all those love-em-and-leave-em guys."[78] The "memoir," purportedly written by two stewardesses, was actually written by an airline public relations man.

By the late 1960s and early 1970s, the slutty stewardess had become standard fare in porn flicks and sexploitation films such as *Spread Eagles* (1968), *The Daisy Chain* (1969), *Fly Now, Pay Later* (1969), and *The Naughty*

Southwest Airlines stewardesses in go-go boots and miniskirts,
early 1970s. Author's collection.

Stewardesses (1975). *The Naughty Stewardesses*, a story of four "sexy flight
attendants as they live out their wildest fantasies," became an erotic cult
classic. Cornelius Wohl and Bill Wenzel's *How to Make a Good Airline
Stewardess* (1972) featured illustrations of thirty-seven stewardesses from
various airlines both in uniforms and completely nude.

In the late 1960s, *Playboy* featured several playmates who were either
ex-stewardesses or aspiring stewardesses. In fact, some women who worked
as bunnies at Playboy clubs in the 1960s went on to become stewardesses.
Playboy's creator, Hugh Hefner, also selected some bunnies to enroll in stew-

ardess school to become "Jet Bunnies" on his private jet.[79] The stewardess had gone from prudish wife to legendary American sex object.

In cultivating a sexier stewardess image in advertising, ad agencies absorbed and adapted aspects of youth counterculture and the sexual revolution to sell air travel to mainstream middle-class consumers. By poaching aspects of the counterculture of the 1960s, airline ads transformed radical concepts into commercial images and slogans. Airlines revamped countercultural proclamations for sexual liberation, which hinged on sexual equality for men and women, into sexually objectified images of women.[80]

This behind-the-scenes story of the airline ad campaigns reveals how and why advertisers produced certain ad images. In fact, multiple (and often conflicting) individuals, corporate interests, technological innovation, and cultural factors shaped the stewardess's evolution from airborne homemaker to aerial sex kitten. Various factors played a role in the rise of the sexy stewardess, including creative trends in the advertising industry, the personal interests of airline industry executives, the tense relationship between advertising creative teams and airline executives, the advent of the jumbo jet, the rise of new travel markets, the popularity of youth-derived fashion trends, and American social and cultural shifts (such as the sexual revolution and the youth counterculture).

But the industry and advertising side of the stewardess icon offers only part of the story. In fact, stewardesses responded to these provocative images in innovative and unexpected ways. These women were not dupes waiting to be awakened by feminism—they were women on the verge of revolt.

7

Beautiful Beehives
and Feminist Consciousness

WHEN AIRLINES were on the brink of hiking up stewardess' hemlines, twenty-five-year-old Patricia Griffith O'Neill interviewed for a position. Her father had been a World War I ace, and she had always idolized stewardesses as "pioneers abroad" with "cachet" and "respect." Blonde-haired, blue-eyed O'Neill had also graduated from a one-year modeling program at the John Robert Powers modeling school. The Pan Am supervisor who interviewed O'Neill found her "honest" and "intelligent" with a "good presence," but O'Neill was a few pounds too heavy according to airline standards. So, the supervisor advised O'Neill to lose weight and reapply. Following a fad diet, O'Neill managed to drop the weight by drinking iced saffola oil with protein powder twice a day. She reinterviewed and got hired in March 1964. Her recorded height: 5′6″. Her weight: 135 pounds—the maximum weight for her height, according to Pan Am's stewardess standards.[1] She flew to Miami for Pan Am's six-week training program.

Stewardess school was notoriously hellish. Women were booted daily for breaking rules and not meeting draconian airline standards. "Every day, you'd see another empty desk. If you smiled wrong, you were out. It was boot camp with white gloves and lipstick. We lived in fear," said one former stewardess. "It was like the military—so strict in every way."[2] In addition to written exams on numerous aviation topics, stewardess trainees had weekly weigh-ins and "personal appearance" checks. Being one pound overweight could mean dismissal. Airlines allotted three pounds for clothing so on weight-check day stewardesses in training wore their flimsiest, lightest-weight outfits. For personal appearance checks, these women queued up in their swimsuits and one by one were admitted into a room, where they strutted around for a grooming supervisor, who took meticulous notes on every aspect of their appearances—from nail polish color to bone structure.

O'Neill shined at stewardess school. "By all odds, the best student in the class," her instructors swooned in admiration. But they also cautioned: "she must watch her weight as she is inclined toward heaviness." Her training evaluation noted that she had a "large bone structure and rib cage. Wide

TWA stewardesses staging demonstration, 1965.
© Bettman/CORBIS.

rib cage. High waisted, low slung derriere. Long thigh line and short calf line. Must get down to 135 pounds." Her weekly weight checks in stewardess school were meticulously recorded in her personnel file. Week one: 139 pounds. Week two: 140 pounds. Week three: 142 pounds. Despite her weight gain, the airline allowed her to graduate.[3] But like all rookie stewardesses, she would have to be on regular weight-check during her first six months on the job. That did not bother O'Neill a bit—she was on cloud nine.

Donning her pristine white gloves, O'Neill jetted to exotic destinations—from Bangkok to Sydney. "It was so genteel—it was the proper way to fly. Everyone respected Pan Am. It was the first airline to serve chateaubriand. I was so proud to be part of it," she recalled. "I thought: I'm stylin'. I'm here. This is going to be fantastic."[4] O'Neill prided herself on her high customer service standards—she even went on to receive thirteen commendation letters from passengers on one delayed flight that she handled gracefully and Pan Am sent her a dozen roses in thanks.[5]

O'Neill cherished being stationed in Pan Am's first-class cabin, where she got to cavort with celebrities and sample cherries jubilee, chocolate mousse, and fancy cheeses. But that's when the trouble started. Tasting the gourmet feasts in first class on a regular basis, O'Neill started gaining weight. She tried to skirt routine weight checks by working night flights, when supervisors were off duty, but this strategy would not save her for long. Management would soon crack down and weight would become her Achilles heel. It would ultimately endanger the career she adored.

Undercover grooming supervisors would secretly ride flights to evaluate stewardesses' looks and behavior. Less than ten months after Patricia O'Neill was hired, in December 1964, Pan Am's medical department sent an ominous "weight slip" to the grooming supervisor regarding O'Neill's weight: now 149 pounds. That day, Jane Gottschall, the grooming supervisor, issued O'Neill a formal warning. The memo stated that Pan Am's weight chart indicated O'Neill's maximum weight for her height of 5'6" was 136 pounds, but Gottschall also noted that O'Neill's frame might require more weight and suggested she see the company doctor for advice. Gottschall ordered O'Neill to report for weight checks every two weeks.[6]

That was just the beginning of O'Neill's trouble. The next year, O'Neill received a series of nine "grooming discrepancy reports" cataloguing her appearance infractions. Her hair was the first problem: it had "very poor texture—does not hold curl," "should be kept neater," "too long," "too bouffant and untidy looking," and "below jaw line—must cut." Her uniform skirt was "too big," and "enormous." On top of it all, her pantyhose were "a shade too dark."[7]

Meanwhile, her weight problem escalated. To make matters worse: Pan Am lowered the weight limits for stewardesses. On November 13, 1968, the flight service base supervisor admonished O'Neill for weighing 143 pounds—11 pounds over Pan Am's new even lower weight maximum of 132. The supervisor issued an ultimatum: O'Neill had to lose eleven pounds in nine weeks, or she would be suspended. She had to report for weight checks on November 25, 1968, December 20, 1968, and January 7, 1969. Her weight loss deadline: January 7, 1969. But O'Neill was always on the go and found it nearly impossible to keep up an exercise regime with her erratic work schedule. O'Neill sent a letter to her supervisor claiming that she did not have a weight problem, but that, in fact, she just had "poor posture."[8] She did not show up for her scheduled weight checks, but this strategy would only get her so far. Would she find a way to save her job?

O'Neill loved being part of Pan Am's stylish stewardess fleet. Like most stewardesses of this era, she was wildly in love with her career. Flying was not just about earning money—it was a profession she treasured that was integral to her identity. But airline policies threatened to quash her career dreams. Airlines required stewardesses to have Barbie-doll physiques and to wear girdles at all times—and those who did not comply were subject to dismissal. Airlines forced thousands of stewardesses into early retirement (and fired them) for a host of reasons, including getting married, getting pregnant, reaching the decrepit age of thirty-two, and gaining weight. O'Neill knew the rules—and she knew she was a damn good stewardess. She hoped that a minor physical flaw would be overlooked, since she was such a service-oriented standout. But like many stewardesses, O'Neill was at risk of losing the career that meant the world to her . . . and she would not go quietly.

O'Neill would ultimately enter a protracted legal battle with the airline. Her case represents one of many attempts by stewardesses to stand up against discriminatory policies. On first glance, these postwar women, who wore girdles and primped to perfection, appear to have been unwitting victims of sexism; but upon closer inspection, we see that these pretty iconic women were, in fact, conscious of—and unhappy about—gender inequality long before the U.S. women's movement of the late 1960s offered a language and context for their complaints. While stewardesses conformed to conservative gender stereotypes in some ways, they simultaneously expressed dissatisfaction with restrictive gender norms and gender-based policies at work. Even at a time when the happy housewife reigned supreme, many stewardesses vociferously defended their choice to relinquish wedding rings for their true love: the sky.

How did these women develop a nascent feminist consciousness at a time when the American media was saturated with images of happy homemakers? The profession transformed the way these women saw themselves and their attitudes about gender in important ways. While airlines required stewardesses to comply with demeaning beauty requirements and increasingly portrayed them as sex objects, the profession simultaneously offered a space for these young women to see themselves as capable, independent, and ambitious professionals. The position provided a unique opportunity for young women to travel far beyond the domestic arena and to forge a strong female-oriented community. As well-respected professionals, they enjoyed public prestige and came to see themselves as career women, worthy of respect. In addition, since these women were required to resign upon marriage, many experienced a jarring disjuncture between their lives as career women and their lives as full-time homemakers, which further contributed to their awareness of gender inequality. Together, these various aspects of the profession made these women starkly aware of gender-based policies and fostered what I call a "proto-feminist" consciousness—an awareness of gender inequality that predates the rise of second-wave feminism in America.

Stewardesses' frustration with airline policies led them to ask questions about gender inequality and mobilized them to marshal powerful challenges to the status quo. Inspired by their love of flying, these women would rise up against airline policies that jeopardized the job they loved. Driven by a deep passion for their work, stewardesses would challenge gender discrimination, including age limits, no-marriage policies, weight limits, higher wages for male pursers, and sexualized advertising. They would organize a formidable female labor union, file landmark lawsuits against workplace discrimination, secretly break the rules, protest, picket, and launch media campaigns—all while looking pretty and feminine.[9] This militant rebellion surfaced after consciousness about gender inequality had been gathering steam among stewardesses for decades.

Ditching Diamonds for the Sky

At the time, O'Neill had not even given the weight limit a second thought—after all, stewardesses had to be pretty . . . and pretty was thin. When O'Neill first got hired as a stewardess, the journalist Betty Friedan had just published *The Feminine Mystique*, a best-selling feminist critique of American culture, but feminism had not yet become a widespread movement in America. O'Neill had never read the thought-provoking tome, nor had she been exposed to feminist thinking. She had gone to a junior college, lived in the suburbs, and traveled internationally, but the embryonic women's movement had not yet made it onto her cultural radar. O'Neill had, however, noticed that many burly male pursers (an in-flight service position similar to stewardess) were never reprimanded by airline management for their weights. She found this unfair but was not angered by it until much later.

Like most working women of this era, O'Neill, of course, had experience dealing with sexist office environments. Before becoming a stewardess, she had worked briefly as a "girl Friday" for a chamber of commerce, where she was routinely leered at and grabbed. She was generally afraid to be alone with any of her bosses. Her stewardess position felt like a welcome reprieve from this brand of harassment. At Pan Am, she felt respected and professional. "The first time I wore the Pan Am uniform, I felt amazing. I felt like I'd come home," said O'Neill. "It was such a feeling. Everybody looked up to us. We were internationally admired."[10]

Another former stewardess, who had worked at the Library of Congress, where a supervisor had tried to rip her clothes off, and as a waitress, where managers expected her to "cooperate sexually," was shocked to find that sexual harassment was not part of the airline work environment. "Here was finally an opportunity to be free, glamorous, beautiful, respected, and, yet, untouchable. I also felt respected because nobody in a position of power took advantage of me. I was finally not at the mercy of a man!"[11]

Stewardesses of this era generally felt respected by airline management, the public, and passengers. It was a high-status position. Stewardesses also enjoyed a measure of independence with respect to their social lives, including dating. Although airlines maintained rigid rules about dating (stewardess trainees were usually not allowed to date), some stewardesses were housed at hotels rather than on-site training schools, which allowed them a greater degree of romantic autonomy during training. After graduating, many stewardesses felt they were able to date for the first time without parental interference. A stewardess who flew with Western from 1961 to 1971 relished her newfound freedom: "re: dating, it gave a woman a certain freedom. . . . It gave one a little bit of an edge in the dating world."[12]

They savored a sense of independence from corporate monotony and control as well. "You could bid different trips and schedules to give you a variety in your work and if you didn't like working with someone, it was only for one month," one former stewardess recalled. They exerted more control over their work schedules than those in nine-to-five jobs. Airlines used a bidding system, which allowed stewardesses to choose their time off and destinations each month.[13]

Stewardesses also experienced some financial independence. "I managed to buy my own home as a single woman and got in two years of college while flying. I was independent before I started flying, however I become more so and very self-sufficient, even buying my own home as a single person in my twenties, which was not done in those days," said a stewardess who flew with Capital Airlines and United from 1959 to 1969. "I made my own decisions!"[14] Another former Pan Am stewardess said she earned approximately $7,000 per year in 1964, "which was great at that time!"[15]

As these young women struck out on their own, they found new support and connection through the tight-knit stewardess community. "There is definitely a bond. We're protective of one another. There is an understanding, even if we worked for different airlines—we all know there is a sisterhood," said a former stewardess. After an intense bonding experience in stewardess training school, usually between four and six weeks long, fledgling stewardesses moved to new cities and usually moved into apartments with fellow stewardesses—five stewardesses would often share a two-bedroom apartment. These women worked together, lived together, and even spent most of their free time together.[16]

As these women spent time together exploring unknown cities, dining together, sleeping in shared hotel rooms, and living together in apartments, they developed an intimate world of female friendship. These bonds were central to stewardess culture. Former stewardesses consider their relationships with fellow stewardesses pivotal not only to their work experience but also to the rest of their lives. In some cases, the intensity of these relationships resembled romances. Peggy Casserta, who was rock star Janice Joplin's long-term lover, had a lesbian affair with the former head cheerleader at her college when they worked as stewardesses together in the early 1960s. Although we do not know how common it was for these women to have sexual contact with each other, we do know that these young women developed intimate, long-lasting bonds.[17]

A former American Airlines stewardess called the relationships between stewardesses "very special": "we all understand our job more than the other non-flight attendant friends." A former Western Airlines stewardess summed up the camaraderie: "the relationships formed were similar to family/sibling and . . . often continued forever."[18] This female-oriented world would play an important role in stirring up stewardess rebellion.

Shaped by their experiences as respected, independent career women, stewardesses did, indeed, brew unconventional ideas about gender. For the most part, these women did not buy into the full-time homemaker fantasy celebrated in postwar culture. Sherry Waterman, who worked as a stewardess from 1949 to 1956, dedicated the final chapter of her memoir "to all the college girls who see life as something more than the usual progression of fraternity pin, engagement ring, wedding band, dishpan, and diapers."[19] She wrote: "Finding a short, socially acceptable all-purpose answer to the maddeningly frequent question 'How come you aren't married?' would be the greatest boon to the stewardess since the advent of pressurized aircraft. In the meantime, I suppose the girls will have to go on smiling sweetly through clenched teeth when they hear that familiar sentence—and there will always be a few who will answer, just lucky, I guess!"[20]

Connie Bosza, who flew during the mid-1940s, also loathed the pervasive assumption that she should abandon her career for marriage: "'I've had enough of your remarks. Did it ever occur to you that I may not WANT to get married? That I may love flying? That I may not want the first man that comes along?'"[21]

Chapter 7

Stewardesses vociferously defended their career ambitions at a time when American feminism was practically nonexistent. Nearly extinguished when it became associated with anti-Americanism during the red scare of the late 1940s, feminism lay shriveled and dormant throughout the 1950s and the early 1960s. However, outbursts from stewardesses (and other rebellious women) reveal that radical ideas about gender were gathering storm below the surface.[22]

Just four years after the aviation enthusiast Connie Bosza started flying, she faced the typical marriage/work conundrum. She wanted to get married, but she also wanted to continue working. Since airlines required stewardesses to resign upon marriage, Bosza reluctantly resigned from her coveted stewardess position at the age of twenty-four.

But Bosza's heart still belonged to the sky. Even as a full-time homemaker, she clung to the world of aviation. She became the editor of the newsletter for former United Airlines stewardesses and a volunteer speaker at high schools for United's stewardess recruitment program. "Flying was definitely in my blood stream and still is!" she wrote. She spent the first six years of her marriage writing a four-hundred-plus-page tome in which she described her own "deep, deep love for this flying experience." "This intense feeling is still so much a part of me that even though I am divinely happy as a housewife, who waits impatiently for her husband to come home every day," Bosza wrote, "I can't escape from the life I knew as an airline stewardess."[23]

In the unpublished memoir she completed in 1952, she betrayed how much she missed her career: "Weeks after I had left the airlines to be married, I kept both summer and winter uniforms all cleaned and pressed in the advent that the airline was so desperate for stewardesses there would be a chance of my taking out a flight. We lived just four miles from the airport and I used to lay out in the sun watching the trips fly overhead. Living so near the field, they didn't have time to gain much altitude and the plane numbers were visible. I'd see no. 062 and say to myself . . . why, you old rascal, are you still flying? And always, I'd know the trip number and in which direction it was heading."[24]

After enjoying a sense of community, respect, independence, and participation in the world through flying, many stewardesses found marital

194

life alienating and isolating. The change from female companionship to the sometimes isolated, lonely life as a full-time homemaker living in a suburban home with a working husband was a painful transition for many of these women.[25]

This disjuncture between stewardesses' lives as career women and their lives as full-time homemakers heightened their awareness of gender inequality. But it also inspired these women to take action. In 1950, four years after Connie Bosza was forced to resign from United, she founded the San Francisco Chapter of Clipped Wings, a club for former United Airlines stewardesses. Forcibly retired stewardesses organized these associations to reconnect with their community. These ex-stewardess organizations cropped up in cities around the world in the 1940s and 1950s, and quickly grew to tens of thousands of members. They organized annual conferences, staged uniform fashion shows, produced newsletters, and held monthly chapter meetings. Through these organizations, stewardesses found the companionship they missed. The newsletters and meetings offered a space for these women to mourn the loss of their careers and to express their dissatisfaction with forced retirement. Perhaps more importantly, these associations would serve as a base for fomenting unconventional ideas about gender roles, and for organizing a way to fight for their jobs.

Pretty Women Fight Back

Expressing discontent with gender inequality and challenging gender-based rules was nothing new for stewardesses. In fact, stewardesses began bucking gender-based policies in the 1940s. In 1944, several United Airlines stewardesses took action against airline policies. Ada Brown, a nurse stewardess who had been flying with United for four years, began organizing a stewardess union. She was soon joined by a fellow United stewardess, Edith Lauterbach, who had developed her pro-union activist thinking at the University of California at Berkeley in the early 1940s, where she majored in journalism and political science. At Berkeley, Lauterbach had established her intellectual commitment to unionization. She described Berkeley as "the factory that turned out some of the most rebellious people." In fact, in the early 1940s, when Lauterbach attended the school, Betty Friedan—who would later become a key figure in catalyzing the second-wave feminist movement in America— was also a student there. Berkeley had spurred Friedan's progressive politics and her feminist thinking, which would become integral to her influential manifesto on gender in America.[26]

But the prospect of unionizing stewardesses was rife with obstacles at the time. In 1946, Republicans won control of Congress and labor's political power waned. Unions were also stifled by the rising anti-Communist tide in the United States. Women were still far less likely to organize than their male counterparts.[27] In fact, airlines had initially hired female flight attendants partly for this reason. Further, airlines attempted to forestall stewardess unionization by implementing resignation regulations (such as age limits and the no-marriage rule) to secure a temporary workforce that would be less likely to organize.

Also, these young, white women, who were usually fresh out of college, considered themselves middle class, and they associated unions with working-class militancy and radicalism. Stewardesses were often from "upper echelon families and their daddies didn't want them to be in a union," said Edith Lauterbach. "It was very difficult to convince women they had a right to have a union and that there was a need for it."[28]

Lauterbach and her fellow organizers found clever ways to navigate these obstacles. Since "union" was considered a "bad word to a great deal of society," they chose the term "association" instead.[29] By 1945, they had managed to sign up three hundred stewardesses for the "association"— thereby founding the Air Line Stewardess Association (ALSA), the first stewardess union.

With Ada Brown as president, the ALSA signed the first collective bargaining agreement for stewardesses in 1946. The contract won stewardesses a pay raise from $125 per month to $155 per month, a limit of eighty-five flying hours per month, and reimbursement for half of their uniform expenses. But more importantly, the contract also won stewardesses the right to see their personnel files (which they wanted in order to prevent indiscriminate firing), and established a grievance mechanism for stewardesses to challenge disciplinary actions and unjust dismissals.[30] While the contract was a victory for stewardesses, the union had not yet won the policy changes that could save Ada Brown's job. In 1947, just two years after organizing the union, Brown was forced to resign when she married because of United's no-marriage policy for stewardesses.

Following Brown's departure, the fledgling union struggled with meager funding for several years because it lacked backing from a more established union. In 1946, the powerful, well-funded Air Line Pilots Association (ALPA) had established the Airline Stewards and Stewardesses Association (ALSSA) in direct competition with the existing ALSA. After several years, in 1949, the ALSA merged with the ALSSA in order to gain support from the influential pilots' union.[31] But the support of the ALPA had its downside: the leaders of the ALPA had unilateral power to get involved in negotiations of the ALSSA, which the ALPA subsidized, and the ALPA protected pilots' interests first. The ALPA's policy on stewardess strikes, for example, was to cross the picket lines. During the first stewardess union convention in 1951, the ALSSA established the union as a regular charter of ALPA, restating the authority of pilot leaders over the stewardesses. At the same convention, the ALSSA established the goal of applying to the American Federation of Labor (AFL) for a charter to become an independent union. As the ALSSA grappled to gain more rights and status, tension with the pilots mounted.

Meanwhile, the ALSSA won pay increases of nearly 150 percent, but the most important battles were still on the horizon.[32] At the time, one of the primary threats to stewardesses' jobs was the no-marriage rule; the vast majority of stewardesses were forced to resign for marriage. The stewardess union tried to tackle this policy head-on. In 1948, a stewardess filed the first grievance against the no-marriage rule at Pan Am and the stewardess union fought to repeal the marriage ban throughout the 1950s. The efforts were a bust. Airlines were intransigent. Leaders of the stewardess union hoped that by forcing grievance proceedings into arbitration, individual stewardesses would effectively challenge the marriage ban, but throughout the 1950s and the early 1960s arbitrators repeatedly sided with airlines. Thousands of stewardesses were being forced into early retirement. The situation was looking grim.

The other major stickler for stewardesses was the age maximum of thirty-two, which airlines imposed during the early 1950s. The ALSSA tried to bargain the age limits away, but negotiations were contentious and airlines would not budge. To counter the policy, stewardesses pulled out their secret weapon: beauty. They used their stylish looks as a publicity stunt to protest the age limit. When American Airlines announced a new age limit of thirty-two for stewardesses in 1953, stewardesses also played up their prettiness to garner public support and media attention. Aging stewardesses did not attack the ageism or sexism head-on, but instead argued that they were still pretty enough to fly. One stewardess was quoted in *Aviation Week* saying, "[It is] unfair for American to imply that when we reach 32, we all become unattractive, surly and anti-social." In a press conference about the same issue years later, the thirty-five-year-old union activist Barbara Roads would ask the press, "Do I look like an old bag?"[33] The implication was that being old was not the problem—*looking* old was.

The ALSSA managed to save the jobs of sixty-four American Airlines' stewardesses, who were thirty-two years old, by negotiating the right for existing stewardesses to work past the age of thirty-two. But it was a minor victory. The age limit still applied for new stewardesses at American Airlines and most other major airlines upheld age limits for all stewardesses.

Stewardesses also used their good looks to oppose corporate control over their physical appearances. In 1962 fifteen airline stewardesses in Los Angeles called a press conference to fight for the right to be a bottle blonde. Blonde hair dye was still banned by airlines. Reporting on the event, *Newsweek* professed that blonde hair was no longer associated with sexual promiscuity: "In the horse-and-buggy days, only a brazen hussy would dare appear in public with her hair dyed. But in the jet age, perfectly respectable young ladies change hair color faster than the speed of sound—unless they happen to be airline stewardesses. The airlines forbid their 'coffee, tea or milk' girls to be anything but mousey about mousey-brown hair." The reporter called the stewardesses "spiritual descendants of Susan B. Anthony," quoting one stewardess saying, "I had dull, drab hair before I changed it to ash-blond. My supervisor insisted I return to my natural color." Jumping on the opportunity to further normalize hair dye, the Clairol corporation suggested that airlines allow an "impartial board to set hair coloring standards acceptable to the stewardesses and their employers."[34]

While stewardesses challenged corporate control over their bodies, they did not undermine the whole concept of beauty as an important professional and feminine attribute. When it came to beauty, stewardesses treaded a paradoxical line—beauty objectified these women, yet it also advanced their public images as well as their private lives.[35] "Being free to be glamorous without being taken advantage of gave me a sense of empowerment," said one former stewardess.[36] Stewardesses relished their beauty—at times, they benefited from calling upon it, but they also were acutely aware of its exploitative aspects. Beauty was both a beast that jeopardized their jobs and a powerful weapon they wielded in their plight.

Instead of flatly rejecting the physical appearance standards imposed by airlines, the ALSSA promoted stewardesses as pretty, feminine women and used their attractiveness to gain respect as they protested discriminatory practices in the airline industry. The ALSSA's newsletter, *Service Aloft*, seamlessly blended articles and photographs celebrating stewardesses' physiques with union organizing details.[37] Even as stewardesses fought major battles against airline gender discrimination, they still insisted on looking "feminine" and attractive.

For example, in 1958 thirty-two stewardesses at Lake Central Airlines, a small Midwestern airline, walked off the job for eleven days to demand better conditions. During the strike, stewardesses wore their stylish uniforms adorned with sashes akin to those worn in beauty pageants to protest and to pose for media photographers.

"We definitely took pride in our appearances. We were programmed to look good. And to this day, I still [think] it's important to look good and be well-groomed in order to get on in this world—personally, professionally, socially," said one former Pan Am stewardess, who flew from the mid-1960s through the mid-1970s.[38]

Regardless of their good looks, by the late 1950s, stewardesses' efforts to end discriminatory policies had largely failed. These women's sustained efforts to continue working after marriage and beyond the age of thirty-two illustrate that they actively challenged traditional gender norms even during the conservative postwar years. Stewardesses did not fully buy into traditional gender norms and beauty standards. When organized resistance failed, they mounted subtle resistance against airline regulations that exerted control over their bodies and threatened their jobs. They hid pregnancies, circumnavigated weight rules by tailoring their uniform skirts, and secretly breached appearance rules. "I had a roommate who married and became pregnant right away but flew, secretly, through her 7th month of pregnancy!" noted one former stewardess. Another former stewardess confessed to lying to her supervisor: "Of course I did not have on my girdle. Was she crazy or something? How could I work a trip clear to Hollywood in a girdle? All that bending and stooping. I had suffered inexorably with binding girdles long enough."[39]

Finally, union organizers devised another strategy for bullying airlines: if stewardesses could obtain licenses, they would have more power to threaten airline operations with a strike. In 1961 the ALSSA proposed an amendment to the Federal Aviation Act of 1958 to include stewardesses in the definition of "airman" and to require stewardesses to receive certification for safety qualifications from the Federal Aviation Administration (FAA). Union organizers testified in hearings before the House Interstate and Foreign Commerce Committee in 1962, but stewardesses lost. Bulldozed yet again, they would need to find yet another way to go up against airlines. But first they would need to create a more powerful, autonomous union.[40]

After eight years of struggling for autonomy from the ALPA, the ALSSA was desperate to gain independence. The leaders of the ALPA had undermined stewardesses' efforts because, at times, their interests conflicted with pilots' interests. The final offense came in 1959, when the AFL ruled that the ALSSA was "part of" the ALPA and that the ALSSA could not be granted an independent charter without the ALPA's consent. In 1960 the ALSSA announced that it was severing all ties to the ALPA. This spiraled into an intense skirmish for control of the ALSSA that resulted in fifty-two lawsuits and countersuits that continued into the mid-1960s. Since the ALSSA had been denied an independent charter with the AFL, the union appealed to the Transport Workers Union (TWU) and in 1961 the ALSSA secured its affiliation with the TWU, thereby establishing itself as independent from the pilots. Now, the ALSSA was autonomous and it had grown from 3,300 members in 1951 to 9,000 in 1961.[41]

In 1964, the larger, newly independent stewardess union was bolstered by a critical, new piece of legislation: the Civil Rights Act. Title VII of the Civil Rights Act, which forbade employers from discriminating on the basis of "race, color, religion or national origin," and "sex," finally gave teeth to stewardesses' grievances. The Civil Rights Act supported aspiring African American stewardesses who had been entangled in long-term struggles to get hired in this coveted position. The bill also created the Equal Employment Opportunities Commission (EEOC) to investigate compliance with new antidiscrimination laws starting in 1965. In addition to providing the legal backbone necessary to successfully pressure airlines to hire black women as stewardesses, Title VII finally provided the legal muscle that steward-esses needed to challenge gender-based policies that had forced them out of their jobs for years.

"We knew it was unfair. We had talked about it for years. We were not deaf and blind!" said Northwest Airlines stewardess Mary Laffey, who was executive chairman of the ALSSA from 1966 to 1968. "But we had no legal leg to stand on until the Civil Rights Act."[42] Stewardesses would be among to first women in America to use Title VII to take on gender discrimina-tion in the workplace and they would be the first to file sex discrimination complaints with the EEOC. Stewardesses voiced frustration to their union and demanded that the EEOC set things straight. But these women were not aiming to achieve milestones for feminism; all they really wanted was to keep their jobs. Their first hot-button topics: the age limit and the marriage ban. But despite an outpouring of grievances from stewardesses, the EEOC did not take action on their behalf. During its first few years of operation, the EEOC failed to enforce Title VII regarding sex. Stewardesses refused to tolerate it. They wrote letters, picketed, and continued to pursue legal action through the EEOC.

Instead of waiting for the EEOC to take action, stewardesses devised other ways to dispute the no-marriage policy. In 1964, Betty Bateman, who had been a stewardess with Braniff since 1959, was fired when supervisors learned that she had been secretly married for a year and a half. With the Civil Rights Act now offering some legal backing for stewardess lawsuits against no-marriage regulations, Bateman filed a complaint with the union and sued. A board representing Braniff and the union was appointed to settle the case. When the board became deadlocked, the U.S. District Court in Dallas appointed an arbitrator. In September 1965, the arbitrator ruled in favor of Bateman and ordered the airline to rehire her with seniority and benefits. In October 1965, the *AFL-CIO News* reported: "Stewardess keeps job—and a husband."[43] The case touched off a series of similar cases from other stewardesses, but for most airlines the marriage ban still applied.

While stewardess union organizers were deeply engrossed in challenging airline marriage policies, they were also becoming involved in new feminist organizations that were cropping up around the nation. During the late 1960s, stewardesses lived with the prominent feminist Alice Paul in Washington, D.C. and helped her rally for the Equal Rights Amendment on Capitol Hill.[44] Colleen Boland, the president of the stewardess union, was a founding member of the National Organization for Women (NOW), established in 1966, which became the nation's largest feminist organization. In fact, one of the major catalysts for founding NOW was the EEOC's failure to investigate and bust sex discrimination in the workplace—which stewardesses had experienced firsthand.[45] As feminism coalesced into a definable movement by the late 1960s, stewardess union organizers began linking their labor concerns with the burgeoning women's movement. Stewardesses were pioneers in the women's movement, but the movement also buttressed their cause by offering a framework for thinking about issues they had been complaining about for decades. Stewardesses also cleverly rallied powerful supporters from the national women's movement, such as Gloria Steinem, who founded the feminist *Ms Magazine*. In addition, some stewardesses became active members of NOW, including Patricia Ireland, who started as a stewardess with Pan Am in 1968 and ultimately went on to become NOW's president.[46]

NOW took up stewardess discrimination as one of its first causes. The organization marshaled its resources to attack airline industry discrimination and to enforce stewardesses' rights as workers under Title VII. Backed by the nation's leading feminist organization, stewardesses became the poster children for sex discrimination in the United States. The partnership between NOW and stewardesses was mutually beneficial—by supporting this brigade of glamour girls, the budding feminist organization put a pretty face on the women's movement and received substantial national media attention. The publicity was a win for stewardesses too, who used the limelight to rally support for their cause. The collaboration between feminist organizations and stewardesses would prove instrumental in busting airlines' staunch, discriminatory policies.

But stewardesses' style of feminism was not universally approved within the larger feminist movement. In particular, stewardesses' involvement in beauty culture created an uneasy alliance between stewardesses and the women's movement. For stewardesses, feminism and beauty often went hand in hand and stewardesses' brand of feminism used beauty to give their claims more clout. In 1969, for example, one Eastern Airline stewardess gave a speech to Congress calling for women's equal rights in the workforce—the same year she competed in two beauty pageants.[47] Some stewardesses considered beauty central to advancing the cause of women's rights. "When most women in the movement were not good looking, men could just blow off the whole movement," one former Pan Am stewardess said.[48]

"I became very active in NOW and I found the women involved to be horrible. A group of us were middle class, employed, and straight. Some of these radical dykes were really awful to us. They asked me if it was part of my job to sleep with pilots. They said, 'You must be very shallow if you wear make-up'—that kind of thing. Some of them definitely had problems with anyone who shaved their legs. Ultimately, these people drove me out of the women's movement," said Anne Sweeney, who had read *The Feminine Mystique* in college, become a Pan Am stewardess in 1964, and joined NOW in the early 1970s. In response to her unwelcome greeting at her local NOW chapter, Sweeney dragged a cadre of Pan Am stewardesses to join the organization and they voted her in as the vice president of NOW's PR department.[49]

Mary Laffey, the executive chairman of the ALSSA, said that feminist organizers from larger women's liberation groups who tried to help stewardesses with their discrimination cases were often "too radical," by which she meant they had "butch haircuts" and were "butchy type of women."[50] Looking "butchy" was particularly dangerous at the time because masculine looks reeked of Communism. In an era when American identity was defined by consumerism, and American womanhood relied on consumer beauty goods, stewardesses were especially devoted to looking feminine and pretty. This was an era when the American press lambasted Soviet women for looking mannish based on their lack of lipstick and their wage work. Stewardesses skirted the possibility of being considered masculine—and, by association, Communist—by perfectly enacting American-style femininity and beauty. Feminine charm and beauty would ultimately pay off in their fight for equal rights.

Finally, in 1967, after an onslaught of stewardess complaints, the EEOC hosted a courtroom showdown between stewardesses and airline management. During the hearing, stewardesses testified about the abuses they endured as a result of age and marriage restrictions. Stewardesses also called in heavy-hitter allies from the women's movement to testify, including Betty Friedan, a founder of NOW, and Marjorie Marcous of the National Women's Party—both of whom used their clout to support stewardesses. The EEOC found in favor of the stewardesses.[51]

Meanwhile, the ALSSA lined up other attacks. "We were thrilled when I became educated about what the Civil Rights bill really said," said Mary Laffey, the union chairman. With Laffey at the helm, the stewardess union refused to sign a new contract until thirty-two-year-olds were allowed to come back to work. Then, in 1964, the ALSSA decided to bring in bigger guns: it filed a complaint with the New York State Commission on Human Rights, which launched an official investigation regarding age discrimination at the airlines. At the same time, the thirty-six-year-old president of the ALSSA, Colleen Boland, who had been forced to retire from her stewardess position, filed a class-action lawsuit. The following year, Laffey and Boland testified before the House Labor Committee along with sixteen other stewardesses, who faced early retirement because of the maximum age policy for stewardesses. In the class-action lawsuit, stewardesses charged that airlines violated Executive Order 1114 of 1964, which prohibited age discrimination by federal contractors.[52] In 1967, the committee ruled that airlines had to reinstate stewardesses fired for reaching the age of thirty-two after 1965.

At the same time, stewardesses were turning up pressure on airlines about the marriage ban. Ultimately a string of lawsuits forced some airlines to bow to union demands and end the ban on marriage. In 1967 Northwest Airlines signed a stewardess contract that reinstated married stewardesses and allowed them to continue flying. Secret marriages had become so common that Northwest supervisors placed bets on how many stewardesses would turn themselves in for being married once the new contract was signed. One United stewardess, for example, kept her marriage a secret until she was discovered when a hidden wedding ring fell out of her pocket and rolled down the hallway floor in front of a senior captain. She was fired. In spite of the new contract at Northwest, some stewardesses were still afraid to admit their marriages to the airline. Laffey said, "It was scary. I got calls, asking 'Do you really think it's okay to say I'm married?'"[53]

In November 1968, United Airlines also reached an agreement with the ALSSA regarding the marriage ban. United agreed that all married stewardesses could request a change in marital status without penalty. Stewardesses who had been discharged because of marriage and had filed a grievance with the EEOC would be reinstated with the same seniority but without back pay.[54]

Federal courts, however, still ruled in favor of airlines because the court considered marriage a factor beyond sex and, therefore, ruled it exempt from Title VII protection. After a series of crushing legal defeats in 1970, a federal court found airlines' marriage ban illegal under Title VII and, finally, the tide turned.[55]

In spite of these victories over age limits and marriage bans, many stewardesses were still deeply embroiled in crisis as airlines continued to fire them. These women would have intense clashes ahead to win the right to keep their jobs—especially with respect to weight restrictions imposed on stewardesses. "Weight check was a big issue. You could be grounded without a salary. This made many stewardesses neurotic—they would starve themselves for three days before a weight check and hope they would come out the right weight. It was quite traumatic. It was unreasonable because we had fat men flying, who were never on weight check," said Mary Laffey, who was executive chairman of the ALSSA.[56]

Patricia O'Neill, for example, was on the verge of losing her job for weight gain. O'Neill's deadline to lose weight came and went, but her weight continued to creep up. In May 1970, Pan Am removed her from the payroll and suspended her for her weight, stating that she was required to reduce her weight from 163 pounds to 133 pounds by October 30, 1970, in order to return to work.[57] She was grounded without pay until she could lose the weight.

In a letter to Pan Am on July 2, 1970, O'Neill argued that in 1968 she had fallen in a galley and injured her back, which was why she had gained a whopping thirty-three pounds. She asked to have the weight suspension removed from her record because it was actually an on-the-job injury that had caused her weight gain. Pan Am denied her request. Her supervisors did not buy her "alleged illness" and she remained grounded without pay. In July and August, O'Neill was required to weigh in at the grooming supervisor's office, but she never showed up. On October 8, the Pan Am grooming supervisor sent O'Neill a letter informing her that if she failed to show up for her weight check on October 30, Pan Am would terminate her employment. By the time her weight loss deadline rolled around on October 30, O'Neill had taken a medical leave. But while her meteoric weight gain threatened her job, there was also a big secret that she was keeping from the airline . . . a secret that would definitely get her fired.

What airline management did not know was that O'Neill's dramatic weight gain, was, in fact, pregnancy weight. In September 1970, just four months after Pan Am removed her from the payroll for weight gain, O'Neill gave birth to her first baby. Since most airlines still required stewardesses to resign upon pregnancy, O'Neill, like many stewardesses of the era, hid her pregnancy because she wanted to keep her job. In October 1970, when O'Neill was slated to return to work if she met the weight requirements, she took a medical leave of absence, claiming that her back was bothering her. She had to keep the birth a secret if she wanted to keep her job.

When O'Neill gave birth to her first child, most airlines still required pregnant stewardesses to resign. However, under extensive pressure from the ALSSA as well as mounting discrimination lawsuits, some airlines began to revamp this policy by the early 1970s. In 1971, National Airlines, for example, modified its maternity clause so that pregnancy was no longer a cause for discharge, but pregnant women were required to inform their supervisors of their pregnancies and go on leave without pay immediately. They were also required to return to work within sixty days of giving birth unless National's medical examiner concluded they needed extra time. O'Neill, however, had to hide her pregnancy because Pan Am still required pregnant stewardesses to resign.

Through a series of leave extensions, O'Neill managed to stay on medical leave for nearly three years, during which time she kept her baby a secret from the airline and she surreptitiously gave birth to a second child. On March 14, 1973, just a few weeks after O'Neill's second child was born, Pan Am informed her that her medical leave would expire in thirty days. Pan Am had a policy of a maximum three-year leave of absence. Just before O'Neill's second baby was born, however, Pan Am had been persuaded to change its maternity policy so pregnant stewardesses were no longer forced to resign.

They were now required to go on leave without pay immediately. Aware of Pan Am's new maternity policy, O'Neill wrote back to her supervisor to reveal that she had just given birth and to request maternity leave.

The airline called her into a hearing before a panel of five men. Since she was breast-feeding her newborn, O'Neill brought her baby to the hearing. Having given birth to two children in three years, O'Neill was still over Pan Am's weight limit for stewardesses. She asked the panel for a few extra months to lose the baby weight. She showed them her commendation letters. She elaborated on her love of flying and her desire to keep her prized position. The panel inspected her file. Pointing to her previous weight infractions, the panel declined her request to keep her job. On May 1, 1973, Pan Am fired O'Neill. She was devastated.

In May 1973 O'Neill had filed a grievance with the TWU in an attempt to get her job back. It took the union a year to process her complaint and, ultimately, in May 1974, the union denied that she had been wrongfully terminated.

This was a double whammy in terms of sex discrimination. O'Neill's story was standard fare for stewardesses at the time. Even after the passage of the Civil Rights Act, airlines routinely forced pregnant stewardesses to resign and fired stewardesses for being over airline weight limits. This, however, was hazy legal territory. Title VII of the Civil Rights Act protected women from sex discrimination in the workplace, but whether courts would consider weight and pregnancy protected arenas was still unknown. Stewardesses were determined to find out. By 1974, a year after O'Neill was fired, the stewardess union had filed maternity and weight complaints with the EEOC against twenty airlines.[58] Both the weight limit and mandatory retirement upon pregnancy would become major points of contention for the stewardesses and other working women in America during the 1970s and beyond.

Stewardess Feminism Flowers

By the early 1970s, the industry and the stewardess position had changed in important ways. First, the advent of Boeing's 747, nicknamed the jumbo jet, in 1970 heralded the large-scale democratization of air travel. As stewardesses were expected to serve even more passengers, the position became more strenuous. Critics predicted that the jumbo jet would become an aerial Greyhound bus—mass transportation without much fanfare or elegance. With the rise of mass air travel, the number of stewardesses also shot up. In 1965 there were fifteen thousand stewardesses working for U.S. airlines; by 1974 that number had grown to forty thousand.[59] This even larger legion of working women would amp up their protests against airline discrimination during the 1970s.

Now bolstered by the flourishing American women's movement, stewardesses responded to industry discrimination by becoming increasingly militant during the early 1970s. Fed up with the hypersexualized stewardess image that airlines propagated in advertising campaigns, two stewardesses, who had taken Eastern Airlines to court on charges of discriminatory weight and grooming regulations, formed an association called Stewardesses for Women's Rights (SFWR) in 1972. The SFWR aimed to help stewardesses who had been wrongly fired get their jobs back, to protest sexualized airline advertising, to change discriminatory policies at airlines, and to raise awareness about women's rights among stewardesses. In 1974 the group filmed a commercial to protest National's "Fly Me" campaign, which attempted to dispel the smutty stewardess image.[60] The SFWR also produced a newsletter informing members of sexist advertising and fought company discrimination by serving as a legal liaison that connected stewardesses who had been discriminated against with lawyers. The women challenging the "Fly Me" campaign confronted the airline head on—they even went on strike twice, once for more than a hundred days, which took a serious bite out of profits.[61] When stewardesses assembled against sexualized advertising campaigns, their powerful collaboration with NOW would pay off. The National Organization for Women filed a complaint with the Federal Trade Commission and publicly attacked National Airlines ads as deceptive and derogatory to women.

Beyond stewardesses' highly visible activism during the 1970s, individual stewardesses also filed a slew of lawsuits to take down airlines' unequal pay practices, maternity policies, and severe beauty rules. Stewardesses were tired of watching men get hired for higher-status, higher-paid purser positions, which involved the same duties as stewardesses. Plus, male pursers could fly until the age of sixty or sixty-five. Using the Civil Rights Act of 1964 and the

Equal Pay Act of 1966, Mary Laffey, the executive chairman of the ALSSA, spearheaded a class-action suit against Northwest Airlines. In 1973, the court ruled for equal pay and raised stewardess salaries to purser level. *Mary Laffey et al. v. Northwest Airlines* became a landmark case for equal pay.[62] Laffey, who started flying in 1958, went on to work as a stewardess for 42 years.

Meanwhile, many forcibly retired stewardesses were still adrift, seeking ways to reconnect and to relive their flying days. In 1973, shortly after being fired, Patricia O'Neill felt very alone. She attended a World Wings International meeting (an organization of former Pan Am stewardesses) in Boston to find a pipeline to other former stewardesses. The sorority-like club hosted social gatherings for ex-stewardesses—many of whom had been forced to resign. As these women mingled over cocktails, "everyone talked about how much they missed flying," recalled O'Neill. "A couple of them said, 'Why don't you fight for it? You're not going to take this lying down.' They said, 'Come on, fight for it,'" said O'Neill. "They told me they knew other girls who were fighting for their jobs back."[63]

Emboldened by fellow former stewardesses, O'Neill began flipping through the yellow pages and cold-calling lawyers. Each lawyer told her, "You're going up against big guys, I'm just small potatoes." One by one, they turned her down. "I just wanted my job back. I wasn't asking for a lot of money or something," O'Neill said. Finally, she found a lawyer willing to take her case.[64]

She then followed the exact steps necessary for pursuing a discrimination lawsuit against Pan Am. In 1974, she filed an unlawful employment practice complaint with the Massachusetts Commission against Discrimination. She alleged that Pan Am had terminated her when she asked for maternity leave/ extended medical leave due to complications with childbirth. She claimed that Pan Am had denied her even though it had a maternity policy in effect at the time. Soon after, she filed a complaint with the Commission on Human Rights of the City of New York. Sixty days after this complaint was filed, the EEOC issued her a notice of her right to sue within ninety days. In August 1976, she filed a motion in the U.S. District Court, claiming that under Title VII of the Civil Rights Act she was a "victim of employment discrimination based on her sex. Specifically, that Pan Am requires unreasonable weight standards for female flight attendants, unequally enforced between men and women."[65] Her second claim was that she had been wrongfully terminated, the airline had miscalculated her leave by including her weight suspension, and, therefore, she should be reinstated.

Meanwhile, the feminist movement burgeoned and American women fought employment policies that discriminated against them. Ultimately, Congress backed them. In 1978, Congress passed the Pregnancy Discrimination Act, an amendment to Title VII, which protected working women's right to maternity leave and benefits. O'Neill figured she now had a legal right to get her job back. "I felt it was discrimination—I was a new mother," she said. O'Neill's primary goal, however, was to get her beloved job back—not to incite feminist rebellion.

Stewardess lawsuits like O'Neill's were springing up around the country, but while these women employed aspects of the broader feminist movement in their fights to keep their jobs, they also upheld seemingly conservative gender ideals. From a contemporary post-feminist perspective, postwar stewardesses seem perplexing. Initially, these women who wore girdles and lost weight to conform to airline policies appear to have been archetypical incarnations of the mythical, quiescent "happy housewife" of the 1950s and unwitting victims of gender oppression. But at the same time, these women were fighting assertively for women's equal rights in the workforce.

Stewardesses' participation in beauty culture threatens to obscure their budding feminist impulses and activism. Beauty operated in complex—often contradictory—ways in the evolution of the stewardess image and in stewardesses' real lives. On the one hand, beauty objectified and standardized these women—it operated as an oppressive set of standards that reified gender, race, and class norms. On the other hand, these women used beauty to legitimize themselves as they expanded their public roles.[66] Beauty was a galvanizing force that united these women, a point of professional pride that fostered self-respect, and a weapon in their war against gender discrimination. By representing a beautiful vision of American femininity, stewardesses gained respect and status around the world. These women legitimized their claims for gender equality by looking like pretty, heterosexual, "all-American" women.

Although stewardesses did not radically overturn the notion that women should look pretty and feminine, they did renegotiate dominant understandings of beauty. For example, African American stewardess applicants (like Patricia Banks and Marlene White) challenged airlines' definition of the "typical American girl" and gracefully claimed that black women could be included in mainstream conceptions of feminine beauty. Stewardesses also protested airlines' age limits by showing that women older than thirty-two could still be pretty. In this way, stewardesses subtly used beauty to carve out a more expansive role for women in the workforce and, ultimately, they employed the beauty codes that had oppressed them as tools in their fight for equality.

Looking Back

While Patricia O'Neill assembled her case against Pan Am, other steward-esses also argued that weight standards constituted a form of sex discrimination and that weight should be restricted only if it impaired their physical abilities to perform their duties. However, these complaints failed to get much traction. Courts continued to rule that airlines could impose weight appearance standards without infringing on Title VII. Despite a few minor victories, this scuffle continued for decades and stewardesses remained subject to weight monitoring and the threat of termination for their weights. But the horde of forcibly retired stewardesses fired for being "overweight" and for being pregnant continued to fight for their jobs back.

Stewardesses around the country filed maternity-related discrimination lawsuits. Marilyn White, a stewardess with National Airlines who had informed her supervisors when she was more than five months pregnant, was fired for not informing them immediately. White had hidden her pregnancy for many months because she wanted to continue flying, instead of having to comply with the airline's policy of immediately grounding pregnant stewardesses without pay. In 1974, White filed a complaint with the EEOC. With several other former National employees, White then filed a class-action lawsuit against National Airlines/Pan Am World Airways, alleging that the airline's maternity-leave policies and practices were discriminatory on the basis of sex and therefore violated Title VII of the Civil Rights Act. In 1983, after fighting for her job back for more than ten years, White was reinstated with seniority. The twelve-year lawsuit resolved in 1987 when

White and the other women who sued National won $1.9 million in back pay—and their jobs back.[67]

Some of the stewardesses who fought discriminatory airline policies legally won the right to keep their jobs—others were not so lucky. Patricia O'Neill pursued her lawsuit in hopes of getting her job back. But every time her lawyer tried to set up a hearing and to access her files, Pan Am told him the person with access to her files was out on vacation or that her files had been misplaced. Pan Am found ways to thwart her every step. "The case just went drip, drip, drip," said O'Neill. Finally, by the 1980s, the case was officially dead. Pan Am had managed to stall her out and effectively kill the case. "I just thought I was in the right and I naively thought I was going to get my job back," O'Neill said. "It never happened."[68]

As stewardesses aggressively pushed to get their jobs back through legal action, major changes were also afoot in the airline industry and a new image of the stewardess was emerging. In 1978, the same year Congress passed the Pregnancy Discrimination Act, Congress also instituted the Airline Deregulation Act, which removed government control over air fares, routes, and the entry of new airlines. This would have a massive impact on the industry and on stewardesses' role in it. Dozens of small airlines surfaced around the country. In this intensely competitive new world of aviation, many airlines would file for bankruptcy; several would recover after corporate restructuring. Some of the nation's biggest players would ultimately go out of business. In this new business atmosphere, airlines no longer had to out-sex their rivals—they could now compete primarily on the basis of cheaper fares. By the early 1980s, customers saw more flight service routes and lower ticket prices. No-frills service became the norm. Glamour took a precipitous nose dive.

Reflecting these changes in the industry, stewardesses also began to insist on the gender-neutral term "flight attendant." Recalibrated as safety professionals, the new flight attendants routinely mobilized strikes and assertively defended their rights as safety professionals. Flight attendant uniforms became androgynous, professional-looking pantsuits with blouses buttoned to the collar and ties. Knees and necklines were covered. At the same time, the profession was also going coed. In 1967, 96 percent of the more than twenty-three thousand U.S. cabin attendants were women and no carriers were hiring male stewards. However, in 1971, a federal court had ruled that sex was not a legal occupational qualification for cabin crew and declared it illegal for airlines to hire only women for the position. By the early 1980s, men constituted 17 percent of the flight attendant workforce.[69] With the rise of the safety-oriented coed flight attendant and barebones service, the golden era of travel had ended.

Flight attendants continued to forge new legal rights for working women in America—as they struggled to keep their jobs and to upgrade working conditions in the 1980s and 1990s. In 1989, flight attendants' strong stance and militancy successfully beat the tobacco industry by winning a federal smoking ban on domestic flights six hours or longer—it was the first federal legislation that regulated workplace smoking. By the early 1990s, flight attendants had also managed to pressure airlines into eliminating (or, at least relaxing) weight standards. In 1991, American Airlines settled flight attendant lawsuits by agreeing to relax weight standards and to reinstate flight attendants who had been dismissed for their weights. In 1994, U.S. Air agreed to abandon weight charts and paid damages to women fired for being "overweight" in a lawsuit filed by the EEOC.[70]

Since September 11, 2001, air travel has spiraled into the antithesis of glamour with degrading security searches, stale pretzels, interminably long lines, and grumpy flight attendants. Air travel is finally truly accessible to the masses—inviting a motley crew of travelers in sweat pants. The once idolized women who serve in the sky have been largely demoted to airborne waitresses—without any special social status or respect. But the women who flew during the bygone days of glamour and pomp still relish their memories of what flying used to be.

For many of these women, the zest for flying never waned. Thousands of former stewardesses—even those who only worked for a year during the mid-1940s, still feel intensely connected to the world of aviation. Decades after retiring, former stewardesses still gather, travel the world for airline-related conventions, model their old uniforms at charity functions, publish ex-stewardess newsletters, and collect aviation memorabilia.[71]

These women kindly spent hours telling me their stories and sharing their memories about this glorious era of air travel. More than fifty-seven years after Lynne Mertes started flying, she still longs for the sky: "Those of us who really loved it, still miss it . . . airplane cabins still smell the same as they did fifty years ago."[72]

More than fifty years after her tenure as a stewardess, Connie Bosza still owns numerous artifacts from her flying days—from stacks of airline newsletters to moth-ball-scented uniform hats. Decades later, after the demise of a marriage, two children raised, broken hips suffered, other jobs taken—her five-year tenure as a stewardess still animates her. In her eighties, she lives alone in a large, sparsely decorated home in rural North Carolina. Her life as a young stewardess is contained in boxes that she opens for curious visitors. Like many stewardesses who worked during the heyday of the profession, Connie created scrapbooks.[73] The worn cover of her first scrapbook is decorated with meticulously cut out images of airplanes. Cracking open the broken binding reveals that the inside is stuffed full of brittle newspaper clippings, letters of praise from passengers, letters from airline management, dozens of passenger business cards, postcards from luxury hotels, and photographs of her posing in front of tourist landmarks with fellow stewardesses.

Patricia O'Neill, one of the many women who fought unsuccessfully to keep their jobs, still daydreams about flying more than thirty years after she was fired. She saved her uniform and Pan Am travel bag as treasured mementos of her glamorous life. She still faithfully reads the airline employee newsletters, attends World Wings International meetings, and travels with other former Pan Am stewardesses. In a recent interview, she said: "To this day, I burst into tears when I think about Pan Am. I miss it every day. I so wish it could have continued. I still miss it terribly."[74]

NOTES

Introduction

1. Passengers on U.S. airlines increased from 3.4 million in 1941 to 38 million in 1955. William Leary, "Airplanes and Air Transport," in *The Oxford Companion to U.S. History*, ed. Paul Moyer (New York: Oxford University Press, 2001), 22.

2. I use the term "stewardess" instead of "flight attendant" because it was the dominant term used during the golden era of flying and the women who flew during this era prefer it. One former stewardess said, "I appreciate your use of the word 'stewardess.' Most of us who flew back then prefer this word to the generic 'flight attendant.' To us, the word 'stewardess' denoted glamour, adventure, and intrigue." Clare Christiansen, former Pan Am stewardess, "Stewardess Questionnaire," author's unpublished form, Summer 2004.

3. William Bary Furlong, "Mostest with the Hostess," *New York Times Magazine*, May 15, 1960, 73; "Glamour Girls of the Air," *Life*, August 25, 1958, 68. For stewardesses' cultural significance, see Furlong, "Mostest with the Hostess." The stewardess Mildred Adams attended a party at Natalie Guggenheim's house. Mildred Adams (former Pan Am stewardess), interview, Pan American Airlines Oral History Project, Special Collections, SFO Library, San Francisco Airport Museum, San Francisco, Calif. On stewardess hostesses at Nixon's inaugural ball, see Gloria Ohlinger, "They're Making a List, Checking It Twice," 1969 and Fran McDowell, interview by the author, August 15, 2009. Girls in their early teens wrote to airlines and to the nation's first airline stewardess, Ellen Church, for advice on scoring stewardess positions. See, for example, Bunny Scott Laird, "Stewardess Questionnaire," author's unpublished form, Summer 2004; Janet Jones to Ellen Church, April 19, 1950, Ellen Church Collection, United Airlines Archives, Chicago; Carol Armstrong Gurdak, "Stewardess Questionnaire," author's unpublished form, Summer 2004.

4. This book is primarily concerned with the golden era of flying from 1945 to 1970, when stewardesses were still international beacons of glamour and air travel's allure had not yet waned. The story ends in the early 1970s, when a new era in air travel was dawning. By the early 1970s, the stewardess position had changed in important ways with the introduction of jumbo jets, court rulings that required airlines to hire male stewards, and organized stewardess backlashes against sexualized advertising. By the 1970s, stewardesses' militant activism had changed the working conditions and the image of the stewardess. Marking a new phase of the profession, stewardesses began using the gender-neutral term "flight attendant" instead of "stewardess."

5. For more on this trend, see Joanne Meyerowitz, "Women, Cheesecake, and Border-line Material: Responses to Girlie Pictures in the Mid-Twentieth Century U.S.," *Journal of Women's History* 8, no. 3 (1996): 13.

6. For more on this, see Lizabeth Cohen, *A Consumers' Republic: The Politics of Mass Consumption in Postwar America* (New York: Knopf, 2003).

7. At its core, the Cold War was also a war of ideas, and politicians on both sides competed to win hearts and minds around the world. In April 1950, President Truman described the Cold War as a "struggle, above all else, for the minds of men" and the U.S. government invested in publicity campaigns showcasing the glories of the American way in efforts to stem Communism's sprawl. Quoted in Richard Pells, *Not Like Us: How Europeans Have Loved, Hated, and Transformed American Culture since World War II* (New York: Basic Books, 1998), 65. For more on the global propaganda war and images of the "good life," see Walter Hixson, *Parting the Curtain: Propaganda, Culture, and the Cold War, 1945–1961* (New York: St. Martin's Press, 1997). For more on the relationship between tourism and national identity, see Shelley Osmun Baranowski and Ellen Furlough, eds., *Being Elsewhere: Tourism, Consumer Culture, and Identity in Modern Europe and North America* (Ann Arbor: University of Michigan Press, 2001). For more on the broader significance of travel during the early Cold War, see Christina Klein, *Cold War Oriental-ism: Asia in the Middlebrow Imagination, 1945–1961* (Berkeley: University of California Press, 2003). For Pan Am's stewardess training motto, see G. Roiz Logan, "Flight Service Uniform Regulations," handwritten grooming lecture notes from stewardess training, February 2, 1960, Box 28, Folder 278, World Wings International Collection, Otto Richter Library, University of Miami, Coral Gables, Fla.

8. For a discussion of how beauty pageant contestants represent an idealized vision of national identity, see Colleen Cohen, *Beauty Queen on the Global Stage* (New York: Routledge, 1996).

9. She represented U.S. stewardesses in this speech, which was recorded in the *Congressional Record*. Fran McDowell, "Lucretia Mott Memorial Speech," *Congressional Record* (1969). She was a contestant in the Miss Universe pageant and an airline stewardess beauty pageant, in which she won a trip for two to Greece.

10. Until recently, the predominant historical portrait of gender in postwar America has focused on the June Cleaver ideal and other factors that limited women's participation in the public realm based on Betty Friedan's ground-breaking book. Betty Friedan, *The Feminine Mystique* (New York: Doubleday, 1963). Recent historical literature has challenged this approach by exploring the many ways that postwar women resisted and subverted the domestic ideal. See, for example, Joanne Meyerowitz, "Beyond the Feminine Mystique: A Reassessment of Postwar Mass Culture," in *Not June Cleaver*, ed. Joanne Meyerowitz (Philadelphia: Temple University Press, 1994); Susan Hartmann, "Women's Employment and the Domestic Ideal in the Early Cold War Years," in *Not June Cleaver*; Dorothy Sue Cobble, "Recapturing Working-Class Feminism: Union Women in the Postwar Era," in *Not June Cleaver*; and Susan Douglas, *Where the Girls Are: Growing up Female with the Mass Media* (New York: Random House, 1994). Despite the cultural significance of tourism in twentieth-century America and the stewardesses' far-reaching iconic status, stewardesses have received scant attention in the historical scholarship on technology, international

politics, and gender. While numerous scholars have traced the development of the airline industry, technological innovation, and pilots, stewardesses have received minimal critical investigation. Kathleen Barry's pioneering *Femininity in Flight* offers the first academic history of stewardesses, which focuses on stewardesses' union organizing in the United States. Kathleen Barry, *Femininity in Flight: A History of Flight Attendants* (Durham, N.C.: Duke University Press, 2007). There are numerous pictorial histories of stewardesses written by former stewardesses, a sociological study on stewardesses, an anthropological study of Japanese American stewardesses, and several doctoral dissertations devoted to the topic. See Cathleen Marie Dooley, "Battle in the Sky: A Cultural and Legal History of Sex Discrimination in the United States Airline Industry, 1930–1980" (Ph.D. diss., University of Arizona, 2001); Suzanne Lee Kolm, "Women's Labor Aloft: A Cultural History of Airline Flight Attendants in the United States, 1930–1978" (Ph.D. diss., Brown University, 1995); Drew Whitelegg, *Working the Skies: The Fast-Paced, Disorienting World of the Flight Attendant* (New York: New York University Press, 2007); and Christine Yano, *Airborne Dreams: "Nisei" Stewardesses and Pan American World Airways* (Durham, N.C.: Duke University Press, 2011). While *The Jet Sex* is a solid entrée into the world of stewardesses, it also examines the larger cultural world of which they were a part, considering these icons internationally, and paying attention to what the stewardess image tells us about broader American cultural, social, and political change. This book also draws on a new cache of sources that have never before been used by scholars to explore airline industry executives' motivations for concocting each stewardess incarnation, as well as representations of stewardesses in popular culture, and intimate stories from stewardesses themselves.

Chapter 1

1. Franz Reichel and the Futurists quoted in Dom Pisano, "The Airplane as a Cultural and Aesthetic Symbol" (unpublished paper, National Air and Space Museum, Washington, D.C., 2005), 2, 5.

2. Jeffrey Meikle, *Twentieth Century Limited: Industrial Design in America, 1925–1939* (Philadelphia: Temple University Press, 1979), 4; Robert Lynd and Helen Lynd, *Middletown in Transition: A Study in Cultural Conflicts* (New York: Harcourt Brace, 1937), 469; Joseph Corn, *The Winged Gospel* (New York: Oxford University Press, 1983), 136.

3. Katherine Milner (former TWA stewardess), interview by Mauree Jane Perry, May 14, 1999, Oral History Program, Special Collections, SFO Library, San Francisco Airport Museum, San Francisco, Calif. Female passengers were also enthused about the rush of flying. One wrote a letter to her family in 1929 about her transcontinental journey aloft that betrayed her elation: "Very entertaining to be flying along 7000 feet up in a blue, blue sky, eating your lunch off a tray. Oh, it is such fun!" she wrote. "I think no matter how many times I do it, I shall never get over the thrill of landing, it is too wonderful." Helen Campbell Robertson to her family, 1929, Western Air Services File, National Air and Space Museum, Washington, D.C.

4. These stunts were common for women barnstormers and they were dangerous. In 1920, "Ethel Dare" died during a plane-to-plane transfer via a hanging rope ladder, a stunt she performed regularly. In 1921, Laura Bromwell set a women's loop-the-loop record with

199 consecutive loops—she subsequently crashed and died while looping a plane. Kathleen Brooks-Pazmany, *United States Women in Aviation, 1919–1929* (Washington, D.C.: Smithsonian Institution Press, 1991), 4.

5. United Airlines, press release, August 1948, 4, Ellen Church Collection, United Airline Archives, Chicago.

6. Ultimately, the materials were too expensive to make this a viable option. Corn, *The Winged Gospel*, 95.

7. In 1913 one aviator carried passengers between San Francisco and Oakland and in 1914 the first scheduled passenger airline began service in the United States flew between Tampa and St. Petersburg, Florida. Henry Ladd Smith, *Airways: The History of Commercial Aviation in the United States* (Washington, D.C.: Smithsonian Institution Press, 1991), 84, 106. In 1926, U.S. airlines carried less than six thousand passengers. Rich Freeman, "The Pioneering Years: Commercial Aviation, 1920–1930," U.S. Centennial of Flight Commission, http://www.centennialofflight.gov/essay/Commercial_Aviation/1920s/Tran1.htm. For more on early attempts to make passenger air travel profitable, see Smith, *Airways*, 113.

8. On the other end of the range, the trip by railroad could cost as much as $230 round trip—depending on the railway company, berth size, and class of service. General Passenger Traffic Manager, "Standard and Tourist Pullman Car Fares," brochure, 1930, California State Railroad Museum, Sacramento, Calif. Southern Pacific, "Four Great Routes," brochure, 1930, California State Railroad Museum, Sacramento, Calif.

9. In the months following serious airplane crashes, air passenger traffic plummeted. Smith, *Airways*, 343. For more on pilots' bad reputation and the airline industry's campaign to revamp it, see Corn, *The Winged Gospel*, 75.

10. In 1909, Maxwell-Briscoe sponsored Alice Ramsey, the first woman to drive across the United States. Virginia Scharff, *Taking the Wheel: Women and the Coming of the Motor Age* (New York: Free Press, 1991), 76. For more on how airlines used women pilots to prove that flying was safe and easy, see Corn, *The Winged Gospel*, 71–90. Even though women only constituted a small percentage of air travelers at the time, airline marketing officials designed special women's departments to convince women that flying was safe because they believed that wives influenced their businessman husbands' decisions about whether to fly or take the train. Suzanne Lee Kolm, "Women's Labor Aloft: A Cultural History of Airline Flight Attendants in the United States, 1930–1978" (Ph.D. diss., Brown University, 1995), 153. Curtiss-Wright, one of the largest aircraft manufacturers, created a women's department in 1929 to send promotional mailings to "all women who pilot planes, who fly in planes, or who are interested in flying." Newsletter, United Airlines Archives, Women's Department, Curtiss-Wright Corp., August 3, 1930.

11. Women were the primary sales force for private-market planes. Corn, *The Winged Gospel*, 76–77.

12. For more on women in the 1920s, see Lois Banner, *Women in Modern America: A Brief History*, 2nd ed. (San Diego: Harcourt Brace Jovanovich, 1995).

13. R. E. G. Davies, *Airlines of the United States since 1914* (London: Putnam, 1972), 582.

14. German and English airlines first hired "cabin boys" in 1922. Smith, *Airways*, 113. Since Stout Air Services carried fewer than 150 passengers per month on this route, service

was quickly discontinued. Stout was ultimately taken over by United Airlines. Pan Am hired male stewards in 1929. Most of this small steward corps in the United States was eliminated around 1930. Helen McLaughlin, *Footsteps in the Sky: An Informal Review of U.S. Airlines Inflight Service 1920s to the Present* (Denver, Colo.: State of the Art, Ltd., 1994), 2–8.

15. Steve Stimpson to Adrian Delfino (United Airlines historian), August 11, 1969, Steve Stimpson Collection, United Airlines Archives, Chicago.

16. Claudia Mitchell and Jacqueline Reid-Walsh, eds., *Girl Culture: An Encyclopedia* (Westport, Conn.: Greenwood, 2007), 215; Dorothy Verrill, *The Sky Girl* (New York: Century, 1930).

17. Suzanne Kolm, "'Who Says It's a Man's World?' Women's Work and Travel in the First Decades of Flight," in *The Airplane in American Culture*, ed. Dom Pisano (Ann Arbor: University of Michigan Press, 2003), 147. In 1937, railroads, which had used African American porters, began hiring young, white female nurses as "stewardesses" too. See Eunice Peterson Hoevet, R.N., "Nurse Stewardesses: Nursing Takes to the Railroad," *American Journal of Nursing* 37, no. 1 (1937); Kathryn Cogley, "Girl on the Train," *American Magazine*, June 1942; "Women on Wheels," *Time*, August 10, 1937. Steve Stimpson, "Couriers," memo to A. G. Kinsman, passenger traffic manager at Boeing Air Transport, February 24, 1930, Steve Stimpson Collection, United Airlines Archives, Chicago.

18. In 1969, there was some debate over whether Stimpson was the first to propose the idea of stewardess service. United's corporate historian A. G. Delfino exchanged letters with Steve Stimpson to try to clarify this issue. Kinsman later claimed to have proposed the idea first.

19. Steve Stimpson, "Young Women Couriers," memo to A. G. Kinsman, passenger traffic manager at Boeing Air Transport, February 24, 1930, Steve Stimpson Collection, United Airlines Archives, Chicago.

20. Patricia Patterson Dudley, interview by the author, August 31, 2011.

21. The story of the stewardesses' origin rings of PR puff, and there have been enough rumblings to suggest that there is more to the story than offered by Boeing's PR department. Two decades later, J. E. Schaefer, who was an employee of Boeing during the 1930s, refuted this version of the story, which was published in *U.S. Air Services* magazine in 1955. In a letter to the magazine's editor, Schaefer claimed that he was in the office with George Wheat, the vice president of Boeing, Harold Carry, Boeing's director of traffic, and Phil Johnson, then the president of Boeing, discussing how to remove wives' objections to men flying and someone in the office suggested female attendants. Schaefer claimed the idea originated there and somehow seeped into United's publicity department. Letter from J. E. Schaefer to Earl Findley, *U.S. Air Services*, Washington, D.C., June 24, 1955, Ellen Church Collection, United Airlines Archives, Chicago. More than ten years after Schaefer stepped forward, a Mr. Kipfer claimed that *he* was the one who first proposed female nurse stewardesses to Steve Stimpson. In 1968, Adrian Delfino, the United Airlines corporate historian, wrote to Stimpson on this matter, to which Stimpson replied: "I definitely do not recall ever hearing any suggestions or ideas from Mr. Kipfer or anyone else, that we start and get going with the first stewardess service. You know where it all started—United Air Lines offices in the St. Francis hotel, San Francisco." Stimpson then added: "At this late date, this sort of gives me a headache."

Letter from Steve Stimpson to Adrian Delfino, Oct. 16, 1968, Steven Stimpson Collection, United Airlines Archives, Chicago. United's corporate historian responded by telling Stimpson that the stewardess origination story would officially remain as it was unless Mr. Kipfer could provide more evidence to substantiate his claim for conceiving the idea. Subsequently, another person who was intimately involved with United at the time also wrote United's historian to set the record straight. This letter writer (whose name is illegible in the handwritten missive) claimed that Ellen Church had not gone to the office to ask for a position as a pilot, but rather to ask about ticket prices to visit Iowa, and that a Robert Sterling had come up with the idea of crediting both Ellen Church and Steve Stimpson for the stewardess idea. Claiming to be a close friend of Mary O'Connor (a famous chief stewardess at United who started in 1933 and worked until 1960), this person asserted that O'Connor believed Steve Stimpson had considered women, but not nurses. Handwritten letter from unknown person, n.d., Ellen Church Collection, United Airlines Archives, Chicago.

22. U.S. Department of Labor, Bureau of Labor Statistics, *Wages and Hours of Labor*, table 319 (1932). Kathleen Barry notes that airlines were willing to pay female stewardesses as much as male stewards, but I have not seen evidence of this, such as pay stubs for male stewards in the 1920s or 1930s. Kathleen Barry, *Femininity in Flight: A History of Flight Attendants* (Durham, N.C.: Duke University Press, 2007), 22.

23. Plus, airline executives were worried that their employees would unionize because other transportation service workers, such as railroad porters, had organized powerful unions. Even though African Americans, who constituted the majority of railroad porters and maids, had been barred from the American Railway Union, they successfully organized a militant union in 1925. Georgia Nielsen, *From Sky Girl to Flight Attendant: Women and the Making of a Union* (New York: Cornell University Press, 1982), 26–30. For more on the ALPA, see George Hopkins, *The Airline Pilots: A Study in Elite Unionization* (Cambridge, Mass.: Harvard University Press, 1971), 179.

24. Memo from Steve Stimpson to Mr. Humphries, "Re: young women stewardesses," April 8, 1930, Steve Stimpson Collection, United Airlines Archives, Chicago.

25. "Stewardess Instructions," training manual, 1936, American Airlines Collection, Special Collections, C. R. Smith Museum, Fort Worth, Tex.

26. Ellen Church, "The Nurse in Aviation," *Pacific Coast Journal of Nursing* 26, no. 9 (1930): 578. Press release, written by Ellen Church, Boeing air transport, undated (ca. 1930), Ellen Church Collection, United Airlines Archives, Chicago.

27. "Boeing System Stewardess Manual," training manual, 1931, Boeing Corporation, Special Collections, Boeing Corporate Archives, Seattle, Wash. Duties were also listed in *Davis' Nursing Survey: A Publication Devoted to the Educational Problems of the Nursing Profession* 2, no. 5 (1938), 82-83.

28. Train travel from Chicago to New York in 1930 took approximately twenty hours compared to twenty-eight hours for coast-to-coast airplane flights, but flights were unpredictable and could be delayed for days. For train times, see *The Official Guide of Railways and Steam Navigation Lines of the U.S.* (New York: National Railway, 1930), 131.

29. Letter, from Mr. Knutson to William Patterson, "Re: Airport Trip West April 7 to 13, 1935," April 15, 1935, Ellen Church Collection, United Airlines Archives, Chicago.

30. Ellen Church quoted in Press release, United Airlines, August 1948, Ellen Church Collection, United Airlines Archives, Chicago.

31. Hiring statistics in "U.S. Airways Lists 135 Stewardesses," *New York Times*, March 9, 1935; "5,000 Seek 20 Jobs as Air Stewardesses," *New York Times*, October 17, 1935.

32. On stewardesses' wages and wage comparisons, see Barry, *Femininity in Flight*, 29. Pullman porters earned approximately $75 to $90 (plus tips) in the 1930s. U.S. Department of Labor, *Wages and Hours of Labor*. For more on wage comparisons, see also Kolm, "Women's Labor Aloft," 88–89 and Mary Elizabeth Pidgeon, *Women in the Economy of the United States of America* (Washington, D.C.: U.S. Department of Labor, Women's Bureau, 1937), 125–28.

33. Karen Saucier Lundy and Sharyn Janes, *Community Health Nursing: Caring for the Public's Health* (n.p.: Jones and Bartlett, 2001), 88.

34. Mary O'Connor, *Flying Mary O'Connor* (New York: Rand McNally, 1961), 24.

35. Mary Roberts (the editor of the *American Journal of Nursing*) to Robert Johnson (at Boeing Air Transport), July 8, 1931, Boeing Corporation, Special Collections, Boeing Corporate Archives, Seattle, Wash.

36. Steve Stimpson, memo to United Airlines, January 25, 1936, Ellen Church Collection, United Airlines Archives, Chicago.

37. Historians such as Joseph Corn and Kathleen Barry have also argued that airlines hired female nurse stewardesses as part of their campaigns to convince the public that flying was safe. Steve Stimpson sent a memo to Boeing's vice president noting that stewardesses would be publicized as "institutionally trained," rather than nurses. See Steve Stimpson, "Re: Stewardesses," memo to Mr. Humphries, April 22, 1930, Steve Stimpson Collection, United Airlines Archives, Chicago. Boeing's first press release announced stewardesses as "young women, who have had institutional training." Ellen Church, "Boeing Air Transport," press release, n.d., ca. 1930, Ellen Church Collection, United Airlines Archives, Chicago; Harold Gray, Boeing's director of traffic, interdepartmental memo to Ellen Church, November 19, 1930, Ellen Church Collection, United Airlines Archives, Chicago.

38. Mr. Knutson, "Re: Airport Trip West April 7 to 13, 1935," letter to William Patterson, April 15, 1935, Ellen Church Collection, United Airlines Archives, Chicago.

39. I reviewed hundreds of airline ads from the 1930s. Occasionally, these ads mentioned "stewardess service" in lists of perks offered, but stewardesses were seldom mentioned in the ads and the nursing qualification was not mentioned. See, for example, the early Boeing ad printed in William Garvey and David Fisher, *The Age of Flight: A History of America's Pioneering Airline* (Greensboro, N.C.: Pace Communications, 2002), 46.

40. Lundy and Janes, *Community Health Nursing*, 88. See films such as *War Nurse* (1930), *Night Nurse* (1931), *Once to Every Woman* (1934), and *The White Parade* (1934). The popular career novel *Jane, Stewardess of the Airlines* (1934), for example, tells the story of a stewardess who boldly risks her life to save the male pilots during a plane crash. Ruthe S. Wheeler, *Jane, Stewardess of the Air Lines* (Chicago: Goldsmith, 1934). See also Chrissie Brodigan, "Flying Girls, Super Sleuths, and Sex Goddesses: The Transformation and Disappearance of the Airborne Heroine in Popular Fiction 1911–1982," George Mason University, http://chnm.gmu.edu/cabinandcrew/essays/heroines/p10.html.

41. Alice Kessler-Harris, *Out to Work: A History of Wage-Earning Women in the United States* (New York: Oxford University Press, 1982), 254; Elaine Tyler May, *Pushing the Limits: American Women, 1940–1961* (New York: Oxford University Press, 1998), 21.

42. Airlines might also have wanted to create a wholesome stewardess image because if the stewardesses appeared to be sexually available, then this might have alienated wives, who influenced their husbands' decisions to fly. Popular culture in the 1930s also reflected the wholesome stewardess image. In 1937, a cartoon in the *New Yorker*, for example, depicted a stewardess being grabbed by a male passenger and a male pilot, but she resisted their advances. The tag line read: "er-please sir. We mustn't interpret the word 'hostess' too broadly." Cartoon reprinted in Peter Arno, "Boy Meets Girl—on the Airways," *Life*, March 29 1937, 18, TWA File, National Air and Space Museum, Washington, D.C.

43. Velma Maul, flight diary, April 17–September 6, 1933, Entries May 17, May 30, Velma Maul Tanzer Collection, National Air and Space Museum, Washington, D.C.; "Stewardess Instructions," American Airlines Collection, Special Collections, C. R. Smith Museum, Fort Worth, Tex.

44. Boeing, "Stewardess Circular No. 1: Traffic Memorandum to the Girls," May 15, 1930, Boeing Corporation, Special Collections, Boeing Corporate Archives, Seattle, Wash.

45. "Stewardess Instructions," American Airlines Collection, Special Collections, C. R. Smith Museum, Fort Worth, Tex.

46. O'Connor, *Flying Mary O'Connor*, 115; Kolm, "'Who Says It's a Man's World?,'" 152. For another example of a stewardess who slapped a male passenger, see also Patricia Patterson Dudley, interview by the author, August 31, 2011. During this interview, Patricia Patterson Dudley, the daughter of William Patterson, the president of United, mentioned that her father would never have allowed male passengers to get fresh with stewardesses—he was too gentlemanly to accept that kind of behavior.

47. After the Civil Aeronautics Board (CAB) began imposing fare regulations in the late 1930s, images of stewardesses started cropping up for the first time in airline advertisements. The first images of stewardesses in airline ads appear in the late 1930s and early 1940s. The CAB and its impact on stewardesses' role in the industry are discussed in the next chapter.

48. Nielsen, *From Sky Girl to Flight Attendant*, 16.

49. Kolm, "'Who Says It's a Man's World?,'" 151.

50. These numbers are approximations. See, Barry, *Femininity in Flight*, 41; Freeman, "The Pioneering Years"; Smith, *Airways*, 106.

51. This included a few male pursers and stewards. Nielsen, *From Sky Girl to Flight Attendant*; Kolm, "'Who Says It's a Man's World?,'" 153.

52. Seven domestic lines used hostesses; one domestic line and two lines extending to foreign countries used male stewards. Eastern hired female stewardesses in 1931, according to *Air Legion Weekly*, December 4, 1931, 7. But Eastern went back to male attendants and then hired women again in the 1940s. Statistics from the Bureau of Air Commerce quoted in *Boeing News*, September 1937, Boeing Corporation, Special Collections, Boeing Corporate Archives, Seattle, Wash. In 1937, 105 male stewards and 286 stewardesses worked on American-operated airlines. "Contact," *New York Times*, July 11, 1937; Bureau of Air Commerce, *Boeing News*, 1937, Boeing Corporation, Special Collections, Boeing Corporate Archives, Seattle, Wash. For more on male waiters, see Dorothy Sue Cobble,

Dishing It Out: Waitresses and Their Unions in the Twentieth Century (Chicago: University of Illinois Press, 1992), 18.

53. In 1943, more than 486,000 women worked in aviation (as riveters, aeronautical engineers, and other positions) and constituted 36.5 percent of aviation industry workers. Deborah Douglas, *American Women and Flight since 1940* (Lexington: University Press of Kentucky, 2004), 20. Women also worked in the military as pilots through the Women Airforce Service Pilots (WASP); they flew military aircraft and tow targets, taught flight instruction, and ferried planes. Reina Pennington, "Clipped Wings: The Rise and Fall of the Women Airforce Service Pilots of World War II," *Minerva: Quarterly Report on Women and the Military* (February 1998): 28.

54. Betty Baxter Anderson, *Peggy Wayne, Sky Girl: A Career Story for Older Girls* (New York: Cupples and Leon, 1941), 110.

55. The stewardess Mary O'Connor, for example, took leave to enlist as a Navy nurse, where she organized air service evacuation for the Navy during the war. Some women became stewardesses after serving in the army. Mary O'Connor, *Flying Mary O'Connor* (New York: Rand McNally, 1961). Bev Bennis, for example, enlisted in the U.S. Navy WAVES then became a stewardess for Eastern in 1946. Bev Bennis, "Stewardess Questionnaire, author's unpublished form, Summer 2004. Student pilot license issued to Ellen Church, May 21, 1935, Ellen Church Collection, United Airlines Archives, Chicago.

56. In 1934, when Central Airlines hired Helen Richey, the first female copilot for a commercial airline, as a short-term publicity stunt, the all-male pilots' union complained to airline management and to the Air Commerce Department that Richey was physically too weak to fly in bad weather. Douglas, *American Women and Flight*, 9, 176. The department had previously considered grounding all female pilots during their menstrual periods, and it backed the male pilots' association by limiting women pilots to flying only when the weather was good. Corn, *The Winged Gospel*, 80; Douglas, *American Women and Flight*, 110–12. Commercial airlines in the United States did not hire another female pilot until 1973, when Frontier Airlines hired the copilot Emily Warner. While precise data do not exist on how many stewardesses had previously trained as pilots, it was not uncommon for stewardesses hired during the 1930s, 1940s, and 1950s to have pilot licenses or at least some training flying planes. Grace Burt Walker was a WASP pilot then became a stewardess. Valerie Lester, *Fasten Your Seat Belts!: History and Heroism in the Pan Am Cabin* ([McLean, Va.]: Paladwr Press, 1995), 98. A young woman named Serafina Dickerman, who formed an aviation club at her high school in the 1930s, went on to train as a pilot for the Civil Aeronautics Authority. She graduated as a pilot in 1941 then went on to become an Eastern Airlines stewardess in 1943. Serafina Dickerman Collection, National Air and Space Museum, Washington, D.C. My questionnaires and interviews with former stewardesses revealed more stewardesses with pilot training: Darlene Deichler, hired by Western Airlines in the mid-1960s, trained to fly on a Cessna 150. Linda Groves Fuller, an Eastern stewardess starting in the early 1960s, trained as a pilot. Jean Smith Fuller, who became a Pan Am stewardess in 1958, had a pilot's license for a twin engine and flew her own plane for twenty years. Carolyn Goff, who became a Pan Am stewardess in 1956, had six hours of training in a Cessna 152 toward a license. Tori Johnson-Kelso, who worked with Pan Am starting in 1960, was also trained to fly on a Cessna 150.

Chapter 2

1. By 1960, that percentage had risen to 20.2 percent. Myron Gutmann, Sara Pullum-Pinon, and Thomas Pullum, "Three Eras of Young Adult Home Leaving in Twentieth-Century America," *Journal of Social History* 35, no. 4 (2002): appendix B.

2. Norma Gaskill Travis, "Stewardess Questionnaire," author's unpublished form, Summer 2004; For a similar take on the position, see Sylvia Ortleib, "Stewardess Questionnaire," author's unpublished form, Summer 2004. Many new stewardesses, especially those starting in the mid-1940s and the 1950s, had never left their hometowns before starting their careers. By the 1960s, more stewardesses had experienced living away from home for college prior to stewardess work, but some had never left home before flying. For example, Linda Peddy had never stayed in a hotel until she interviewed with Braniff in 1968. Linda Lowrey Peddy, "Stewardess Questionnaire," author's unpublished form, Summer 2004.

3. Suzanne Lee Kolm, "Women's Labor Aloft: A Cultural History of Airline Flight Attendants in the United States, 1930–1978" (Ph.D. diss., Brown University, 1995), 166. In the 1950s, there were 18,000 applicants one year for 511 stewardess positions at American Airlines. Mildred Jackson, stewardess scrapbook, 1950s, Mildred Jackson scrapbook, Kiwi Club, Dallas, Tex.

4. For example, in 1956, four major airlines rejected Constance Mazarella before Pan Am hired her for a stewardess position. Constance Mazarella, "Stewardess Questionnaire," author's unpublished form, Summer 2004. See also Betty Lou Ruble Snyder, "Stewardess Questionnaire," author's unpublished form, Summer 2004.

5. Requirements varied slightly for different airlines. In 1946, Pan Am required stewardess applicants to be twenty-one to twenty-seven years old, single, 5'3" to 5'7" tall, weigh less than 130 pounds, and have "good posture" and an "attractive appearance" (including a "good figure" and "natural" color hair). D. E. Mills, "P.A.A. Passenger Service Memo," circular traffic memo, March 13, 1946, 1, Pan Am World Airways Collection, Otto Richter Library, University of Miami, Coral Gables, Fla. See also Press release, American Airlines Archives, January 5, 1945, 1, American Airlines Collection, Special Collections, C. R. Smith Museum, Fort Worth, Tex.; *Senior Scholastic*, February 10, 1947.

6. *Chicago Daily Tribune*, June 7, 1957, B5; Olga Curtis, "Formula: Snaring Hubby Easy Trick, Airline Stewardesses Prove," magazine article, June 18, 1956, Mildred Jackson, personal collection; Kay Canfield, "Expert Tells How to Pack Your Cosmetics," *Chicago American*, May 26, 1953. In 1954, NBC-TV's daily *Home Show* featured an interview with Jackson on training air hostesses. American Airlines, press release, 1949, Mildred Jackson scrapbook, Kiwi Club, Dallas, Tex.; American Airlines, "Biographical Notes—Mildred Jackson," press release, n.d., ca. 1953, Mildred Jackson scrapbook, Kiwi Club, Dallas, Tex.

7. Estelle Atwell, "What to Wear," *Chicago Sunday Tribune*, July 19, 1953; "Pogue's: Teens! Here They Are . . . Our 3 'Try-out' Judges," newspaper clipping, n.d., Mildred Jackson scrapbook, Kiwi Club, Dallas, Tex.

8. Curtis, "Formula."

9. Barbara Rafferty, "Stewardess Trainer Debunks Theory Flying Leads to Romance," *Chicago Daily Tribune*, July 5, 1956.

10. Bill Styles, "She Likes a Job 'Plane 'n Fancy,'" *Chicago Sun-Times*, December 11, 1955; Betty Walker, "Sky's No Limit for Her," *Chicago Sun-Times*, March 28, 1950; Marge

Varner, "Eight Careerists Honored at 2nd Annual Observance," newspaper clipping, 1957, Mildred Jackson scrapbook, Kiwi Club, Dallas, Tex.; Ruth MacKay, "She Sets Three Goals and Reaches All of Them," *Chicago Daily Tribune*, April 2, 1956; "Miss Mildred Jackson, '46, Wins Contest; Is No. 1 Saleswoman for American Airlines," *Baylor Line*, newspaper article, 1954, Mildred Jackson scrapbook, Kiwi Club, Dallas, Tex.; "Supervisor of Air Line Stewardess Training to Speak Twice Here Today," *Chicago American*, newspaper clipping, Mildred Jackson scrapbook, Kiwi Club, Dallas, Tex.

11. For example, she gave a speech at the sales executives club in Chicago, in 1952, titled "How to Get a Girl" on her employee recruitment strategies. Unknown author (from American Airlines department headquarters) to Art Hetherinton Jr. (regional direction PR), February 27, 1956, Mildred Jackson scrapbook, Kiwi Club, Dallas, Tex.

12. Lizabeth Cohen, *A Consumers' Republic: The Politics of Mass Consumption in Postwar America* (New York: Knopf, 2003), 122; Juliann Sivulka, *Ad Women: How They Impact What We Need, Want, and Buy* (New York: Prometheus Books, 2008).

13. For more on how expanding consumer needs precipitated women moving into the workforce and for the number of women wage-workers in 1960, see Alice Kessler-Harris, *Out to Work: A History of Wage-Earning Women in the United States* (New York: Oxford University Press, 1982), 302. In 1940, 27.4 percent of American women were in the workforce; the percentage rose to 35 percent in 1944 and fell to 29.8 percent in 1947. For statistics on women in the workforce during this era, see Leila Rupp and Verta Taylor, *Survival in the Doldrums: The American Women's Rights Movement, 1945 to the 1960s* (New York: Oxford University Press, 1987), 13. In 1950, American women made up 29 percent of the workforce; in 1965 they made up 35 percent. Kessler-Harris, *Out to Work*, 301. For more on the disjuncture between real-life working women and idealized housewives, see Susan Douglas, *Where the Girls Are: Growing up Female with the Mass Media* (New York: Random House, 1994).

14. Frances Aves Smith, *Opportunities for Youth in Air Transportation*, Air-Age Education Research (New York: American Airlines, 1944), 6.

15. At the time, airlines were still targeting primarily wealthy businessmen. An American Airlines survey of 1953 found that more than 30 percent of air travel passengers had incomes over $15,000 per year and 79 percent of first-class passengers were men (60 percent in coach). Passenger survey, 1953, American Airlines Collection, Special Collections, C. R. Smith Museum, Fort Worth, Tex. In 1955, Pan Am's ad agency remarked on a definitive link between income, education, and the desire for foreign travel. The agency described Pan Am travelers as "college graduates" with family incomes of at least $5,000 per year (more often over $7,500 per year), "pleasure bent with cultural interests," and "averaging 40 years old." For the data on Pan Am's passengers, see the following documents in the J. Walter Thompson Collection, John W. Hartman Center for Sales, Advertising and Marketing History, Duke University, Durham, N.C.: "Pan Am World Airways Script for System Sales Meeting," meeting agenda, December 6, 1955, Review board records, box 23, folder: meetings 1955–56; "Advertising Plan for 1957," meeting minutes, 1957, Meetings Pan Am Minutes 1957, box 23. For passenger mile statistics, see Deborah Douglas, *American Women and Flight since 1940* (Lexington: University Press of Kentucky, 2004), 112.

16. In 1948 the CAB permitted Capital Airlines to reduce fares to match Pullman fares as a way to compete against trains. Other airlines followed suit. It was not until 1953 that airlines surpassed railroads in carrying Americans distances of two hundred miles or more. Kolm, "Women's Labor Aloft," 134.

17. This number included a few stewards. From 1945 to 1955, the U.S. stewardess corps increased by four thousand. Suzanne Kolm, "'Who Says It's a Man's World?' Women's Work and Travel in the First Decades of Flight," in *The Airplane in American Culture*, ed. Dom Pisano (Ann Arbor: University of Michigan Press, 2003), 153.

18. Since nursing was a low-paid, low-status position, early nurse-stewardesses were often from working-class backgrounds. Stewardess positions appealed to nurses in the years after the Depression partly because many nurses were desperate for a steady income. See Susan Reverby, *Ordered to Care: The Dilemma of American Nursing, 1850–1945* (New York: Cambridge University Press, 1987), 212; Susan Reverby, "The Search for the Hospital Yardstick: Nursing and the Rationalization of Hospital Work," in *Health Care in America: Essays in Social History*, ed. Susan Reverby and David Rosner (Philadelphia: Temple University Press, 1979). Reverby argues that by the late 1910s and the 1920s, nursing was attracting more working-class than middle-class women to its ranks. Statistics about the types of work stewardesses' parents held do not exist; however, questionnaires completed by former stewardesses for this study suggest that many stewardesses hired from 1945 to 1969 had mothers who were full-time homemakers and fathers who worked in professions such as law, medicine, education, engineering, and the like. See, for example, Diane Johnson, "Stewardess Questionnaire," author's unpublished form, Summer 2004; Bev Bennis, "Stewardess Questionnaire," author's unpublished form, Summer 2004; Mazarella, "Stewardess Questionnaire." On the ideal stewardess, see Jack Stark, *Air Hostess*, Vocational and Professional Monographs 69 (Boston: Bellman, 1946), 7.

19. Airline executives, travel writers, air transportation policymakers, and travel boosters tapped this vision of America's role in the world and promoted air travel as a key component of this global project. The U.S. State Department encouraged American tourists to see themselves as ambassadors of U.S. foreign policy overseas and urged travel writers to approach tourism as an educational project with foreign policy implications, rather than merely a leisure pursuit. See Christopher Endy, *Cold War Holidays: American Tourism in France* (Chapel Hill: University of North Carolina Press, 2004). In 1945, John Budd, the publisher of *Air Transportation*, called aviation a "winged ambassador of democracy" that promised that "our American way of life, our economy, our political set-up, our culture, are going to have a far greater effect upon the world than ever before." John Budd, transcription of a speech by the publisher of air transportation for Northwest Airlines to the New York Board of Trade, June 22, 1945, Northwest Airlines Collection, Minnesota Historical Society, St. Paul, Minn. At the christening of the Clipper America in 1949, sponsored by Margaret Truman, Juan Trippe, the president of Pan Am, called the new aircraft "the symbol of the prestige, strength and goodwill of the American Flag on the airways of the world." Juan Trippe, "Jet Clippers Fulfilling Mass Transportation Philosophy," speech at the christening of the Clipper America, March 5, 1949, Pan Am Airlines Collection, Historical Museum of Southern Florida, Miami, Fla. See also Juan Trippe, "Post-War Air Transport and the Average Man," speech at the National Institute of

Social Sciences, May 19, 1943, Pan Am Airlines Collection, Historical Museum of Southern Florida, Miami, Fla.; W. Averell Harriman, transcription of a speech by the Secretary of Commerce, read at the takeoff of Pan Am's first scheduled flight around the world, June 17, 1947, United States Department of Commerce; Juan Trippe, "Sound Foreign Trade and World Aviation," speech at the Associated Industries of Massachusetts, October 23, 1953, Pan Am Airlines Collection, Historical Museum of Southern Florida, Miami, Fla. This advertising strategy regarding tourism had a long history in America. Beginning in the 1890s, the emerging tourist industry promoted tourism as a ritual of American citizenship and a patriotic duty. Marguerite S. Shaffer, *See America First: Tourism and National Identity, 1880–1940* (Washington, D.C.: Smithsonian Institution Press, 2001). Airline leaders also collaborated with Cold War tourism initiatives of the U.S. government because the airlines had a vested interest in maintaining good relationships with government officials given that the airlines relied heavily on the government for various aspects of business—such as negotiating airport landing rights, controlling passport requirements, determining route assignments, and conducting publicity campaigns. Endy, *Cold War Holidays*. In fact, the expansion of America's commercial aviation routes around the world served the interests of U.S. airlines, U.S. corporations, and U.S. foreign policy, but by representing air travel as an enterprise that promised universally desirable results (or "progress") for the world, airline executives advanced their corporate interests and found a compelling way to sell tickets. Airlines tied their corporate images to America's emerging postwar national identity and America's military victory in public relations campaigns and ads partly because they were jockeying to win status as the nation's "flag carrier" airline. While other nations offered government funding for a single national airline, in the United States airlines competed for dominance. According to the aviation scholar Jennifer Van Vleck, "The 'logic of the air' embodied the universalizing aspirations of American foreign policy, yet also signified what was exceptional about the United States; aviation both instantiated American empire and denied that it was such." Jennifer Van Vleck, "The 'Logic of the Air': Aviation and the Globalism of the 'American Century,'" *New Global Studies* 1, no. 1 (2007).

20. A wide range of economic interests were concerned that consumer reluctance to spend might precipitate another depression after World War II, so they heavily promoted consumption as central to the nation's postwar well-being. For more on this, see Cohen, *A Consumers' Republic*.

21. The modeling mogul John Robert Powers, who supplied models for many national advertising campaigns, claimed to have invented the image of the girl next door in the 1940s. Powers proclaimed: "Today's American girl" is "the Girl Next Door." John Robert Powers, *The Powers Girls: The Story of Models and Modeling and the Natural Steps by Which Attractive Girls Are Created* (New York: Dutton, 1941), 63, 26. See also Jennifer Craik, *The Face of Fashion: Cultural Studies in Fashion* (New York: Routledge, 1994), 79. The status and wages of American models also increased substantially during the postwar era. Another modeling career guide of the era also claimed that "breeding, education and intelligence" counted, rather than merely external beauty. Olga Malcova, *Wanted: Girl with Glamour, Careers in Modeling* (New York: Duell, Sloan and Pearce, 1941), 157.

22. The historian Eileen Boris argued that postwar stewardess uniforms evoked the military "to quell fears of flying by associating the practice with an image of strength."

Eileen Boris, "Desirable Dress: Rosies, Sky Girls, and the Politics of Appearance," *International Labor and Working-Class History* 69 (2006): 123–42. Mary Murray, *Skygirl: A Career Handbook for the Airline Stewardess*, 2nd ed. (New York: Duell, Sloan and Pearce, 1953), 21. An article in *Flying* echoed this image by calling today's pilot "a scientist." Chuck Myers, "What Is a Good Pilot?," *Flying* (September 1959): 36.

23. See, for example, *Chicago Daily Tribune*, August 30, 1956, N5; Rafferty, "Stewardess Trainer Debunks Theory Flying Leads to Romance"; "Irene Glaze, Airline Stewardess," press release, November 27, 1946, 9, American Airlines Collection, Special Collections, C. R. Smith Museum, Fort Worth, Tex.; Jack McPhaul, "Airline Stewardesses Attend Midway School," *Chicago Sun-Times*, April 25, 1952; Richard Thruelsen, "Airline Hostess," *Saturday Evening Post*, May 24, 1947. Airline press releases consistently distanced the pilot from rebellious masculinity. Later, representations of the astronaut mimicked those of the pilot. Angie Holdeman, "The NASA Man: The Astronaut Image and Masculinity in the 1960s" (paper presented at the annual meeting of the Pacific Coast Branch of the American Historical Association, July 25, 2007).

24. For more on the masculinity crisis, see Steven Cohan, *Masked Men: Masculinity and the Movies in the Fifties* (Bloomington: Indiana University Press, 1997); Barbara Ehrenreich, *The Hearts of Men: American Dreams and the Flight from Commitment* (New York: Random House, 1983); K. A. Cuordileone, *Manhood and American Political Culture in the Cold War* (New York: Routledge, 2005); Michael Davidson, *Guys Like Us: Citing Masculinity in Cold War Poetics* (Chicago: University of Chicago Press, 2003); Robert Corber, *Homosexuality in Cold War America: Resistance and the Crisis of Masculinity* (Durham, N.C.: Duke University Press, 1997); Tom Pendergast, *Creating the Modern Man: American Magazines and Consumer Culture, 1900–1950* (Columbia: University of Missouri Press, 2000); David Savran, *Taking It Like a Man: White Masculinity, Masochism, and Contemporary American Culture* (Princeton, N.J.: Princeton University Press, 1998); Margaret Marsh, "Suburban Men and Masculine Domesticity, 1870–1915," *American Quarterly* 40 (1988), 165-86; James Gilbert, *Men in the Middle: Searching for Masculinity in the 1950s* (Chicago: University of Chicago Press, 2005); Bill Osgerby, *Playboys in Paradise: Masculinity, Youth and Leisure-Style in Modern America* (Oxford: Berg, 2001); Ramona Barth, "What's Wrong with American Men?," *Reader's Digest*, November 1949, 23-25; Gilbert, *Men in the Middle*, 69, 4; Michael Kimmel, *Manhood in America: A Cultural History* (New York: Free Press, 1996), 253.

25. Cohan, *Masked Men*, xii. During the 1950s, the British film critic Raymond Durgnat wrote, "There is a haunting fear that a 'liberal' policy towards communism is a policy of men who are, not exactly feminized, but neutered, castrated, by their scruples." Quoted in Rebecca Bell-Metereau, *Hollywood Androgyny* (New York: Columbia University Press), 101.

26. "Executive Flight," *Playboy* (April 1955): 10; Press release, 1957, United Airlines Archives, Chicago; Richard Gehman, "Toupees, Girdles, and Sun Lamps," *Cosmopolitan* (May 1957): 39–42. From 1962 to 1969, the load factors on these flights declined significantly and the service was cancelled in 1970.

27. "Executive Flight," *Playboy* (April 1955): 10; Press release, 1957, United Airlines Archives, Chicago.

28. See Laura Hobson, "Planes for Men Only Ire Lady Writer," *Los Angeles Herald Express*, February 9, 1954; Dorothy Kilgallen, "The Voice of Broadway: Girls, Arise! Now Flight's

Only for Men," *New York Journal-American*, April 19, 1957, 16. Hobson also criticized the men on the flight by saying they had a right to decide to fly on all-male flights, since "half of them probably haven't made any other decision all day." Susan Aven, "I Was a Steward-ess on an All-Male Flight," *Mainliner* (August 1957). United's marketing team may even have intended to stir up controversy by inviting this female reporter to pose as a stewardess.

29. There was some question as to whether the claim was real or a publicity stunt. "Woman Fights Airline on Flights for Men Only," *Los Angeles Times*, January 26, 1958, Executive Flight Folder, United Airlines Archives, Chicago. I have not seen any evidence of a lawsuit. The corporate archives of United Airlines contained multiple articles on this, including a handwritten note on the article cited above mentioning that there were ques-tions about whether this was a publicity stunt.

30. Burke, Dowling, and Adams Advertising Agency, *Dottie—This Is Delta* (Delta Airlines, 1951), promotional film, National Air and Space Museum, Washington, D.C.

31. Sherry Waterman, *From Another Island: Adventures and Misadventures of an Airline Stewardess*, 2nd ed. (New York: Chilton, 1962), 16; Murray, *Skygirl*, 49, 18, 20.

32. Elaine Tyler May, *Homeward Bound: American Families in the Cold War Era* (New York: Basic Books, 1988).

33. The stewardess was popularly depicted as a model postwar wife and mother—usu-ally shown serving food to male passengers and feeding babies. For example, the cover of one issue of the *Atlantic Journal Magazine* was a photo of a smiling stewardess holding a baby. Marguerite Steedman, "Beauty Flies the Airways," *Atlantic Journal Magazine*, May 6, 1945. See also *Douglas Airview*, March 1946, 23, Delta Archives, Delta Air Transport Heritage Museum, Inc., Atlanta, Ga.

34. Murray, *Skygirl*, 36; "Irene Glaze, Airline Stewardess," American Airlines Collec-tion, Special Collections, C. R. Smith Museum, Fort Worth, Tex. "A modern sky girl does more than just serve meals . . . and the title 'hostess' is exactly fitting the definition of her duties," according to one vocational guide. The profession now required an enactment of feminine expertise, including "charm, poise, speech, bearing and make-up in addition to becoming a brilliant conversationalist. Thus the name air hostess." Stark, *Air Hostess*, 7. Stark was a representative for TWA.

35. Airlines capitalized on women's roles in their noncommercial relationships to cultivate customer service that benefited airlines' corporate interests. In this way, airlines imported supposedly "feminine" qualities into the corporate environment, where they functioned as valuable commodities. Arlie Russell Hochschild, *The Managed Heart: Com-mercialization of Human Feeling* (Berkeley: University of California Press, 1983). "Student Stewardess: Supplementary Training Manual," training manual, 1954, American Airlines Collection, Special Collections, C. R. Smith Museum, Fort Worth, Tex.

36. Stark, *Air Hostess*, 5.

37. Murray, *Skygirl*, 48.

38. Barth, "What's Wrong with American Men?"; Leland Stowe, "What's Wrong with American Women?," *Reader's Digest*, October 1949; Betty Friedan, *The Feminine Mystique* (New York: Doubleday, 1963), 53.

39. The Women Army Corps campaign invented the female soldier as white, middle class, educated, and heterosexual in order to evoke links between race, class, and sexual

respectability to stave off public anxiety. Leisa D. Meyer, *Creating G.I. Jane: Sexuality and Power in the Women's Army Corps During WWII* (New York: Columbia University Press, 1996), 54.

40. For mid-century debates, see, for example, Mary C. Lyne and Dorothy Tuttle, "Soviet Attack on Women's Minds," *McCall's*, August 1953, 44-45; William J. Jorden, "Portraits of the Soviet Woman," *New York Times Magazine*, February 3, 1957, 11-13; Welles Hangen, "Closeup of the 'Soviet Woman,'" *New York Times Magazine*, March 11, 1956, 26, 67. For a later assessment, see May, *Homeward Bound*.

41. Some carriers allowed stewardesses to work until the age of thirty-five.

42. Rafferty, "Stewardess Trainer Debunks Theory Flying Leads to Romance." In addition, airlines established the stewardess position as "feminine" by marking it as white-collar work, rather than "masculine" manual labor that resembled wartime Rosie-the-Riveter positions. An American Airlines press release in 1950 summed up this vision: "Donna admits she approached The Stewardess Training School in Chicago with some trepidation. She had been told it was in American's hangar at the airport and had visions of a classroom surrounded by oil drums and quarters resembling the back of a machine shop. Once established in the school, Donna soon learned that any similarity between the machine shop and The Stewardess Training Center was purely coincidental and . . . she would never realize she was not living and studying at a fashionable girls' academy." Press release, April 27, 1950, American Airlines Collection, Special Collections, C. R. Smith Museum, Fort Worth, Tex.

43. Aleene Barnes, "Miss Skyway Pauses Here During Tour," *Los Angeles Times*, February 20, 1956.

44. "Airline Hostess Life Offers Fun, Romance," *Los Angeles Times*, April 26, 1951; "Berit Strengall, Airline Stewardess," press release, November 1, 1947, 6, and "Irene Glaze, Airline Stewardess," both in American Airlines Collection, Special Collections, C. R. Smith Museum, Fort Worth, Tex.; Waterman, *From Another Island*, 76; McPhaul, "Airline Stewardesses Attend Midway School."

45. McPhaul, "Airline Stewardesses Attend Midway School"; "Eight Lovelies," *Los Angeles Examiner*, October 11, 1953; "What Airline Girls Are Made Of or, There's No Place Like Home," *New York Sales Executive Weekly*, March 31, 1953.

46. State of Minnesota Fair Employment Practices Commission, report on Vivian Chavis, n.d., 35, Marlene White Files, Northwest Airlines Collection, Minnesota Historical Society, St. Paul, Minn.

47. *Chicago Daily Tribune*, August 30, 1956, N5; Murray, *Skygirl*, 50.

48. Joan Herrold, "It's Personality, Not Beauty That Counts in Airline Work," *Pittsburgh News*, newspaper clipping, 1956, Mildred Jackson scrapbook, Kiwi Club, Dallas, Tex.; Untitled press release, American Airlines, 1945, American Airlines Collection, Special Collections, C. R. Smith Museum, Fort Worth, Tex. Airlines also administered lengthy intelligence tests to prospective stewardesses and instructed new recruits to be informed citizens, capable of "intelligent conversation." In 1946, Pan Am required stewardess applicants to score "above average on Otis test." Ronald Akana, interview, n.d., 1, Oral History Project, United Airlines Archives, Chicago. Training manuals instructed stewardesses to "keep up with the level of the informed modern individual" and considered the ability to

converse intelligently "the essence" of stewardess work. "Student Stewardess," and "Irene Glaze, Airline Stewardess," 6, both in American Airlines Collection, Special Collections, C. R. Smith Museum, Fort Worth, Tex.; Murray, *Skygirl*, 49.

49. Thomas Snyder, "120 Years of American Education: A Statistical Portrait" (Document, U.S. Department of Education, Office of Educational Research and Improvement, 1993), 17. In 1958, women made up 33 percent of all college students; by the mid-1950s, 60 percent of female college students dropped out to marry. Lois Banner, *Women in Modern America: A Brief History*, 2nd ed. (San Diego: Harcourt Brace Jovanovich, 1995), 141; statistics based on Pan Am Airways Personnel Records calculated for this book by Lynne Pinkerton, National Institute of Occupational Safety and Health, Atlanta, Ga., 2005. Statistics on education levels for stewardesses with other major airlines do not exist. I have based this assessment on my sources such as airline press releases, stewardess applications, interviews, and oral histories. Pan Am had a larger applicant pool because it flew the most international routes and was one of the most sought-after airlines for stewardess employment; thus, it could be even more selective in hiring.

50. McPhaul, "Airline Stewardesses Attend Midway School." See also "City, County Brass to Host Hostesses," newspaper clipping, n.d., Mildred Jackson scrapbook, Kiwi Club, Dallas, Tex.

51. One stewardess hopeful drove to Boston from a small town in Massachusetts three times a week to a "reducing salon" and got braces on her teeth. "I set out to achieve my goal. I wanted to fly around the world," she said. "I still had braces on when I interviewed, but I told them they'd be off in a month. I guess because I was so determined, they considered me a good candidate." Beverly Reid, "Stewardess Questionnaire," author's unpublished form, Summer 2004. Because the position was so competitive, merely getting hired gave these young women a strong sense of accomplishment. Stewardesses did not consider themselves wives in training—they viewed themselves as an elite cadre who had achieved a challenging career goal. The former stewardess Mildred Pluto Delp also noted that the stewardess image was "that of someone special and of someone whose job was hard to get." Mildred Delp, "Stewardess Questionnaire," author's unpublished form, Summer 2004.

52. Peddy, "Questionnaire."

53. After being rejected by several airlines, she pressed airline interviewers to find out why. A supervisor told her that she was five pounds overweight, had too many blemishes on her face, and had no college education—all strikes against her. She reapplied. After two interviews, American Airlines agreed to "take a chance" on her because she was so "determined." Johnson, "Questionnaire." Diane Johnson to her family (#6), 1960; (#3), 1960; (#4), August 7, 1960, all Diane Johnson, personal collection.

54. One former Pan Am stewardess, who flew from 1954 to 1956, said, "The proper woman was supposed to stay home and take care of the children and serve them," but she "wanted to see the world" instead, so she became a stewardess. Eugenia McColl, "Stewardess Questionnaire," author's unpublished form, Summer 2004. A former stewardess who flew from 1959 until 1969 said, "I wanted to . . . do something with my life besides getting married and having children." Sonia Coyle, "Stewardess Questionnaire," author's unpublished form, Summer 2004. Another said she became a stewardess because it sounded "better and

more exciting than marriage." Carol Novak Morgan, "Stewardess Questionnaire," author's unpublished form, Summer 2004.

55. Birdie Bomar (a former Delta stewardess who worked from 1940 to 1941), interview, August 31, 1999, Oral History Project, Delta Archives, Delta Air Transport Heritage Museum, Inc., Atlanta, Ga.; Carolyn Richter Goff, "Stewardess Questionnaire," author's unpublished form, Summer 2004; Artha Hornbostel, personal diary, September 29, 1953, Artha Hornbostel, personal collection.

56. Connie Bosza, "21 Seats and a Head—How to Toss Your Cookies" (unpublished memoir, 1952), 136, Connie Bosza, personal collection.

57. Kathleen Barry, *Femininity in Flight: A History of Flight Attendants* (Durham, N.C.: Duke University Press, 2007), 65. For example, one stewardess, who was hired in 1946, wrote to Pan Am informing the company of her intention to marry in 1952 and her desire to continue working. Pan Am terminated her employment anyway in accordance with company policy. Patricia Ann Collins to Pan American Airlines, 1952, Collins File, Pan Am Airways Personnel Records, National Institute of Occupational Safety and Health, Atlanta, Ga.

58. Paul Deutschman, "Hostess on Flight 408," *Holiday* (June 1958): 66. In the prewar era, airlines did not consider good looks key to stewardess hiring, but by the postwar era, beauty was central to hiring. See Karolyn Dixon, "Delta Passenger Service," *Delta Digest*, October 1946, employee magazine, Delta Airlines Archives, Atlanta, Ga.; "Berit Strengell, Airline Stewardess," press release, November 1, 1947, American Airlines Collection, Special Collections, C. R. Smith Museum, Fort Worth, Tex. An American Airlines press release of 1946 proclaimed that the stewardess class included "40 of the nation's most attractive girls." Press release, September 15, 1946, 1, American Airlines Collection, Special Collections, C. R. Smith Museum, Fort Worth, Tex. A Delta pamphlet for grade-school teachers noted that aspiring stewardesses should be "well above average in attractiveness." "The Air Age in Education," pamphlet for teachers, ca. 1950, Delta Airlines Archives, Atlanta, Ga. Airlines held beauty pageants for stewardesses and employee newsletters published photographs of those crowned as beauty queens. In 1946, stewardesses from fourteen airlines competed in the "Miss Airline Queen" pageant, which included a swimsuit competition. *Capitaliner*, September 1946, Capital Airlines File, National Air and Space Museum, Washington, D.C. Industry press releases also bragged that 80 percent of stewardesses held titles awarded for beauty and personality like "Sweetheart of Sigma Chi," "Snow Queen," or "Prom Queen." *Chicago Daily Tribune*, January 3, 1956, B3; "Irene Glaze, Airline Stewardess," 2, American Airlines Collection, Special Collections, C. R. Smith Museum, Fort Worth, Tex.

59. "Dottie Lamour Is the No. 1 Pin-up Girl of the U.S. Army," *Life*, July 7, 1941, 34. From 1942 to 1946, *Esquire* printed 9 million copies of the magazine and sent them to American troops. Maria Elena Buszek, *Pin-up Grrrls: Feminism, Sexuality, Popular Culture* (Durham, N.C.: Duke University Press, 2006), 210; Joanne Meyerowitz, "Women, Cheesecake, and Borderline Material: Responses to Girlie Pictures in Mid-Twentieth Century U.S.," *Journal of Women's History* 8, no. 3 (1996): 12.

60. The "pin-up girl" antecedents were illustrated by George Petty and printed in *Esquire* magazine's first issue in 1933. Buszek, *Pin-up Grrrls*, 203, 12, 198, 207; Meyerowitz, "Women, Cheesecake, and Borderline Material."

61. In 1953, *Playboy* magazine published its first issue featuring Marilyn Monroe as the centerfold. But Monroe exemplified a childlike sexuality that encapsulated both the "girl next door" and the foxy vixen—her sweet childish voice allowed her to soften the sexual threat of the World War II pin-up. Lois Banner, *Marilyn Monroe: The Passion and the Paradox* (New York: Bloomsbury Press, 2012); Tamar Christensen, "The Golden Age of the American Pin-up, 1942–1957: Cultural Representation and Relevance" (master's thesis, California State University, Long Beach, 2007), 33; Robert Westbrook, "'I Want a Girl, Just Like the Girl That Married Harry James,'" *American Quarterly* 42, no. 4 (1990): 600.

62. During the war, the military and U.S. public health campaigns deemed out-of-control female sexuality a powerful threat to the war effort and launched campaigns that warned the American public about dangerous, loose "victory girls," who might convey secrets to the enemy and infect the troops with venereal diseases. The military's attempts to manage soldiers abroad also prominently featured cautions against homosexuality. Miriam Reumann, *American Sexual Character: Sex, Gender, and National Identity in the Kinsey Reports* (Berkeley: University of California Press, 2005), 20, 21; Meyerowitz, "Women, Cheesecake, and Borderline Material," 15; Banner, *Marilyn Monroe*.

63. See Reumann, *American Sexual Character*, 34; May, *Homeward Bound*, 93; David Johnson, *The Lavender Scare: The Cold War Persecution of Gays and Lesbians in the Federal Government* (Chicago: University of Chicago Press, 2004).

64. In 1951, an American expert on the Soviet Union also reported that the Soviets viewed Americans as having "sunk so low that we are interested only in sexual pathology. Our family has decayed, our morals have disintegrated." Reumann, *American Sexual Character*, 45, 46.

65. *Continental Eagle*, October 1945, Continental Airlines File, National Air and Space Museum, Washington, D.C.

66. Powers, *The Powers Girls*.

67. Airlines even employed former Powers models as stewardesses and grooming instructors. In 1945, one reporter called stewardesses "winged Powers models." Steedman, "Beauty Flies the Airways."

68. Powers, *The Powers Girls*, 26.

69. Erik Bergaust, "They Broke the Fear Barrier," *Flying*, May 1955, 27, 76–77.

70. Edan Wright, "It's All Rough and Tumble in Air Stewardess Class," *Chicago Daily News*, March 12, 1951.

71. "Berit Strengell, Airline Stewardess," 5; Press release, May 8, 1956; and "Irene Glaze, Airline Stewardess," all in American Airlines Collection, Special Collections, C. R. Smith Museum, Fort Worth, Tex. The Miss America beauty pageant used the interview sections of the competition to make the pageant "respectable." Sarah Banet-Weiser, *The Most Beautiful Girl in the World* (Berkeley: University of California Press, 1999).

72. Untitled press release, American Airlines, 1956, American Airlines Collection, Special Collections, C.R. Smith Museum, Forth Worth, Tex.

73. Lois Banner, "The Meaning of Glamour in the Twentieth Century" (unpublished manuscript, 2007), 1.

74. Liz Willis, "Hollywood Glamour: Sex, Power, and Photography, 1925–1939" (Ph.D. diss., University of Southern California, 2007).

75. Banner, "The Meaning of Glamour in the Twentieth Century."

76. See, for example, Rafferty, "Stewardess Trainer Debunks Theory Flying Leads to Romance"; McPhaul, "Airline Stewardesses Attend Midway School"; "Irene Glaze, Airline Stewardess," American Airlines Collection, Special Collections, C. R. Smith Museum, Fort Worth, Tex.; Thruelsen, "Airline Hostess"; Mary Ann Callan, "High-Hiking Air Line Stewardess Takes Earth When She Finds It," *Los Angeles Times*, January 10, 1949; *Three Guys Named Mike*, directed by Charles Walters (Culver City, Calif.: Metro-Goldwyn-Mayer, 1951).

77. Pan American Airways, Latin American Division, "Flight Service Training Manual," stewardess training manual, December 4, 1945, 3, Pan Am World Airways Collection, Otto Richter Library, University of Miami, Coral Gables, Fla.; "Pan American Airlines Pilot Manual," training manual, September 1, 1945, Box 21, Pan Am Airlines Collection, Historical Museum of Southern Florida, Miami, Fla.

78. Patricia Patterson Dudley, interview by the author, August 31, 2011.

79. Edith Lauterbach, interview by Barbara Hanson, April 16, 2002, United Airlines, Oral History Program, United Airlines Archives, Chicago.

80. *Women Air Service Pilots World War II: Wearing the Wasp Uniform* (U.S. Army Airforces Regulations, February 14, 1944).

81. A stewardess manual of 1956 mandated that a hat "shall be worn at all times when in uniform . . . [and] shall be worn at a slight angle to the right." Lillian Fletcher, *Stewardess/Hostess Training Manual* (Newton Center, Mass.: Mount Ida Junior College, 1956), 7. For more on blondes, see Banner, "The Creature from the Black Lagoon."

82. Donna Steele, *Wings of Pride: T.W.A. Cabin Attendants, a Pictorial History, 1935–1985* (Marceline, Mo.: Walsworth, 1985), 156; "Stewardess Supervisor's Handbook," training manual, 1954, American Airlines Collection, Special Collections, C. R. Smith Museum, Fort Worth, Tex. Another manual noted, "The natural color of hair is not to be altered by bleaching or dying." Fletcher, *Stewardess/Hostess Training Manual*, 7.

83. Fletcher, *Stewardess/Hostess Training Manual*, 6. Pan Am also prohibited excess rouge and lipstick. See also Harold Houston, "Pan American Airlines System Passenger Service Manual," training manual, 1944, Box 435, Folder 9, Pan Am World Airways Collection, Otto Richter Library, University of Miami, Coral Gables, Fla. Stewardesses were also instructed on which fingernail polish colors were acceptable: "clear red shades for TWA" (Certainly Red by Revlon); other airlines mandated a natural or slightly colored polish (such as Sun Rose). In 1945, Pan American's training manual declared: "Any over-use which lends toward stagey make-up appearance is prohibited." Airways, "Flight Service Training Manual," 1, Pan Am World Airways Collection, Otto Richter Library, University of Miami, Coral Gables, Fla. In 1947, United Airlines also instructed stewardesses "do not wear extreme make-up." "United Airlines Stewardess Manual," training manual, February 1, 1947, 2, United Airlines Archives, Chicago. Kathy Peiss, *Hope in a Jar: The Making of America's Beauty Culture* (New York: Henry Holt, 1998), 167. John Powers, who claimed to have invented the girl-next-door look, rejected aspiring models for being "artificial," by which he meant "bleached hair, heavily made-up eyes, enough rouge and lipstick to supply a regiment of women." Powers, *The Powers Girls*, 49. This heavily made-up look

was standard for the outdated Ziegfeld glamour girl, who had previously been a dominant beauty icon in America. Ziegfeld girls were "show girls, languorous sophisticates, heavily artificial types" and "creatures of glamour," who wore "extreme make-up." Powers, *The Powers Girls*, 63. Powers' credo: "naturalness is more attractive than artificiality." Powers, *The Powers Girls*, 50. See also Linda Mizejewski, *Ziegfeld Girl: Image and Icon in Culture and Cinema* (Durham, N.C.: Duke University Press, 1999). The most "charming girl" was "the most 'natural' one, the typical American girl, pretty, healthy, vivacious, self-reliant." Powers, *The Powers Girls*, 24.

84. Reflecting this edict, airlines conjured the "natural" look not only because it suggested sexual respectability, but also because it was a mark of American identity. "Naturalness" had become integral to the "American look," which now required a heavy dose of skillfully applied cosmetics. Stewardess training included detailed instructions on how to achieve the natural look by applying just the right eye shadow, mascara, lipstick, powder, eyebrow pencil, rouge, and foundation. "Student Stewardess," American Airlines Collection, Special Collections, C. R. Smith Museum, Fort Worth, Tex.

85. Between 1940 and 1946, cosmetics sales in the United States rose by 65 percent. Craik, *The Face of Fashion*, 161. During World War II, the attractive, made-up woman became a potent symbol of the American way and American women wore lipstick as a badge of national identity. The historian Kathy Peiss observed that American women wore lipstick to signify "the 'red blood of the true American woman.'" Wartime cosmetics advertisements made consumption essential to accessing feminine identity. Peiss, *Hope in a Jar*, 239, 40, 45.

86. Charm school ads referred to themselves as "finishing schools for models and career girls" and promised to teach "charm, poise, streamlined figure and beautifully groomed model look that opens doors to career and social success!" The Patricia Stevens charm school in Chicago billed itself as the "training headquarters for 'glamour jobs'" (including stewardess positions). Print advertisement, *Chicago Daily Tribune*, February 18, 1951, American Airlines Collection, Special Collections, C. R. Smith Museum, Fort Worth, Tex.

87. Historians have described the postwar era as a time when America evolved into a consumer nation, in which mass consumption became a civic duty. Cohen, *A Consumers' Republic*.

88. "Cloud Nine," *Playboy* (July 1957): 35; "Untitled Article," *Playboy* (October 1957): 9

Chapter 3

1. *Marlene White v. Northwest Airlines, Inc.*, Exhibit 1, 2 (1961); "Stewardess Supervisor's Handbook," training manual, 1954, American Airlines Collection, Special Collections, C. R. Smith Museum, Fort Worth, Tex.

2. Patricia Banks, interview by the author, March 7, 2008.

3. Banks, interview by the author, March 7, 2008.

4. Howard Woods, "Airlines Admit Jim Crow on Chicago Planes," *Chicago Defender*, March 10 1945; "Sues Airlines, Charges Bias," *Pittsburgh Courier*, August 16, 1947, 1.

5. When Bosza told fellow stewardesses about the flight, they expressed reluctance to serve black passengers as well. One stewardess told Bosza that she would have refused

the trip. Although stewardesses were service workers, they claimed prestige and elite professional status partly by associating with the typical air travel clientele of wealthy businessmen, celebrities, and political dignitaries. Serving African American passengers threatened their elite professional status. Connie Bosza, "21 Seats and a Head—How to Toss Your Cookies" (unpublished memoir, 1952), 262, Connie Bosza, personal collection.

6. "Delta Airlines Hostess Rude to Actress," *Los Angeles Sentinel*, November 13, 1947, 1; "Ella Fitzgerald Sues Airline Company," *Pittsburgh Courier*, January 15, 1955, 1; "Ella Fitzgerald Settles Airline Suit for $7000," *Los Angeles Sentinel*, January 31, 1957, A1.

7. Wilfred Leland to Governor Orville Freeman, August 25, 1958, Northwest Airlines Collection, Minnesota Historical Society, St. Paul, Minn.

8. Sheridan Prasso, *The Asian Mystique: Dragon Ladies, Geisha Girls, and Our Fantasies of the Exotic Orient* (New York: Public Affairs, 2005), 88; Christine Yano, *Airborne Dreams: "Nisei" Stewardesses and Pan American World Airways* (Durham, N.C.: Duke University Press, 2011).

9. Fair Employment Practices Commission, *Marlene E. White v. Northwest Airlines, Inc.*, June 19, 1962, 2; and State of Minnesota Fair Employment Practices Commission, "Status Report on Marlene White," unpublished investigation report, August 11, 1959, both in Marlene White Files, Northwest Airlines Collection, Minnesota Historical Society, St. Paul, Minn.

10. Suzanne Lee Kolm, "Women's Labor Aloft: A Cultural History of Airline Flight Attendants in the United States, 1930–1978" (Ph.D. diss., Brown University, 1995). See, for example, Carol Pursell, *Technology in Postwar America: A History* (New York: Columbia University Press, 2007). In an effort to modernize its image, Pullman trains, which initially employed African American male porters and African American female maids, followed airlines in 1948 when they eliminated train maids and began hiring exclusively white women to perform the duties of both porters and attendants. Only Southern railroad lines continued to employ African American maids on trains. Melina Chateauvent, *Marching Together: Women of the Brotherhood of Sleeping Car Porters* (Chicago: University of Illinois Press, 1998), 121.

11. Banks, interview by the author, March 7, 2008.

12. "Merit Employment in the Airline Industry," January, 1958, 5, Marlene White Files, Northwest Airlines Collection, Minnesota Historical Society, St. Paul, Minn.

13. "Airline Integration Project," 1954, NAACP Collection, Manuscripts Division, Library of Congress, Washington, D.C.

14. Dom Pisano, ed., *The Airplane in American Culture* (Ann Arbor: University of Michigan Press, 2003); Penny Von Eschen, "Who's the Real Ambassador? Exploding Cold War Racial Ideology," in *Cold War Constructions: The Political Culture of United States Imperialism, 1945–1966*, ed. Christian Appy (Amherst: University of Massachusetts Press, 2000); *Russian Civil Aviation Magazine* (January 1966); James Rorty, "The First Colored Air Hostess," *The Crisis* (June–July 1958): 339.

15. Mary Dudziak, *Cold War Civil Rights: Race and the Image of American Democracy* (Princeton, N.J.: Princeton University Press, 2002), 56.

16. "Negro Air Hostess Resigns," *New York Times*, July 11, 1958, 28; Letter from Lounneer Pemberton (the executive director of the Urban League of Kansas City, Mo.) to Richard

Fox (the assistant director of the FEPC), July 10, 1959, Marlene White Files, Northwest Airlines Collection, Minnesota Historical Society, St. Paul, Minn.

17. "TWA Hires First Negro Air Hostess," 37. TWA was pressured into hiring Tiller in July 1959. She also appeared in a photograph in *Jet* magazine on December 17, 1959.

18. New York State Commission against Discrimination, *Patricia Banks v. Capital Airlines, Inc.*, July 14, 1959, Patricia Banks Collection, Schomburg Center, New York Public Library.

19. Ibid., 54A.

20. Ibid., 333.

21. For more on how black women have historically been portrayed as the antithesis of American conceptions of beauty and womanhood, see K. Sue Jewell, *From Mammy to Miss America and Beyond* (New York: Routledge, 1993), 36; Karen Brodkin, *How Jews Became White Folks and What That Says about Race in America* (New Brunswick, N.J.: Rutgers University Press, 1999), 86; Ruth Feldstein, *Motherhood in Black and White: Race and Sex in American Liberalism, 1930–1965* (Ithaca, N.Y.: Cornell Press, 2000), 99; Rickie Solinger, *Wake Up Little Susie: Single Pregnancy and Race before Roe v. Wade* (New York: Routledge, 2000); Stephanie Coontz, *The Way We Never Were: American Families and the Nostalgia Trap* (New York: Basic Books, 1992).

22. FEPC investigators studied Vivian Chavis's case during Marlene White's trial. *Marlene White v. Northwest Airlines, Inc.*

23. White's lawyer set out to challenge these cultural assumptions about African American women by asserting that White was an "intelligent, attractive, natural girl." *Marlene E. White v. Northwest Airlines, Inc.*, 11, Marlene White Files, Northwest Airlines Collection, Minnesota Historical Society, St. Paul, Minn.

24. *Patricia Banks v. Capital Airlines, Inc.*, 20, Patricia Banks Collection, Schomburg Center, New York Public Library.

25. "Stewardess Supervisor's Handbook," updated pages, from 1954–63, American Airlines Stewardess Service Division, 1954.

26. Kathy Peiss, *Hope in a Jar: The Making of America's Beauty Culture* (New York: Henry Holt, 1998), 258, 6–10. The market researcher David Sullivan advised white-run corporations interested in advertising to African American customers to avoid exaggerated black characters with "flat noses, thick lips, kinky hair." David Sullivan, "Don't Do This—If You Want to Sell Products to Negroes!," *Sales Management* 52 (1943): 48, 50.

27. "Velvea Smith Hammer vs. American Airlines," *Race Relations Law Reporter* (Spring 1966).

28. "Stewardess Supervisor's Handbook," American Airlines Collection, Special Collections, C. R. Smith Museum, Fort Worth, Tex.

29. Ibid. In 1965, a stewardess union president said she only knew of one Jewish stewardess. "Stewardesses Accuse Carriers of Discrimination," *Aviation Daily*, September 3, 1965.

30. Peiss, *Hope in a Jar*, 149; Lois W. Banner, *American Beauty: A Social History through Two Centuries of the American Idea, Ideal, and Image of the Beautiful Woman* (New York: Alfred A. Knopf, 1983), 206. Feminist theorists have taken issue with this view of cosmetics as vehicles for self-expression. See Susan Bordo, *Unbearable Weight: Feminism, Western Culture, and the Body* (Berkeley: University of California Press, 1993).

31. Brodkin, *How Jews Became White Folks*, 36; Noel Ignatiev, *How the Irish Became White* (New York: Routledge, 1995); Elizabeth Haiken, *Venus Envy: A History of Cosmetic Surgery* (Baltimore: Johns Hopkins University Press, 1997), 192; Sander Gilman, *Making the Body Beautiful: A Cultural History of Aesthetic Surgery* (Princeton, N.J.: Princeton University Press, 1999), 195; Matthew Frye Jacobson, *Whiteness of a Different Color* (Cambridge, Mass.: Harvard University Press, 1998), 96.

32. *Patricia Banks v. Capital Airlines, Inc.*, 176, Patricia Banks Collection, Schomburg Center, New York Public Library.

33. "Stewardess Supervisor's Handbook," American Airlines Collection, Special Collections, C. R. Smith Museum, Fort Worth, Tex.

34. Quoted in Kerry Segrave, *Suntanning in 20th Century America* (Jefferson, N.C.: McFarland, 2005), 77, 128. For more on tanning, see Peiss, *Hope in a Jar*, 151.

35. Laila Haidarali, "Polishing Brown Diamonds: African-American Women, Popular Magazines, and the Advent of Modeling in Early Postwar America," *Journal of Women's History* 17, no. 1 (2005): 10.

36. *Marlene E. White v. Northwest Airlines, Inc.*, 13, Marlene White Files, Northwest Airlines Collection, Minnesota Historical Society, St. Paul, Minn.

37. Ibid., Appendix, 3.

38. Banks, interview by the author, March 7, 2008.

39. Banks, interview by the author, March 7, 2008.

40. "TWA Hires First Negro Air Hostess," *Ebony* (July 1959): 37.

41. "Open Skies for Negro Girls," *Ebony* (June 1963); "The Catlins Are Northwest Airlines 'Stews,'" *Ebony* (November 1964), 43-50.

42. Banks, interview by the author, March 7, 2008.

43. Banks, interview by the author, March 7, 2008.

44. Banks, interview by the author, March 7, 2008.

45. Banks, interview by the author, March 7, 2008.

46. Banks, interview by the author, March 7, 2008.

47. Kathleen Barry, *Femininity in Flight: A History of Flight Attendants* (Durham, N.C.: Duke University Press, 2007), 117.

48. Dudziak, *Cold War Civil Rights*, 209, 13, 213.

49. Robert Serling, "Negro Hostess Aloft—with No to-Do," *New York World Telegram*, July 21, 1965, 18.

50. Statistics based on Pan Am Airways Personnel Records, calaculated for this book by Lynne Pinkerton, National Institute of Occupational Safety and Health, Atlanta, Ga., 2005.

51. In 1945, an African American market researcher estimated that African Americans were becoming important consumers with incomes amounting to $10.29 billion. Median incomes of "Negroes and other races" climbed from $489 in 1939 to $1,448 in 1947. David Sullivan, "Negro Incomes and How They Are Spent," *Sales Management* (June 14, 1945): 106; Haidarali, "Polishing Brown Diamonds," 4; Stephen Fox, *The Mirror Makers: A History of American Advertising and Its Creators* (Urbana: University of Illinois Press, 1984), 278; Robert Weems Jr., *Desegregating the Dollar: African American Consumerism in the Twentieth Century* (New York: New York University Press, 1998); Jason Chambers, *Madison*

Avenue and the Color Line: African Americans in the Advertising Industry (Philadelphia: University of Pennsylvania Press, 2008).

52. This was the earliest print ad for an airline that I found in a publication catering to the African American population. "Wherever in the World You Travel, You're Better Off with Pan Am," *Ebony*, advertisement, February 1963, Pan American Airlines Files, J. Walter Thompson Collection, John W. Hartman Center for Sales, Advertising and Marketing History, Duke University, Durham, N.C.

53. Eastern Air Lines, "Advertisement: If You're Interested in People, Places and a Prestige Job, Eastern Is Interested in You," June 1967; United Air Lines, "Advertisement: Make Travel Your Career . . . Be a United Air Lines Stewardess," *Ebony* (May 1964); United Airlines, "Advertisement: Should You Be a United Stewardess?," *Ebony* (April 1967); United Airlines, "Advertisement: United Airlines Stewardess Recruitment," *Ebony* (February 1964); Weems, *Desegregating the Dollar*.

54. See, for example, Delta Airlines, press release, March 16, 1967, Delta Archives, Delta Air Transport Heritage Museum, Inc., Atlanta, Ga.

55. Kolm, "Women's Labor Aloft," 346; Susannah Walker, *Style and Status: Selling Beauty to African American Women, 1920–1975* (Lexington: University Press of Kentucky, 2007).

56. "Newest Negro Stewardess," *Jet*, November 8, 1962, 48.

57. "TWA Hires First Negro Air Hostess," 37. TWA was pressured into hiring Tiller in July 1959. She also appeared in a photograph in *Jet* magazine on December 17, 1959.

58. Haidarali, "Polishing Brown Diamonds," 3; Jewell, *From Mammy to Miss America*; Leith Mullings, *On Our Own Terms: Race, Class and Gender in the Lives of African American Women* (New York: Routledge, 1997), 111.

Chapter 4

1. Bernard Glemser, *Girl on a Wing* (New York: Random House, 1960), 18.

2. The term was coined by the gossip columnist Igor Cassini. David Lubin, *Shooting Kennedy: J.F.K. and the Culture of Images* (Berkeley: University of California Press, 2003), 32.

3. United and American rejected her for her height. Christiansen applied when airlines still had a 5′7″ height maximum; most airlines upped it to 5′9″, 5′10″, or 5′11″ with the introduction of jets.

4. Clare Christiansen, "Stewardess Questionnaire," author's unpublished form, Summer 2004.

5. Clare Christiansen, letter to her mother (#1), October 16, 1956, and letter to her mother (#2), October 19, 1956, Clare Christiansen, personal collection.

6. Clare Christiansen, letter to her mother (#3), December 9, 1956, and letter to her mother (#4), December 14, 1956, Claire Christiansen, personal collection.

7. Clare Christiansen, interview by the author, October 31, 2011. Other former Pan Am stewardesses echoed this sentiment. See, for example, Jean Smith Fuller, "Stewardess Questionnaire," author's unpublished form, Summer 2004.

8. Stewardesses felt that airlines treated them like royalty by putting them up at the best hotels. Carolyn Richter Goff, "Stewardess Questionnaire," author's unpublished form,

Summer 2004; Robert Allegrini, *Chicago's Grand Hotels: The Palmer House, the Drake, and the Hilton Chicago* (Chicago: Arcadia, 2005); Mary Laffey Inman, interview by the author, November 14, 2007.

9. Artha Hornbostel, personal diary, September 29, 1953, Artha Hornbostel, personal collection.

10. See, for example, Anne Thomas, scrapbook, Anne Thomas, personal collection.

11. Sylvia Ortleib, "Stewardess Questionnaire," author's unpublished form, Summer 2004.

12. Tori Johnson-Kelso, "Stewardess Questionnaire," author's unpublished form, Summer 2004. See also Patricia O'Neill, "Stewardess Questionnaire," author's unpublished form, Summer 2004.

13. Surveys by the New York Port Authority in 1963 and *SKY* magazine in 1964 also found that 60 percent of airline passengers were on business trips. Quoted in Briefing memo, December 9, 1964, United Airlines Campaign in the 1960s "Friendly Skies" Campaign Collection, Special Collections, Leo Burnett Advertising Agency Corporate Archives, Chicago. In 1960, American men's median income was approximately $4,100 per year. U.S. Bureau of the Census, *A Half-Century of Learning: Historical Census Statistics on Educational Attainment in the United States, 1940 to 2000*, Census 2000 PHC-T-41, Table 2; U.S. Bureau of the Census, *Current Population Reports: Consumer Income*, Series P-60, no. 36. For *Printer's Ink* statistic, see Confidential memo, May 14, 1963, United Airlines Campaign in the 1960s "Friendly Skies" Campaign Collection, Special Collections, Leo Burnett Advertising Agency Corporate Archives, Chicago.

14. Briefing memo, June 12, 1963, United Airlines Campaign in the 1960s "Friendly Skies" Campaign Collection, Special Collections, Leo Burnett Advertising Agency Corporate Archives, Chicago. While 72.7 percent of United's seats were occupied in 1952, by 1962 the percentage of occupied seats had dropped to 53.6 percent. Leo Burnett, "New Horizons in Advertising for United Airlines," proposal, September 21, 1965, United Airlines Archives, Chicago.

15. For more on airline profit predictions, see *Wall Street Journal*, June 4, 1963, Burnett File, United Airlines Archives, Chicago; "Annual System Advertising Plan for Pan Am World Airways 1958," October 17, 1957, Pan American Airlines Files, J. Walter Thompson Collection, John W. Hartman Center for Sales, Advertising and Marketing History, Duke University, Durham, N.C. In fact, in 1962, the return on investment for eleven domestic airlines was only 4.4 percent, less than half the rate the CAB established as "adequate." For this statistic, see "Untitled Report," June 12, 1963, United Airlines Campaign in the 1960s "Friendly Skies" Campaign Collection, Special Collections, Leo Burnett Advertising Agency Corporate Archives, Chicago. For Pan Am's ad team's response to predictions of plummeting profits, see Minutes from review board meeting on Pan Am overseas division of 1961 regarding advertising, November 23, 1961.

16. By the end of 1953, airlines had topped railroads in carrying passengers two hundred miles or more. Suzanne Lee Kolm, "Women's Labor Aloft: A Cultural History of Airline Flight Attendants in the United States, 1930–1978" (Ph.D. diss., Brown University, 1995), 41; James Love, unpublished think piece, June 3, 1963, Special Collections, Leo Burnett Advertising Agency Corporate Archives, Chicago; Phil Schaff, "Memo to Leo Burnett, Re:

My Quick Thoughts Regarding Your Transportation Think-Piece," memo, June 3, 1963, United Airlines Campaign in the 1960s "Friendly Skies" Campaign Collection, Special Collections, Leo Burnett Advertising Agency Corporate Archives, Chicago.

17. The Institute for Social Research at the University of Michigan also reported that 6.7 percent of the adult population in the United States had flown in 1955. Quoted in Briefing memo, June 12, 1963, United Airlines Campaign in the 1960s "Friendly Skies" Campaign Collection, Special Collections, Leo Burnett Advertising Agency Corporate Archives, Chicago.

18. Airline advertising teams noticed these broader shifts in American spending. The advertising team for United Airlines reported that the number of households earning $10,000 per year and over went from 1.2 million in 1950 to nearly 9 million in 1960. Leo Burnett, "Notes on Rationale for 'Courageous Candor' or 'No Hogwash' Series," Leo Burnett Advertising Agency for United Airlines, n.d., Burnett Agency Archives, Chicago, Ill. In 1957, Pan Am's advertising team also highlighted the new trend in American families: in 1950, 12 million families had $4,000 in disposable income after taxes; in 1956, 26 million families did; and, by 1959, 36 million families were expected to have that disposable income. See "Annual System Advertising Plan for Pan Am World Airways 1958;" and "Advertising Plan for 1957," meeting minutes, 1957, Meetings Pan Am Minutes 1957, Box 23, both in J. Walter Thompson Collection, John W. Hartman Center for Sales, Advertising and Marketing History, Duke University, Durham, N.C.

19. "A Study of Attitudes toward Leading American Airlines," report prepared by Elmo Roper and Associates for Lennen and Newell Corporation, November 1958, American Airlines Collection, Special Collections, C. R. Smith Museum, Fort Worth, Tex.

20. Christopher Endy, *Cold War Holidays: American Tourism in France* (Chapel Hill: University of North Carolina Press, 2004), 128; "Advertising Plan for 1957," Meetings Pan Am Minutes 1957, Box 23, J. Walter Thompson Collection, John W. Hartman Center for Sales, Advertising and Marketing History, Duke University, Durham, N.C.

21. U.S. Bureau of the Census, *Statistical Abstract of the United States 1960*, 81st ed. (Washington, D.C.: U.S. Government Printing Office, 1960), 580; Endy, *Cold War Holidays*, 128, 29; Kolm, "Women's Labor Aloft," 41.

22. Schaff, "Memo to Leo Burnett, Re: My Quick Thoughts Regarding Your Transportation Think-Piece," United Airlines Campaign in the 1960s "Friendly Skies" Campaign Collection; Love, unpublished think piece, Special Collections, Leo Burnett Advertising Agency Corporate Archives, Chicago.

23. The Pan Am ad team noted that one-third of all transatlantic passengers had incomes of $5,000 or less. In 1958 the median income for males over the age of fifteen in the United States was $3,743. U.S. Bureau of the Census, *Current Population Survey: Annual Social and Economic Supplements*, Historical Income Tables, Table P-8AR, Age—People, All Races, by Median Income and Sex: 1947 to 2009. On Pan Am's changing advertising strategy and on the demographics of *Life*'s readers, see the following documents in the J. Walter Thompson Collection, John W. Hartman Center for Sales, Advertising and Marketing History, Duke University, Durham, N.C.: "Advertising Plan for 1957," Meetings Pan Am Minutes 1957, Box 23; Pan American Airlines, "Minutes from Review Board Meeting on Pan Am Overseas Division," October 31, 1957. *Life*'s

readership fit this middlebrow demographic: $7,500 annual income, college educated, and metropolitan.

24. This number went from 169 million in 1970 to 240 million in 1977. Kolm, "Women's Labor Aloft," 195.

25. Cornelia Otis Skinner, "Idle in Idlewild," in *The Ape in Me* (Boston: Houghton Mifflin, 1959), 131; Endy, *Cold War Holidays*, 138–41.

26. "Advertising Plan for 1957," Meetings Pan Am Minutes 1957, Box 23, J. Walter Thompson Collection, John W. Hartman Center for Sales, Advertising and Marketing History, Duke University, Durham, N.C.

27. "A Study of Attitudes toward Leading American Airlines," American Airlines Collection.

28. Kolm, "Women's Labor Aloft," 120–25.

29. Briefing memo, June 12, 1963, United Airlines Campaign in the 1960s "Friendly Skies" Campaign Collection, Special Collections, Leo Burnett Advertising Agency Corporate Archives, Chicago. The increasing ad budgets of the airlines reflected larger corporate trends of this era—from 1945 to 1960 U.S. corporations increased their advertising expenditures by 400 percent. Stephanie Coontz, *The Way We Never Were: American Families and the Nostalgia Trap* (New York: Basic Books, 1992), 171.

30. "A Study of Attitudes toward Leading American Airlines," American Airlines Collection.

31. The historian Steven Ross has shown how early movie palaces played on people's dreams of upward mobility by providing luxury that allowed working-class moviegoers to feel middle class. Steven Ross, *Working-Class Hollywood: Silent Film and the Shaping of Class in America* (Princeton, N.J.: Princeton University Press, 1998).

32. "Passenger Reactions to the Boeing 707s and Electras, an Opinion Survey for American Airlines," April 1959, American Airlines Collection, Special Collections, C. R. Smith Museum, Fort Worth, Tex.; Briefing memo, June 12, 1963, United Airlines Campaign in the 1960s "Friendly Skies" Campaign Collection, Special Collections, Leo Burnett Advertising Agency Corporate Archives, Chicago. This fascination with technology was also part of a larger trend in American advertising during the late 1950s and the early 1960s, when advertisements used pride in the American military and technological strength to sell products. For example, Bulova, the watch-making company, announced an army general as the chair of research and development to equate military strength with product quality. Hazel Warlaumont, *Advertising in the 60s: Turncoats, Traditionalists, and Waste Makers in America's Turbulent Decade* (London: Praeger, 2001), 112–13.

33. The space race escalated again in 1961, when the Soviets successfully launched the first manned spacecraft. American politicians took Soviet achievements in space seriously. Seven weeks later, President John F. Kennedy used his state of the union address to announce a gigantic expansion of the U.S. space program (including a plea for a budget of $9 billion over the next five years) and NASA announced its aim to send a three-man team to the moon. Susan Bridger, "The Cold War and the Cosmos: Valentine Tereshkova and the First Woman's Space Flight," in *Women in the Krushchev Era*, ed. Melanie Ilič, Susan Emily Reid, and Lynne Attwood, Studies in Russian and East European History and Society (New York: Palgrave Macmillan, 2004), 222.

34. Quoted in Hon. Warren Magnuson, Congressional Record, April 13, 1959.

35. The RAND Corp., a policy think tank commissioned by the U.S. Navy to study Aeroflot, found that Aeroflot's global air expansion was not motivated by potential profits, but rather to "enhance [the Soviets'] political power" to win "political good will and technological respect, particularly in the underdeveloped world." Hans Heymann, *A Briefing on the Soviet Role in International Civil Aviation* (Santa Monica, Calif.: RAND, November 21, 1957), 23. In 1958, the presidentially appointed Air Coordinating Committee also underscored stewardesses' rising global significance: "The personnel who represent our airlines abroad are proof of the success of the American system." Juan Trippe, transcript of a statement before President Eisenhower's Committee on Facilitation and Promotion of International Travel, 1958, 1, Box 461, F11, 2-23-1950 to 10-8-1959, Pan American Airlines Collection, Otto Richter Library, University of Miami, Coral Gables, Fla.

36. Both the Soviets and the Americans took the propaganda war seriously and launched massive image campaigns abroad. Estimating that the Soviets employed 1.4 million "full-time professional propagandists and agitators" in 1953, President Eisenhower announced the creation of the United States Information Agency (USIA), which was designed to "persuade foreign peoples that it lies in their own interest to take actions which are also consistent with the national objectives of the United States." Walter Hixson, *Parting the Curtain: Propaganda, Culture, and the Cold War, 1945–1961* (New York: St. Martin's Press, 1997), 26.

37. James Winchester, "Glamor on Wings," *American Mercury* (November 1956): 146.

38. This statistic included "pursers"—male flight attendants ranked above stewardesses. Statistics based on Pan American Airways personnel records, calculated for this book by Lynne Pinkerton, National Institute of Occupational Safety and Health, Atlanta, Ga., 2005.

39. "Airline Hostess," *American Youth Magazine* (January–February 1961): 11. See also Recruiting brochure for American Airlines, n.d., ca. early 1960s, American Airlines File, National Air and Space Museum, Washington, D.C.

40. "Win Your Wings as a Pan Am Stewardess," brochure, March 1967, Pan American Airlines Collection, Otto Richter Library, University of Miami, Coral Gables, Fla.

41. "The Jet Age Stewardess," press release, February 28, 1962, 3, American Airlines Collection, Special Collections, C. R. Smith Museum, Fort Worth, Tex.

42. National Airlines press release, August 12, 1965, 1, National Airlines, Pan Am World Airways Collection, Otto Richter Library, University of Miami, Coral Gables, Fla.

43. Statistics based on Pan American Airways personnel records, calculated for this book by Lynne Pinkerton, National Institute of Occupational Safety and Health, Atlanta, Ga., 2005; U.S. Bureau of the Census, *A Half-Century of Learning*.

44. Press release, February 24, 1959, American Airlines Collection, Special Collections, C. R. Smith Museum, Fort Worth, Tex.; "Stewardesses Train at Plush School," *Milkwaukee Journal*, November 26, 1957, 4.

45. "Horizons Unlimited: An Indoctrination Course for Flight Service Personnel," training material, 1961, 57, Norma Gaskill Travis, personal collection; *Pan Am Sales Clipper*, July 1959, Pan American Airlines File, National Air and Space Museum, Washington, D.C.

46. Airlines also began to employ famous industrial designers such as Raymond Loewy to develop color schemes, interior airplane designs, and corporate identities for airlines,

airline logos, and stewardess uniforms. Records, n.d., Raymond Loewy Collection, Manuscripts Division, Library of Congress, Washington, D.C.

47. In 1960, stewardesses were paid between $255 and $355 per month compared to full-time clerical workers in the United States, who earned a median salary of $298 per month at the time. U.S. Bureau of the Census, Series G 372-415, 1982a, Table 55. In 1957, American Airlines estimated it would interview over fifteen thousand women to hire about one thousand stewardesses. Kolm, "Women's Labor Aloft," 134; Kathleen Barry, *Femininity in Flight: A History of Flight Attendants* (Durham, N.C.: Duke University Press, 2007), 111; Marci Nelson and Shirley Motter Linde, eds., *Airline Stewardess Handbook* (Careers Research, 1968), 11.

48. Endy, *Cold War Holidays*, 131.

49. Alice Kessler-Harris, *Out to Work: A History of Wage-Earning Women in the United States* (New York: Oxford University Press, 1982), 302.

50. Helen Gurley Brown, *Sex and the Single Girl* (Fort Lee, N.J.: Barricade Books, 1962), 103.

51. Stephen Gundle, "Hollywood Glamour and Mass Consumption in Postwar Italy," *Journal of Cold War Studies* 4, no. 3 (2002): 111.

52. In January 1961, an American stewardess wrote her mother about this rising female icon: "Mom, what do you think of Jackie Kennedy? I think she's so striking. Don't you like her fashion designer's taste? I love the style coat she started. Jackie looks like a photographer model type—certainly a far cry from the previous first lady type." Diane Johnson, letter to her family (#7), January 25, 1961, 4, Diane Johnson, personal collection; M. Bender, "The Kennedys, in White House a Year, Bring New Look to Domestic Scene," *New York Times*, January 20, 1962. For more on Kennedy's importance for American women, see Susan Douglas, *Where the Girls Are: Growing up Female with the Mass Media* (New York: Random House, 1994), 38–39, 41.

53. Gundle, "Hollywood Glamour and Mass Consumption," 102; Vanessa Schwartz, *It's So French!: Hollywood, Paris, and the Making of Cosmopolitan Film Culture* (Chicago: University of Chicago Press, 2007), 53; Artha Hornbostel, interview by the author, July 5, 2005.

54. Donna Steele, *Wings of Pride: T.W.A. Cabin Attendants, a Pictorial History, 1935–1985* (Marceline, Mo.: Walsworth, 1985); Untitled press release, National Airlines, Pan Am World Airways Collection, Otto Richter Library, University of Miami, Coral Gables, Fla.; "Pan Am Opens International Stewardess College in Miami," press release, November 9, 1965, 2, Pan American Airlines Collection, Otto Richter Library, University of Miami, Coral Gables, Fla.

55. *Toplifter*, October 1957, Northwest Airlines Collection, Minnesota Historical Society, St. Paul, Minn.; Kolm, "Women's Labor Aloft," 337.

56. "Pan Am's Finishing School," *Airways Magazine*, 1969, 14, Box 291, f1, Pan American Airlines Collection, Otto Richter Library, University of Miami, Coral Gables, Fla.

57. Christine Yano, *Airborne Dreams: "Nisei" Stewardesses and Pan American World Airways* (Durham, N.C.: Duke University Press, 2011). Japan Airlines (JAL) wove a similar image of "traditional" Japanese women in its U.S. ads. A 1962 JAL ad, featuring shoji screens and tea accoutrements, read: "The service, too, is delightfully Japanese. In her colorful kimono, your hostess pampers you so graciously you feel like an honored guest in

a Japanese home." These ads proclaimed the best of both worlds: technologically advanced "sleek swift jets" and the "timeless world of classic Japan" via the "kimono-clad Japanese hostesses." JAL focused on describing Japanese hostesses as high-status women with "diplomat fathers" and "international" backgrounds. One ad bragged, "Only her Japanese heritage could endow such an understanding of perfect service" and "you are experiencing 1,200 years of tradition in the art of pleasing others . . . you feel her real desire to please you, and only you. For she satisfies herself only as she succeeds in making you happy." Various advertisements for Japan Airlines, 1960s, Folder J-075000-03, Japan Airlines File, National Air and Space Museum, Washington, D.C. See the following documents in the J. Walter Thompson Collection, John W. Hartman Center for Sales, Advertising and Marketing History, Duke University, Durham, N.C.: Three print advertisements for Japan Airlines in 1956; Print advertisement for Japan Airlines, 1962, Competitive Ads Box; Print advertisement for Japan Airlines, 1968, Competitive Ads Box 37.

58. Yano, *Airborne Dreams*, 18.

59. Peggy Lee Baranowski, "Stewardess Questionnaire," author's unpublished form, Summer 2004. Although the infamous girdle check has become part of airline history, Clare Christiansen, who flew for Pan Am for thirteen years until 1969 and was a stewardess supervisor for thirteen years, said she never had a girdle check and she never gave a girdle check. She said, "They used to ask do you have your girdle on. I was very thin, maybe if you were heavier and had a bulge, they might check, but it wasn't a routine. I can vouch for that because I never had one. It's an urban legend." Clare Christiansen, interview by the author, October 31, 2011.

60. Gundle, "Hollywood Glamour and Mass Consumption," 111.

61. V. P. Roiz, "Grooming Newsletter," memo to all female pursers and stewardesses, September 1959, Box 22, F212, World Wings International Collection, Otto Richter Library, University of Miami, Coral Gables, Fla.

62. Statistics based on Pan Am Airways Personnel Records, calculated for this book by Lynne Pinkerton, National Institute of Occupational Safety and Health, Atlanta, Ga, 2005.

63. "Look of the Leader for Stewardesses," training manual, 1965, 1, and "New Stewardess Wardrobe," press release, August 7, 1967, 3, both in American Airlines Collection, Special Collections, C. R. Smith Museum, Fort Worth, Tex. For more on the relationship between the aesthetic of technology and gender, see Susan Jeffords, *The Remasculinization of America: Gender and the Vietnam War* (Bloomington: Indiana University Press, 1989), 10.

64. "Our Fair Ladies," *Atlantic Service Newsletter*, January/February 1958, Box 22, World Wings International Collection, Otto Richter Library, University of Miami, Coral Gables, Fla. A 1958 Pan Am newsletter announced: "Recently, however, the increasing complexity of our services has tended to make skilled technicians out of our gracious hostesses. Also, because of the divergent speech and cultural background of some of the girls, more emphasis had to be placed on striving for an appearance standard for the group." This rhetoric had been a trend since the mid-1940s. In 1944, Pan Am instructed the stewardess to "know and use the cosmetics which best harmonize with her complexion and uniform." Harold Houston, "Pan American Airlines System Passenger Service Manual," training manual, 1944, Box 435, Folder 9, Pan Am World Airways Collection, Otto Richter Library, University of Miami, Coral Gables, Fla. Another stewardess handbook proclaimed, "Each

stewardess shall choose a coiffure that is most attractive for her own personality and styled to suit her uniform hat." Lillian Fletcher, *Stewardess/Hostess Training Manual* (Newton Center, Mass.: Mount Ida Junior College, 1956), 7.

65. Barbara Ehrenreich, *The Hearts of Men: American Dreams and the Flight from Commitment* (New York: Random House, 1983), 30; Joanne Meyerowitz, "Beyond the Feminine Mystique: A Reassessment of Postwar Mass Culture," in *Not June Cleaver*, ed. Joanne Meyerowitz (Philadelphia: Temple University Press, 1994).

66. Patricia Ann Collins, employment application, August 28, 1946, Collins File, Pan Am Airways Personnel Records, National Institute of Occupational Safety and Health, Atlanta, Ga.; "Hiring Notes on Stewardess Applicant," interviewers' notes for Patricia Ann Collins, September 23, 1946, Collins File, Pan Am Airways Personnel Records, National Institute of Occupational Safety and Health, Atlanta, Ga.

67. The manual also mentioned "personality, educational background, experience with public, and linguistic ability." Exam for Pan American Airlines supervisors in training, 1958, World Wings International Collection, Otto Richter Library, University of Miami, Coral Gables, Fla.

68. "Stewardess Supervisor's Handbook," training manual, 1954, 1, American Airlines Collection, Special Collections, C. R. Smith Museum, Fort Worth, Tex. The section was updated in 1963. In 1965, Pan Am's "philosophy and techniques of stewardess selection" also centered on attractiveness. "Philosophy and Techniques of Stewardess Selection," instructions for supervisors, December 1965, Box 14, series 1, Folder 126, World Wings International Collection, Otto Richter Library, University of Miami, Coral Gables, Fla. See also "Stewardess Supervisor's Handbook," Section 20-15, updated May 1958, American Airlines Collection, Special Collections, C. R. Smith Museum, Fort Worth, Tex.

69. "Stewardess Supervisor's Handbook," American Airlines Collection, Special Collections, C. R. Smith Museum, Fort Worth, Tex. The section was updated July 15, 1960.

70. "Stewardess Recruitor's Notes on Applicants," handwritten notes, March 9, 1960, Box 281, Folder 9, Pan Am World Airways Collection, Otto Richter Library, University of Miami, Coral Gables, Fla.

71. State of Minnesota Fair Employment Practices Commission, "Status Report on Marlene White," unpublished investigation report, August 11, 1959, Marlene White Files, Northwest Airlines Collection, Minnesota Historical Society, St. Paul, Minn.

72. "Philosophy and Techniques of Stewardess Selection," Box 14, series 1, Folder 126, World Wings International Collection, Otto Richter Library, University of Miami, Coral Gables, Fla.

73. Airlines taught supervisors to "always make applicant walk back and forth across the interviewing room." "Stewardess Supervisor's Handbook," 2, American Airlines Collection, Special Collections, C. R. Smith Museum, Fort Worth, Tex. The section was updated in 1960. During an interview with TWA in 1953, Jane Fiser, a stewardess hopeful, was asked to pull her skirt above her knees so the interviewers could see if her "legs were okay." Because Fiser was 5'7¾" tall and weighed 144 pounds, the supervisor advised her to drop down to 138 pounds and return for another interview. Jane Fiser (former TWA stewardess, 1953), interview by Mauree Jane Perry, May 20, 1999, 3, Oral History Program, Special Collections, SFO Library, San Francisco Airport Museum, San Francisco, Calif.

Other stewardesses recalled similar experiences during their interviews: Linda Lowrey Peddy, "Stewardess Questionnaire," author's unpublished form, Summer 2004; Betsy Fowler, "Stewardess Questionnaire," author's unpublished form, Summer 2004.

74. "Stewardess Supervisor's Handbook," American Airlines Collection, Special Collections, C. R. Smith Museum, Fort Worth, Tex. The section was updated in 1963. The manual also included a chart with ideal figure measurements, including bust, hips, height, and weight. "Philosophy and Techniques of Stewardess Selection," Box 14, series 1, Folder 126, World Wings International Collection, Otto Richter Library, University of Miami, Coral Gables, Fla.

75. Statistics based on Pan Am Airways Personnel Records, calculated for this book by Lynne Pinkerton, the National Institute of Occupational Safety and Health, Atlanta, Ga, 2005.

76. On the relationship between class and weight, see Joan Brumberg, "Fasting Girls: The Emerging Ideal of Slenderness," in *Women's America: Refocusing the Past*, ed. Linda Kerber (New York: Oxford University Press, 2004), 393. See also Lois W. Banner, *American Beauty: A Social History through Two Centuries of the American Idea, Ideal, and Image of the Beautiful Woman* (New York: Alfred A. Knopf, 1983), 283–85.

77. When the Equal Employment Opportunities Commission (EEOC) investigated Northwest Airlines, it reviewed one hundred Northwest stewardess applicants and found that the airline was so rigid about weight requirements in stewardess hiring that it cleared the airline of a discrimination charge from an African American stewardess applicant who was denied employment purportedly because she was eight and a half pounds overweight and an inch too short. State of Minnesota Fair Employment Practices Commission, report on Vivian Chavis, n.d., Marlene White Files, Northwest Airlines Collection, Minnesota Historical Society, St. Paul, Minn. See also "Ladies Bridge Club Cindy's Cup of Tea," *Pan Am Clipper*, November 15, 1966, Special Collections, SFO Library, San Francisco Airport Museum, San Francisco, Calif.

78. "Pan American Airlines Overseas Division Manual," training manual, 1960, 4, Box 28, Folder 278, Roiz Logan Papers, World Wings International Collection, Otto Richter Library, University of Miami, Coral Gables, Fla.; "Stewardess Training Notes," training outline, February 15–March 25, 1960, Tori Anderson, personal collection. The stewardess training manual for American Airlines in 1965 contained figure measurement charts, showing the ideal bust, waist, hip, and thigh measurements. "Look of the Leader for Stewardesses," American Airlines Collection, Special Collections, C. R. Smith Museum, Fort Worth, Tex.

79. "Pan American Airlines Overseas Division Manual," Box 28, Folder 278, Roiz Logan Papers, World Wings International Collection, Otto Richter Library, University of Miami, Coral Gables, Fla.; "Stewardess Training Notes," Tori Anderson, personal collection; "Flight Service Manual," training manual, July 18, 1966, 10, 1966 Box 438, Pan Am World Airways Collection, Otto Richter Library, University of Miami, Coral Gables, Fla.

80. "Memo To: All Female Pursers and Stewardesses, Subject: Grooming Newsletter," April 1959, World Wings International Collection, Otto Richter Library, University of Miami, Coral Gables, Fla.; "Rules Covering All Standing Positions," United Airlines train-

ing handout, November 8, 1960, Carol Armstrong Gurdak, personal collection; Grooming Course Outline for Stewardess Trainers, July 30, 1968, Pan American Airlines, World Wings International Collection, Otto Richter Library, University of Miami, Coral Gables, Fla.

81. "Regarding: Pan American Airlines Grooming Program," memo to flight service superintendant, April 24, 1959, Box 22, Folder 212, World Wings International Collection, Otto Richter Library, University of Miami, Coral Gables, Fla. The manual for American Airlines in 1965 still instructed stewardesses to use "cosmetics to enhance natural beauty" because the public "visualize[s] our stewardesses as wholesome, natural looking women." "Look of the Leader for Stewardesses," 4, American Airlines Collection, Special Collections, C. R. Smith Museum, Fort Worth, Tex. "Hard" and "jaded" were terms critics of the Varga girl pin-up used to suggest promiscuity when contrasting her against the wholesome Petty girl pin-up.

82. The study also found that "the woman using outlandish and startling shades of make-up or nail polish admits she does not get sufficient notice—she feels dull, inferior and subconsciously wants attention." Roiz, "Grooming Newsletter," 2, Box 22, Folder 212, World Wings International Collection, Otto Richter Library, University of Miami, Coral Gables, Fla. See also "Flight Service Manual," 11, 1966 Box 438, Pan American Airlines Collection, Otto Richter Library, University of Miami, Coral Gables, Fla. Trans Caribbean airlines also required stewardesses to get company approval for lipstick shades. "Trans Caribbean Operations Manual," training manual, March 1968, 16, American Airlines Collection, Special Collections, C. R. Smith Museum, Fort Worth, Tex.

83. Johni Smith, *How to Be a Flight Stewardess: A Handbook and Training Manual for Airline Hostesses* (North Hollywood: Pan American Navigation Service, 1966).

84. For more on hiring Norwegian blondes, see Press release, 1963, Box 127, Pan Am World Airways Collection, Otto Richter Library, University of Miami, Coral Gables, Fla. In 1967, Pan Am created a substantial publicity hubbub about hiring blonde Norwegian twins, and in the late 1960s, stewardess beauty contest winners were more often blonde, whereas earlier stewardess beauty contest winners tended to be brunettes. In 1968, blonde Miss Miami Airlines represented Miami in the International Airlines beauty pageant. "Regarding: Flight Service Recruitment," memo, 1958, Box 22, World Wings International Collection, Otto Richter Library, University of Miami, Coral Gables, Fla.

85. "Flight Service Manual (1967)," training manual, September 1, 1967, Box 25, Folder 244, World Wings International Collection, Otto Richter Library, University of Miami, Coral Gables, Fla.; "Look of the Leader for Stewardesses," 6-1, American Airlines Collection, Special Collections, C. R. Smith Museum, Fort Worth, Tex.; "Flight Service Manual," 12, 1966 Box 438, Pan American Airlines Collection, Otto Richter Library, University of Miami, Coral Gables, Fla. Pan Am prohibited "long hair, fancy or extreme haircuts (Pixie, Pony Tail, Whirlwind, extreme tendril bangs, etc.)." "Pan American Airlines Overseas Division Manual," Box 28, f278, Roiz Logan Papers, World Wings International Collection. A 1959 Pan Am memo instructed stewardesses who had to wear a "chignon or French twist because of texture" to request permission from the grooming supervisor. Roiz, "Grooming Newsletter," 1, Box 22, Folder 212, World Wings International Collection, Otto Richter Library, University of Miami, Coral Gables, Fla. The memo also contained a list of girls who had permission to wear these hairstyles.

86. Inman, interview by the author. See also Ortleib, "Questionnaire."

87. Helene Hills, personal letters to her mother, 1961–62, Helene Hills, personal collection.

88. Linda Groves Fuller, "Stewardess Questionnaire," author's unpublished form, Summer 2004.

89. Betty Lou Ruble Snyder, "Stewardess Questionnaire," author's unpublished form, Summer 2004; "Flight Service Manual," 10, 1966 Box 438, Pan Am World Airways Collection, Otto Richter Library, University of Miami, Coral Gables, Fla. See also "Look of the Leader for Stewardesses," and "Trans Caribbean Operations Manual," both in American Airlines Collection, Special Collections, C. R. Smith Museum, Fort Worth, Tex.; "Mainliner Stewardess Guide," training manual, 1959, 2, Gayla Kanaster, personal collection; G. Roiz Logan, "Flight Service Uniform Regulations," training manual, February 2, 1960, Box 28, Folder 278, World Wings International Collection, Otto Richter Library, University of Miami, Coral Gables, Fla. A Delta stewardess also recalled that they were required to wear girdles even to their training classes "and that got checked." Jenny Poole (former Delta stewardess), August 30, 1999, Oral History Program, Delta Archives, Delta Air Transport Heritage Museum, Inc., Atlanta, Ga.

90. Helen Figley, scrapbook, Special Collections, SFO Library, San Francisco Airport Museum, San Francisco, Calif. Proficiency report on Patricia Ann Collins, 1948, Collins File, Pan Am Airways Personnel Records, National Institute of Occupational Safety and Health, Atlanta, Ga. Collins's file contains fifteen proficiency reports from 1948 to 1950.

91. Pan Am's evaluations of 1954 still focused on duties performed. Proficiency report on Norma Gaskill Travis, March 12, 1954, Travis File, Pan Am Airways Personnel Records, National Institute of Occupational Safety and Health, Atlanta, Ga. In 1957, however, Pan Am introduced new stewardess evaluation forms, which included increasingly detailed appearance categories, such as hair, weight, height, hose, nails, figure, and girdle. See Proficiency report on Betty Snyder Ruble, 1957, Ruble File, Pan Am Airways Personnel Records, National Institute of Occupational Safety and Health, Atlanta, Ga.; "Stewardess Training Notes," Tori Anderson, personal collection; Pan American Airlines form, 1960, Box 28, Folder 278, Roiz Logan Papers, World Wings International Collection, Otto Richter Library, University of Miami, Coral Gables, Fla. Mary Lou Mackie, who became a United stewardess in 1958, saved many of her evaluation reports, which betray the increasing focus on physical image. Her evaluations in 1958 included categories such as "quality of work, quantity of work, dependability, relationships with others, attitude, judgment, appearance." The "appearance" category was just one out of more than a dozen categories, in which the supervisors usually noted "neat" or "very neat" or "neatly groomed" without further specification; the remainder of the form focused on duties. United Airlines in-flight evaluation reports, 1958–1963, Mary Lou Mackie, personal collection. By 1959, United's evaluations had begun to pay more attention to looks and Mackie had begun receiving more detailed critiques of her appearance, including a criticism for not wearing white gloves and for a lack of nail polish: "would prefer to see your nails polished as it adds a finished touch to your grooming. Since your hands are in constant view of the passengers, this is an important detail." Mary Lou Mackie, personal collection.

92. "1961 Grooming Discrepancy Report," stewardess evaluation, September 6, 1961; "Grooming Discrepancy Report," stewardess evaluation, May 6, 1964; and Robert Klinger to Betty Snyder Ruble, September 22, 1960, all in Ruble File, Pan Am Airways Personnel Records, National Institute of Occupational Safety and Health, Atlanta, Ga.

93. For more on the broader meaning of the fairs, see Robert Rydell, *Fair America: World's Fairs in the United States* (Washington, D.C.: Smithsonian Institution Press, 2000), 133. For the description of the inflatable globe, see "The Biggest Earth on Earth," press release, Box 257, Pan Am World Airways Collection, Otto Richter Library, University of Miami, Coral Gables, Fla.

94. For more on the relationship between tourism and foreign relations, see Endy, *Cold War Holidays*; Trippe, 2, Box 461, Folder 11, 2-23-1950 to 10-8-1959, Pan Am Airlines Collection, Historical Museum of Southern Florida, Miami, Fla.

95. Christina Klein, *Cold War Orientalism: Asia in the Middlebrow Imagination, 1945–1961* (Berkeley: University of California Press, 2003).

96. Gil Troy, *Mr. and Mrs. President: From the Trumans to the Clintons* (Lawrence: University Press of Kansas, 2000), 110. For more on Jackie's international popularity and her role as a diplomat, see Carol Schwalbe, "Jacqueline Kennedy and Cold War Propaganda," *Journal of Broadcasting and Electronic Media* 49, no. 1 (2005), 111-127.

97. Oleg Cassini, *A Thousand Days of Magic: Dressing Jacqueline Kennedy for the White House* (New York: Rizzoli, 1995), 22.

98. Trippe, 2, Box 461, Folder 11, 2-23-1950 to 10-8-1959, Pan Am Airlines Collection, Historical Museum of Southern Florida, Miami, Fla.; "Annual System Advertising Plan for Pan Am World Airways 1958," Pan American Airlines Files, J. Walter Thompson Collection, John W. Hartman Center for Sales, Advertising and Marketing History, Duke University, Durham, N.C. One Midwestern newspaper summed up this sentiment: "Hundreds of all-around American girls will emerge from airline stewardess schools trained in poise, efficiency, courteousness, and the expression of national friendliness so appreciated by those who fly the world's airways." "Sky Is the Limit for Career Girls," *Evansville (Ind.) Sunday Courier and Press*, 1965, Delta Archives, Delta Air Transport Heritage Museum, Inc., Atlanta, Ga.

99. "'Angel-Goddess' Returns from Tibetan Refugee Camp," press release, April 4, 1962, Box 427, and "Pan Am Stewardesses to Aid Tibetan Refugees," press release, November 7, 1961, Box 427, both in Pan American Airlines Collection, Otto Richter Library, University of Miami, Coral Gables, Fla.; U.S. Bureau of the Census. "Two Stewardesses Volunteer for Help to Laotians," *Norwalk Hour*, June 7, 1971, 29.

100. See, for example, "The Refugees' Angel," *San Francisco Chronicle*, April 15, 1962; "The 'Angel Goddess,'" *New York Journal-American*, April 14, 1962; Gay Pauley, "Angel Teacher Brings America to Refugee Tots," *Utica (N.Y.) Observer-Dispatch*, April 6, 1962; Claire Wallace, "Air Stewardess Taught Tibetans," *New York World-Telegram*, April 5, 1962.

101. See, for example, Claire Wallace, "Air Stewardess Taught Tibetans," *New York World-Telegram*, April 5, 1962, which extolled "the pretty blonde lady" for teaching at the refugee school.

102. "'Angel-Goddess' Returns from Tibetan Refugee Camp," Box 427, Pan American Airlines Collection, Otto Richter Library, University of Miami, Coral Gables, Fla. See

also *Fort Lauderdale News*, April 6, 1962, Box 246, f15, Pan American Airlines Collection, Otto Richter Library, University of Miami, Coral Gables, Fla.; Wallace, "Air Stewardess Taught Tibetans."

103. "Image Improvement Is the Name of the Course," *Clipper*, July 1, 1968, Box 291, f1, Pan American Airlines Collection, Otto Richter Library, University of Miami, Coral Gables, Fla.

104. "Clipper System General Office," *Clipper*, October 1961, 6, Pan American Airlines Collection, Otto Richter Library, University of Miami, Coral Gables, Fla.

Chapter 5

1. *Journal of Commerce*, November 21, 1967.

2. The enthusiasm of U.S. airlines for the Moscow route was not driven by profit potential, but rather by "competitive rivalry and national prestige." Hans Heymann, *A Briefing on the Soviet Role in International Civil Aviation* (Santa Monica, Calif.: RAND, 1957), 18.

3. Eugene Rostow, Untitled Speech, 1968, 2, Pan Am World Airways Collection, Otto Richter Library, University of Miami, Coral Gables, Fla; Harold Gray, "Welcome to the USA Speech," November 18, 1968, Pan Am World Airways Collection, Otto Richter Library, University of Miami, Coral Gables, Fla.; Daniel Gilmore, "Blue Skies, Champagne and Caviar Make Cold War Seem Lost to Oblivion," *Newsweek*, July 18, 1968; Holmes Alexander, "An Event to Remember," McNaught Syndicate, July 29, 1968; Harold E. Gray, letter inside menu of first Pan Am flight to Moscow, 1968, Pan Am World Airways Collection, Otto Richter Library, University of Miami, Coral Gables, Fla.; *Air Travel* (July 1968): 11.

4. "Airlines: The Russians Are Coming," *Newsweek*, July 29, 1968. See also *Post Dispatch*, July 9, 1968, Pan Am World Airways Archives, University of Miami; "The Red and the Black (Caviar)," *Newsweek*, July 29, 1968, Pan Am World Airways Archives, University of Miami; "Last Blocks to Air Link about to Fall," *Journal of Commerce*, November 21, 1967; Bob Considine, King Features Syndicate, July 26, 1968. The *San Francisco Chronicle*, for example, reported: "girl-watching air travelers will find the Soviet stewardesses somewhat plainer, bigger around and less inclined to pamper the clientele than her American counterpart as created by capitalist competition." "Jet to Moscow," *San Francisco Chronicle*, July 14, 1968.

5. *McCall's* magazine warned that Soviet propaganda was damaging America's reputation globally and that the Soviets had "devoted an immense proportion of their word war to capturing the hearts and minds of women all over the world." "Objective foreign visitors may all agree that our women are among the best treated in the world, but the Communists will quote an American woman's speech for equal rights to prove that women are abused and oppressed in the United States." Mary C. Lyne and Dorothy Tuttle, "Soviet Attack on Women's Minds," *McCall's* (August 1953): 44.

6. For more on the propaganda campaigns depicting the "good life," see Walter Hixson, *Parting the Curtain: Propaganda, Culture, and the Cold War, 1945–1961* (New York: St. Martin's Press, 1997); Jessica Gienow-Hecht, "Cultural Transfer," in *Explaining the History of American Foreign Relations*, ed. Michael Hogan (New York: Cambridge University Press, 2004).

7. Mildred Jackson, "American Girl Introduces Russian Girl to Lipstick," *Chicago Daily Tribune*, November 28, 1956; Mildred Jackson, "Russian Girl Boasts, 'We're Free People'; Doesn't Act It," *Chicago Daily Tribune*, December 4, 1956; Mildred Jackson, "Chicago Girl Sees Russians Parade Their New Fashions," *Chicago Daily Tribune*, December 8, 1956. In "Russian Girl Boasts, 'We're Free People': Doesn't Act It," Jackson recounted showing her nylon slip to a Russian woman. The Russian woman "gasped," said, "'O, it's beautiful,' and reached down to touch it." Jackson then found out that the Russian woman's silk slip cost 150 rubles, the equivalent of $37.50, whereas Jackson's nylon slip only cost $13.00. She proceeded to ask the Russian woman about bras, girdles, nail polish, and lipstick. The woman told her, "We can say and do what we wish. We are free people in Russia." Jackson found this statement ironic because Russian women were clearly not free enough to buy nylon slips (or other beauty products essential to feminine identity) at reasonable prices.

8. See Lizabeth Cohen, *A Consumers' Republic: The Politics of Mass Consumption in Postwar America* (New York: Knopf, 2003).

9. Lynne Attwood, *Creating the New Soviet Woman: Women's Magazines as Engineers of Female Identity, 1922–53* (New York: Palgrave Macmillan, 1999), 171.

10. Dale Ross Rubenstein, *How the Russian Revolution Failed Women* (Boston: New England Free Press, n.d. [ca. 1970]), 25. The first Soviet Constitution of 1918 proclaimed the equality of all citizens—regardless of sex, race, nationality—and established the right of women to elect or be elected in the Soviet political system. Mary Buckley, *Women and Ideology in the Soviet Union* (Ann Arbor: University of Michigan Press, 1989).

11. Buckley, *Women and Ideology in the Soviet Union*, 133, 113; Gail Warshofsky Lapidus, *Women in Soviet Society: Equality, Development and Social Change* (Berkeley: University of California Press, 1978), 168–69; Susan Bridger, "The Cold War and the Cosmos: Valentine Tereshkova and the First Woman's Space Flight," in *Women in the Krushchev Era*, ed. Melanie Ilič, Susan Emily Reid, and Lynne Attwood, Studies in Russian and East European History and Society (New York: Palgrave Macmillan, 2004), 222–37. This was the same year Betty Friedan's feminist tome was published in the United States.

12. Nina Popova, "Equality of Soviet Women in the Economic Sphere," in *Equality of Women in the U.S.S.R.* (Moscow: Foreign Languages Publishing House, 1957), 119.

13. Elizieveta Popova, "Women's Status in U.S.S.R.," *U.N. Bulletin*, June 15, 1949, 648; N. Popova, "Equality of Soviet Women in the Economic Sphere."

14. While the percentage of U.S. women workers paled in comparison to the percentage of Soviet women workers, American women constituted an increasing proportion of the workforce. In 1960, 80 percent of U.S. women who earned wages worked in stereotypical female jobs. Alice Kessler-Harris, *Out to Work: A History of Wage-Earning Women in the United States* (New York: Oxford University Press, 1982), 303.

15. John F. Kennedy made America's image a campaign issue in 1960 by claiming that a secret USIA poll revealed that world esteem for the United States was slipping.

16. Quoted in Carol Pursell, *Technology in Postwar America: A History* (New York: Columbia University Press, 2007), 102. While American identity relied on consumerism, the Soviet National Exhibition in New York City in June 1959 presented technological prowess through an elaborate display on Sputnik, large industrial appliances, and heavy machinery—such as a nuclear ice-breaker and space capsules.

17. Toni Howard, "The Sorry Life of Soviet Women," *Saturday Evening Post*, December 26, 1959, 70.

18. For more on the Nylon War and the U.S. psychological warfare initiative against the Soviets, see Hixson, *Parting the Curtain*.

19. See, for example, Oriana Atkinson, "My Life Behind the Iron Curtain [Pt. 2]," *Woman's Home Companion* (November 1946): 36–37, 141–42, 44; G. Warren Nutter, "The True Story of Russia's Weakness," *U.S. News and World Report*, March 1, 1957, 46; Audrey R. Topping, "First in Space—but Not in Femininity," *New York Times Magazine*, June 30, 1963, 12; Edgar Snow, "Meet Mr. and Mrs. Russia at Home," *Saturday Evening Post*, December 22, 1945. The American press also contrasted Soviet achievements in aviation, space, and military technology with retrograde consumer technology in Russian homes.

20. Howard, "The Sorry Life of Soviet Women," 70.

21. During the Cold War, U.S. policymakers, anthropologists, psychologists, academics, journalists, and travel writers collectively constructed a discourse of the Soviets as "other" in narratives ostensibly intended to demystify the Soviet people. See, for example, Ed Sullivan, "My Journey to Moscow," *Reader's Digest* (March 1960): 52–56; Francis B. Stevens, "What Things Are Like Inside Russia," *U.S. News and World Report*, August 14, 1961, 54–58; Lou Atzenweiler, "I Lived with a Russian Family," *Look*, August 19, 1958, 19–24. Anthropologists at the Harvard Institute for Russian Studies also developed theories on the "Russian character." These narratives positioned the Soviets as essentially different from Americans and often constructed the Soviet Union as backward, oppressive, and inferior. In this way, American narratives about the Soviet people resembled what the literary theorist Edward Said identified as "orientalism"—a strategy in which Americans constructed the West and East as coherent, distinct, mutually exclusive entities, and systematically depicted the East as backward, traditional, and, at times, inferior to the West. Edward Said, *Orientalism: Western Conceptions of the Orient* (London: Random House, 1979). For references to Soviet women's looks, see "Soviet Women Work Long, Hard at Jobs," *Dallas Morning News*, July 31, 1968; Thomas P. Whitney, "S-X in the Soviet Union," *New York Times Magazine*, January 1, 1956, 11, 44–45; Gunnar D. Kumlien, "Fashion a La Russe," *Commonwealth*, January 17, 1958, 402–4; Welles Hangen, "Closeup of the 'Soviet Woman,'" *New York Times Magazine*, March 11, 1956, 26, 67; Bob Considine, King Features Syndicate, July 26, 1968. The American reporter Thomas Whitney went so far as to describe Soviet women as the opposite of American Petty girls. T. Whitney, "S-X in the Soviet Union"; "Soviet Women Work Long, Hard at Jobs."

22. "Soviet Women Work Long, Hard at Jobs." See also Joseph B. Phillips, "A Typical Woman of Postwar Moscow," *Newsweek*, November 4, 1946, 23.

23. See, for example, Dorothy Thompson, "I Write of Russian Women," *Ladies Home Journal* (March 1956): 11; Gertrude Samuels, "Why Russian Women Work Like Men," *New York Times Magazine*, November 2, 1958, 23. In 1957, G. Warren Nutter, an American economics professor, published a lengthy story on Soviet life in *U.S. News and World Report* that included an explanation of "Why women lack 'feminine qualities.'" The report branded the "elaborate rationalization" for Soviet women's workforce participation "the product of indoctrination," concluding that "the long hours of work leave those not handicapped

by heavy jobs little time for grooming their feminine qualities even if the incentive were there." Nutter, "The True Story of Russia's Weakness," 117.

24. Samuels, "Why Russian Women Work Like Men," 23.

25. Howard, "The Sorry Life of Soviet Women," 21; Julie Whitney, "Women: Russia's Second-Class Citizens," *Look*, November 30, 1954, 114; Samuels, "Why Russian Women Work Like Men," 23; Kumlien, "Fashion a La Russe," 403.

26. For example, U.S. coverage of the first Soviet woman promoted to a high post in the Communist Cabinet fixated on her masculine appearance—highlighting her lack of make-up and her "severe bun," as well as her "man-tailored worsted suit with a mannish white shirt and black string tie." Hangen, "Closeup of the 'Soviet Woman,'" 26; Howard, "The Sorry Life of Soviet Women," 78. For more on the relationship between violating gender norms and lesbianism, see Leisa D. Meyer, *Creating G.I. Jane: Sexuality and Power in the Women's Army Corps During WWII* (New York: Columbia University Press, 1996), 150. Popular articles also called Soviet women "amazons," a code word for lesbian at the time, and occasionally Soviet lesbian villains appeared in Hollywood films of the era, such as the menacing Russian lesbian Rosa Llebb in the James Bond film *From Russia with Love*. In 1950, the Senate Appropriations Committee held widely publicized hearings on the federal employment of homosexuals and other "sex perverts." Robert Dean, *Imperial Brotherhood: Gender and the Making of Cold War Foreign Policy* (Amherst: University of Massachusetts Press, 2001), 60; David Johnson, *The Lavender Scare: The Cold War Persecution of Gays and Lesbians in the Federal Government* (Chicago: University of Chicago Press, 2004).

27. For mentions of ugly Soviet women, see Orianna Atkinson, "My Life Behind the Iron Curtain [Pt. 1]," *Woman's Home Companion* (October 1946): 30–31; Kumlien, "Fashion a La Russe," 404; Stewart Alsop, "Those Smug, Smug Russians," *Saturday Evening Post*, December 31, 1955, 66; Samuels, "Why Russian Women Work Like Men," 23; Hangen, "Closeup of the 'Soviet Woman,'" 26; "It Is Difficult for People like Us to Believe That Even the Heart Is Subject to Regulation in Russia," *McCall's* (June 1960): 106. In 1956, Dorothy Thompson also called Soviet women "poorly and unbecoming[ly] dressed." Thompson, "I Write of Russian Women." Toni Howard, in the *Saturday Evening Post*, described the typical Soviet woman: "Her hair will be the color nature made it, probably brown, but so badly cut and badly permanented that it hangs on her neck like a tangle of frizzled wool." Howard, "The Sorry Life of Soviet Women," 20. See also T. Whitney, "S-X in the Soviet Union."

28. Howard, "The Sorry Life of Soviet Women," 20.

29. This vision represented the Cold War as an opportunity for Americans to forge intellectual and emotional bonds around the globe. This conceptual model for understanding America's role overseas burgeoned during the Cold War because it offered a language for articulating a vision of America as a nonimperial, beneficent presence in the world—which cast American expansion in a positive light. Christina Klein, *Cold War Orientalism: Asia in the Middlebrow Imagination, 1945–1961* (Berkeley: University of California Press, 2003), 99. This model may have served as a cloak for imperialist maneuvers, relying on what Mary Louise Pratt called "narratives of anti-conquest," which legitimated U.S. expansion while denying its imperial nature. Mary Louise Pratt, *Imperial Eyes: Travel Writing and Transculturation* (New York: Routledge, 1992).

30. In the 1930s, when Soviet women began entering the workforce in large numbers, Soviet magazines (which were official organs of the state) suggested that Soviet women had a "natural" desire to look pretty and that hard work was compatible with beauty and femininity. Attwood, *Creating the New Soviet Woman*, 131. For more on Communist fashion, see also Katalin Medvedev, "Ripping up the Uniform Approach: Hungarian Women Piece Together a New Communist Fashion," in *Producing Fashion: Commerce, Culture, and Consumers*, ed. Regina Lee Blaszczyk (Philadelphia: University of Pennsylvania Press, 2008). For more on the relationship between national identity and fashion, see Irene Guenther, *Nazi Chic: Fashioning Women in the Third Reich* (New York: Oxford International, 2004).

31. Quoted in Olga Gurova, "The Art of Dressing: Body, Gender, and Discourse on Fashion in Soviet Russia in the 1950s and 1960s," in *The Fabric of Cultures: Fashion, Identity, and Globalization*, ed. Eugenia Paulicelli (New York: Routledge, 2009), 77. See also Attwood, *Creating the New Soviet Woman*, 164.

32. Susan Reid, "The Krushchev Kitchen: Domesticating the Scientific-Technological Revolution," *Journal of Contemporary History* 40 (2005): 308-9; Susan Reid, "Women in the Home," in *Women in the Krushchev Era*, ed. Susan Reid and Lynne Attwood (New York: Palgrave, 2004); Susan Reid, "Destalinization and Taste, 1953-1963," *Journal of Design History* 10 (1997): 177-78; Susan Reid, "Cold War in the Kitchen: Gender and the De-Stanlization of Consumer Taste in the Soviet Union under Krushchev," *Slavic Review* 61, no. 2 (2002): 211–52; Gurova, "The Art of Dressing," 81. See also Attwood, *Creating the New Soviet Woman*, 165.

33. Kumlien, "Fashion a La Russe," 404; Thompson, "I Write of Russian Women."

34. Bill Osgerby, *Playboys in Paradise: Masculinity, Youth and Leisure-Style in Modern America* (Oxford: Berg, 2001), 142. Soviet women were also supposedly deprived of heterosexual love—a linchpin of American feminine identity. In the American imagination, the Soviet state controlled marriage to serve the regime's agendas, thereby barring women from expressing their true feminine selves through heterosexual relationships. Soviet wedding ceremonies purportedly lacked the fanfare, expense, religious aspect, and genuine sentiment of American weddings. See, for example, "It Is Difficult for People Like Us to Believe That Even the Heart Is Subject to Regulation in Russia," 106. After a trip to the Soviet Union with her husband, the preeminent American journalist Dorothy Thompson wrote in *Ladies Home Journal* that Russians looked "unhappy": "Love—married love, young love, passing gay attraction, or even gentle consideration has obviously not been included in any five-year plan." Thompson, "I Write of Russian Women," 18. See also "It Is Difficult for People Like Us to Believe That Even the Heart Is Subject to Regulation in Russia," 107; Phillips, "A Typical Woman of Postwar Moscow"; Kumlien, "Fashion a La Russe," 404. *U.S. News and World Report* outlined the Soviet woman's lack of heterosexual marriage and domestic life as evidence of her alienation from "her very concept of herself as a woman." Nutter, "The True Story of Russia's Weakness," 70.

35. Tatiana Kolysko (journalist), interview by the author in Moscow, August 16, 2004.

36. Tatiana Filipieva (former Aeroflot stewardess and Aeroflot psychologist), interview by the author in Moscow, August 14, 2004.

37. Many Soviet women found that "equality" was a double-edged sword: it granted them wage-labor rights but also a double burden in terms of household labor. Buckley, *Women and Ideology in the Soviet Union*.

38. Ministerstva Grazhdanskoi Aviatsii C.C.C.P., "Dlia Stiuardov/Stiuardess/Na Samoletakh Vozdushnykh Linii General'nogo Upravleniia Grazhdanskoi Aviatsii," Dolzhnostnaia Instruktsiia, January 8, 1945, Ministry of Civil Aviation Collection, State Economic Archives, Moscow.

39. Ministerstva Grazhdanskoi Aviatsii C.C.C.P., "Po Rabote Bortprovodnikov Samoletov Grazhdanskogo Vozdushnogo Flota C.C.C.P.," Aeroflot stewardess training manual, August 1955, F 1973 O 59 E 69, Ministry of Civil Aviation Collection, State Economic Archives, Moscow.

40. Ibid.

41. Ibid.; Ludmilla Viktorovna Zaviagina (Aeroflot Museum curator and former Aeroflot stewardess), interview by the author in Moscow, August 12, 2004.

42. Nachal'nika Glavnogo Upravleniia Grazhdanskogo Vozdushnogo Flota Pri Sovnarkome C.C.C.P., "Perechen' Predmetov Formennogo Obmundirovaniia, Vydavaemykh Komandiram Korablei, Vtorym Pilotam, Shturmanam, Bortmekhanikam, Bortradistam I Bortprovodnikam Samoletov Mezhdunarodnykh Vozdushnykh Linii C.C.C.P.," order, 1953, F9527 O2 E1278, Ministry of Civil Aviation Collection, State Economic Archives, Moscow.

43. In 1966, the Soviet civil aviation magazine depicted Aeroflot stewardesses at hairstyling salons, primping before a flight, but they were expected to maintain typical Soviet workplace hairstyles. In 1966, Aeroflot stewardesses asked to update their hairstyles, arguing that the required hairstyle was out of fashion, but officials rejected the request, stating that the airplane was a workplace and therefore was no place for fashion. *Grazhdanskoi Aviatsii* (July 1966).

44. Reid, "Women in the Home"; Reid, "Destalinization and Taste, 1953–1963"; Reid, "Cold War in the Kitchen."

45. Hugh McDonald, *Aeroflot: Soviet Air Transport since 1923* (London: Putnam, 1975).

46. Ministerstva Grazhdanskoi Aviatsii C.C.C.P., order, ca. 1958, F4527 O1 E4986, Ministry of Civil Aviation Collection, State Economic Archives, Moscow; "Aeroflot Predicts One-Third Gain in Scheduled Traffic for 1961," *Aviation Week*, March 27, 1961.

47. Filipieva, interview, August 14, 2004.

48. Zaviagina, interview, August 12, 2004. Active Komsomol members generally received privileges and preferences in promotions.

49. Filipieva, interview, August 14, 2004; Zaviagina, interview, August 12, 2004.

50. Filipieva, interview, August 14, 2004.

51. This chapter explores what scholars have called the "cultural transfer" of American and Soviet ideas across borders. While some scholars have preferred the term "cultural imperialism," in order to imply that one nation deliberately attempts to impose its ideology and way of life on another nation, recent scholars in various disciplines have suggested replacing this term with the concept of "cultural transmission," in order to suggest a more fluid and shifting movement of ideas both internationally and within particular nations. See, for example, Gienow-Hecht, "Cultural Transfer."

52. Some American reporters noted that Aeroflot had reinvented itself with a new "competitive image" on par (or nearly on par) with Western airlines. In 1968 *Aviation Week and Space Technology* declared that Aeroflot had "successfully modified its old image." Donald Winston, "New Aeroflot Competitive 'Image' Emerges," *Aviation Week and Space*

Technology, July 22, 1968, 28-30. Lauding Aeroflot's technological accomplishment, these stories praised the Soviet Union's new plane, the IL-62, for speed, capacity, and comfort that rivaled Western jets. Jon Margolis, "East-West Link Has Flying Star," *Newsday*, July 17, 1968.

53. "Airlines: The Russians Are Coming," *Newsweek*, July 29, 1968; Robert Hotz, "Aeroflot Comes to the U.S.," *Aviation Week and Space Technology*, July 22, 1968, 11; Edmund Faltermayer, "Soviet Airline Takes Free Enterprise Tack to Woo Passengers," *Wall Street Journal*, May 14, 1963; "A Fast Ride on Aeroflot's New Jet," *New York Times*, July 21, 1968.

54. A Soviet aviation directive of 1964 mandated service improvements for international passengers. Ministra Grazhdanskoi Aviatsii C.C.C.P. Loginova E, "O Merakh Po Dal'neishemu Ulichsheniiu Obsluzhivaniia Passazhirov Na Mezhdunarodnykh Vozdushnykh Liniiakh," order, May 12, 1965, F 55 O1 E106, Ministry of Civil Aviation Collection, State Economic Archives, Moscow.

55. Zaviagina, interview, August 12, 2004; *Grazhdanskoi Aviatsii*, July 1967.

56. American articles that praised Aeroflot's uniforms noted that Aeroflot stewardesses' skirts were "cut above the knee." Ansel Talbert, "Aeroflot Looks Good on Moscow–New York Service," *Air Transport World* (August 1968).

57. Ministra Grazhdanskoi Aviatsii Loginova E., "O Merakh Po Dal'neishemu Uluchsheniiu Raboty Sluzhby Bortprovodnikov I Povysheniiu Kachestva Obsluzhivaniia Passazhirov Na Bortu Samoletov," order, 1969, F55 O1 E666, Ministry of Civil Aviation Collection, State Economic Archives, Moscow.

58. Gregory Frost, "What Russian Girls Are Like," *New York Times Magazine*, January 24, 1965, 44; Elena Whiteside, "For Soviet Women: A 13-Hour Day," *New York Times Magazine*, November 17, 1963, 28.

59. Olga Carlisle, "The Russian Woman," *Saturday Evening Post*, June 19, 1965, 43. Frost, "What Russian Girls Are Like" also debunked myths about Russian women—namely, that they were "homely," "unfeminine," and "puritanical" (44).

60. My thinking on this was informed by Daniel Horowitz's biography of Betty Friedan, which illustrated links between the American Left, modern feminism, and the Cold War. Horowitz locates the roots of the white, middle-class American women's movement of the 1960s in the world of progressive and labor feminism of the late 1940s and the early 1950s, including the Congress of American Women. Horowitz traces Friedan's affiliation with several radical organizations, including the pro-Soviet Women's International Democratic Federation. Daniel Horowitz, *Betty Friedan and the Making of the Feminine Mystique: The American Left, the Cold War, and Modern Feminism* (Amherst: University of Massachusetts Press, 1998).

61. Oriana Atkinson, "Weaker (?) Sex of Soviet Russia," *New York Times Magazine*, March 3, 1946, 52. Atkinson also presented a favorable vision of women's wage work by depicting Soviet women as pretty and feminine. When she profiled a female Soviet aviator, for example, she wrote: "It is difficult to picture such an impressive woman sitting happily over an embroidery frame and conducting the daily, uninspiring routine of domesticity. But . . . when not on duty with the army she is a feminine person."

62. "A foreigner in Moscow . . . is constantly surprised at the fields of work open to women here. The first reaction is likely to be, 'well, for heaven's sake!' The second is likely to be, 'well, why not?'" Ibid. Marveling at these working women, Atkinson came to the

conclusion that wage work offered women "opportunity," "dignity," "self-respect," and "freedom." Atkinson, "My Life Behind the Iron Curtain [Pt. 2]."

63. These celebratory views of Soviet women's roles in the mainstream press, however, had their roots in the writings of Communist women in America. In 1945 and 1946, American Communist women celebrated Soviet women's workforce participation as a model for women's equality. The American professor Rose Mauer, for example, expounded the virtues of Soviet women in a report for the National Council of American-Soviet Friendship, later criticized by the House Un-American Activities Committee (HUAC), a Communist-ferreting organization, as "the communist party's principal front for all things Russian." The report, which lauded Soviet women for combining work and domestic life, argued that Soviet women showed that "jobs can be combined with happy home life, that children can be secure and satisfied when the mother takes on responsibility outside the home, that women can master 'men's' professions, that masses of women can be intelligently concerned with larger issues, national and international." Mauer quoted a female Soviet pilot saying, "A woman who confines herself purely to domestic life deteriorates mentally and in other ways. She is in danger of becoming an idler, a gossip, and frittering away her time and energies on dull hobbies and useless practices." Beyond claiming that working women could have happy domestic lives, the report also debunked claims that "concern with work and politics makes them less attractive as women" or "hard and unfeminine." A section titled "Heroines Are Lovely Too" went into detail about how Soviet women took "particular pains" with their physical appearances and had "no trace of masculinity." Rose Mauer, *Soviet Women* (New York: National Council of American-Soviet Friendship, 1945), 6, 55, 56.

64. For example, in 1949 the House Un-American Activities Committee published a scathing report on the Congress of American Women (CAW), a pro-Soviet organization advocating for women's rights. The HUAC claimed that the group used women's equality to promote Communist domination of the world. And, by 1950, the CAW had disbanded. Kate Weigand, *Red Feminism: American Communism and the Making of Women's Liberation* (Baltimore: Johns Hopkins University Press, 2001), 63.

65. Exploring stewardesses within the context of Cold War culture also contributes to a growing body of scholarship on gender and international relations. In a pivotal essay, the feminist historian Joan Scott called us to consider gender one of the fundamental ways that "political power has been conceived, legitimated, and criticized." Joan Scott, "Gender: A Useful Category of Historical Analysis," *American Historical Review* 91, no. 5 (1986): 48. While gender and foreign relations have traditionally been cordoned as separate fields, several scholars have taken Scott's challenge seriously by launching provocative inquiries into the relationship between gender and political power, which offer insight into systems of power—particularly, how they are constructed, contested, and legitimated. Several scholars have demonstrated the importance of investigating this relationship by showing, for example, how gendered language has legitimized international hierarchies in dangerous ways. The scholar Emily Rosenberg astutely asked: "What does gender have to do with 9/11? Why did the administration present Laura Bush to publicly express concern about the Taliban's treatment of women?" Rosenberg and others found that these two seemingly disparate concerns are deeply intertwined. Emily Rosenberg, "Rescuing Women

and Children," *Journal of American History* 89, no. 2 (2002): 456–65. Gayatri Spivak, for example, has shown the relationship between gender and colonialism in the texts of British and American women writers. Gayatri Chakravorty Spivak, "Three Women's Texts and a Critique of Imperialism," *Critical Inquiry* 12, no. 1 (1985): 243–61. Andrew Rotter has analyzed how the British characterized Bengali men as effeminate as part of the project of imperialism and how gendered imagery was used to justify and support imperialist projects. Andrew Rotter, "Gender Relations, Foreign Relations: The United States and South Asia, 1947–1964," *Journal of American History* 81, no. 2 (1994): 518–42. Cynthia Enloe traced the connections between masculinity and militarization in the aftermath of the Cold War. Cynthia Enloe, *The Morning After: Sexual Politics at the End of the Cold War* (Berkeley: University of California Press, 1993). See also Cynthia Enloe, *Maneuvers: The International Politics of Militarizing Women's Lives* (Berkeley: University of California Press, 2000); Dean, *Imperial Brotherhood*; K. A. Cuordileone, *Manhood and American Political Culture in the Cold War* (New York: Routledge, 2005); Elaine Tyler May, *Homeward Bound: American Families in the Cold War Era* (New York: Basic Books, 1988); Kristin Hoganson, "What's Gender Got to Do with It? Gender History as Foreign Relations History," in *Explaining the History of American Foreign Relations*, ed. Michael Hogan (New York: Cambridge University Press, 2004); Emily Rosenberg, "Considering Borders," in *Explaining the History of Foreign Relations*, ed. Michael Hogan (New York: Cambridge University Press, 2004); Emily Rosenberg, "Consuming Women: Images of Americanization in the 'American Century,'" in *The Ambiguous Legacy: U.S. Foreign Relations in the "American Century,"* ed. Michael J. Hogan (Cambridge: Cambridge University Press, 1999); Emily Rosenberg, "Gender, a Round Table: Explaining the History of American Foreign Relations," *Journal of American History* 77, no. 1 (1990): 116–24; Emily Rosenberg, "Rescuing Women and Children"; Emily Rosenberg, "Walking the Borders," *Diplomatic History* 14, no. 4 (1990): 565–73.

Chapter 6

1. Leo Burnett Advertising Agency for United Airlines, "There Is Something Special about United. Exactly What Is It?," creative exploration, June 14, 1963, 29, United Airlines Archives, Chicago.

2. Leo Burnett, "New Horizons in Advertising for United Airlines," proposal, September 21, 1965, United Airlines Archives, Chicago.

3. For more on this trend in advertising, see Joanne Meyerowitz, "Women, Cheesecake, and Borderline Material: Responses to Girlie Pictures in the Mid-Twentieth Century U.S.," *Journal of Women's History* 8, no. 3 (1996): 9–35; Tom Reichert, *The Erotic History of Advertising* (Amherst, N.Y.: Prometheus Books, 2003).

4. Stephen Fox, *The Mirror Makers: A History of American Advertising and Its Creators* (Urbana: University of Illinois Press, 1984), 219, 21.

5. Mary Wells Lawrence, *A Big Life (in Advertising)* (New York: Alfred A. Knopf, 2002), 4.

6. Jack Kerouac, "Aftermath: The Philosophy of the Beat Generation," *Esquire* (March 1958).

7. The nation was the youngest it had ever been, with almost half the population under

the age of twenty-five. Mary Cross, ed., *A Century of American Icons* (Westport, Conn.: Greenwood, 2002), 313.

8. Juliann Sivulka, *Ad Women: How They Impact What We Need, Want, and Buy* (New York: Prometheus Books, 2008), 447.

9. Grace Palladino, *Teenagers: An American History* (New York: Basic Books, 1996), xiii; Thomas Frank, *The Conquest of Cool: Business Culture, Counterculture, and the Rise of Hip Consumerism* (Chicago: University of Chicago Press, 1998), 109.

10. Todd Leopold, "When Madison Avenue Was the Center of the Universe," review of *A Big Life (in Advertising)*, by Mary Wells Lawrence, CNN.com, June 19, 2002, http://edition.cnn.com/2002/SHOWBIZ/books/06/19/lawrence.advertising/.

11. Lawrence, *A Big Life (in Advertising)*, 50.

12. Frank, *The Conquest of Cool*, 119; *Madison Avenue Magazine* (June 1967): 22.

13. See also Fox, *The Mirror Makers*, 249.

14. Lois Banner, *Women in Modern America: A Brief History*, 2nd ed. (San Diego: Harcourt Brace Jovanovich, 1995), 165. For more on the sexual revolution as a commercial phenomenon, see Todd Gitlin, *The Sixties: Years of Hope, Days of Rage* (New York: Bantam Books, 1987), 30.

15. Hazel Warlaumont, *Advertising in the 60s: Turncoats, Traditionalists, and Waste Makers in America's Turbulent Decade* (London: Praeger, 2001); Thomas O'Guinn and Chris Allen, *Advertising and Integrated Brand Promotion* (n.p.: South-Western College Publications, 2008), 24.

16. Frank, *The Conquest of Cool*.

17. Leo Burnett Advertising Agency for United Airlines, "Something Special about United," United Airlines Archives, Chicago; Fox, *The Mirror Makers*, 98, 257–58; Leo Burnett Advertising Agency for United Airlines, planning considerations, July 12, 1965, 8, United Airlines Archives, Chicago.

18. Dick Stanwood, interview by the author, June 23, 2005.

19. Phil Schaff, "Memo to Leo Burnett, Re: My Quick Thoughts Regarding Your Transportation Think-Piece," memo, June 3, 1963, United Airlines Campaign in the 1960s "Friendly Skies" Campaign Collection, Special Collections, Leo Burnett Advertising Agency Corporate Archives, Chicago; Leo Burnett Advertising Agency for United Airlines, 7, United Airlines Archives, Chicago.

20. Dick Stanwood, interview by the author, June 23, 2005.

21. Bob Johnson, "Marketing and Services Administration," briefing, n.d., United Airlines Campaign in the 1960s "Friendly Skies" Campaign Collection, Special Collections, Leo Burnett Advertising Agency Corporate Archives, Chicago.

22. Patricia Patterson Dudley, interview by the author, August 31, 2011.

23. Leo Burnett, "Notes on Rationale for 'Courageous Candor' or 'No Hogwash' Series," unpublished report, n.d., United Airlines Campaign in the 1960s "Friendly Skies" Campaign Collection, Special Collections, Leo Burnett Advertising Agency Corporate Archives, Chicago; Leo Burnett Advertising Agency for United Airlines, "Something Special about United," United Airlines Archives, Chicago.

24. Burnett, "New Horizons in Advertising for United Airlines," United Airlines Archives, Chicago; United Airlines slide presentation preceding the film, Burnett Agency, 1965, p. 11.

25. *New York Times*, March 11, 1971, newspaper clipping, Pan American Airlines Files, J. Walter Thompson Collection, John W. Hartman Center for Sales, Advertising and Marketing History, Duke University, Durham, N.C.; Kathleen Barry, *Femininity in Flight: A History of Flight Attendants* (Durham, N.C.: Duke University Press, 2007), 98.

26. By 1970, U.S.-based airlines were carrying 150 million passengers—three times as many as they had in 1960. In 1967, Burnett ad executives and United executives met to discuss whether they should embark on a campaign dealing with the problems of the whole airline industry. "Crucial Years Ahead," unpublished report, July 25, 1967, United Airlines Campaign in the 1960s "Friendly Skies" Campaign Collection, Special Collections, Leo Burnett Advertising Agency Corporate Archives, Chicago. See also *Marketing Magazine*, December 15, 1969, 51, Pan American Airlines Files, J. Walter Thompson Collection, John W. Hartman Center for Sales, Advertising and Marketing History, Duke University, Durham, N.C.; Leo Burnett Advertising Agency for United Airlines, "Something Special about United," 6, United Airlines Archives, Chicago.

27. In the mid-1960s, airlines substantially increased their advertising efforts to expand the market and to improve the image of air travel as it became, in effect, mass transportation. In 1967, the Thompson advertising agency employed 407 people on Pan Am in the United States alone and churned out sixteen thousand ads that year for the airline. *Madison Avenue Magazine* (July 1968): 10, Pan American Airlines Files, J. Walter Thompson Collection, John W. Hartman Center for Sales, Advertising and Marketing History, Duke University, Durham, N.C.. From 1965 to 1968, Pan Am spent $40 million abroad to advertise itself and promote air travel to the United States. Tony Brenna, *Editor and Publisher Magazine*, January 13, 1968, Pan American Airlines Files, J. Walter Thompson Collection, John W. Hartman Center for Sales, Advertising and Marketing History, Duke University, Durham, N.C.

28. "Program for Personal Travel," Schedules and Marketing Development, unpublished report, November 6, 1964, American Airlines Collection, Special Collections, C. R. Smith Museum, Fort Worth, Tex.

29. Briefing memo, December 9, 1964, United Airlines Campaign in the 1960s "Friendly Skies" Campaign Collection, Special Collections, Leo Burnett Advertising Agency Corporate Archives, Chicago. An American Airlines marketing report predicted that lower-income individuals would become the major demographic group of the personal travel market. In 1964, American Airlines focused on appealing to what it referred to as "blue collar" travelers to win the personal travel market. "Program for Personal Travel," American Airlines Collection, Special Collections, C. R. Smith Museum, Fort Worth, Tex. That year, the median family income for year-round, full-time workers was $6,599. U.S. Bureau of the Census, *Current Population Reports: Consumer Income*, Series P-60, no. 36, 1–2. On "'de-formalizing' United's image," see Leo Burnett Advertising Agency for United Airlines, "Something Special about United," 16, United Airlines Archives, Chicago.

30. "Taking Off on a New Sales Pitch," *Business Week*, August 3, 1968, 44.

31. "Youth Market Research Report," unpublished report, 1971, Pan Am World Airways Collection, Otto Richter Library, University of Miami Libraries, Coral Gables, Fla.

32. Alastair Gordon, *Naked Airport: A Cultural History of the World's Most Revolutionary Structure* (New York: Metropolitan Books, 2004); Stanwood, interview by the author, June 23, 2005.

33. Fox, *The Mirror Makers*, 269.

34. Ibid., 270.

35. Lawrence, *A Big Life (in Advertising)*, 60, 23.

36. Ibid., 56.

37. Shirley Kennedy, *Pucci: A Renaissance in Fashion* (New York: Abbeville Press, 1991), 98.

38. One article, for example, stated: "The dominant color in the Soviet Union is gray. But gray if not the national color, is the national mood. Russians walk the streets of Moscow, their faces frozen in gloom." James Cary, untitled article, July 26, 1968. For more references to Soviet gray, see "The Soviet Family," *Atlantic Monthly* (February 1952): 18–20; William J. Jorden, "Portraits of the Soviet Woman," *New York Times Magazine*, February 3, 1957, 11–13; Toni Howard, "The Sorry Life of Soviet Women," *Saturday Evening Post*, December 26, 1959, 20–21, 76–78. See also Kennedy, *Pucci*, 79; Olga Gurova, "The Art of Dressing: Body, Gender, and Discourse on Fashion in Soviet Russia in the 1950s and 1960s," in *The Fabric of Cultures: Fashion, Identity, and Globalization*, ed. Eugenia Paulicelli (New York: Routledge, 2009); Carol Pursell, *Technology in Postwar America: A History* (New York: Columbia University Press, 2007), 102; Karal Ann Marling, *As Seen on TV: The Visual Culture of Everyday Life in the 1950s* (Cambridge, Mass.: Harvard University Press, 1994), 243.

39. Kennedy, *Pucci*, 98; Lawrence, *A Big Life (in Advertising)*, 37.

40. Quoted in Kennedy, *Pucci*, 46.

41. Juliann Sivulka, "Historical and Psychological Perspectives of the Erotic Appeal in Advertising," in *Sex in Advertising: Perspectives on the Erotic Appeal*, ed. Tom Reichert (New York: Routledge, 2002); Meyerowitz, "Women, Cheesecake, and Borderline Material," 12.

42. In the 1960s, *Women's Wear Daily* observed, "The old guard no longer sets fashion . . . the mood is youth-youth-youth." Quoted in Valerie Steele, *Fifty Years of Fashion: From New Look to Now* (New Haven, Conn.: Yale University Press, 1997), 50.

43. Thomas P. Whitney, "S-X in the Soviet Union," *New York Times Magazine*, January 1, 1956, 11.

44. Stanwood, interview by the author, June 23, 2005.

45. Continental's reputation had also been marred by its former president, Bob Six, who was a "flashy" man, according to Burnett's team, because he had been divorced twice (once from the Hollywood star Ethel Merman). Schaff, "Memo to Leo Burnett, Re: My Quick Thoughts Regarding Your Transportation Think-Piece," 2, United Airlines Campaign in the 1960s "Friendly Skies" Campaign Collection. On movies and movie palaces, see Lary May, *Screening out the Past: The Birth of Mass Culture and the Motion Picture Industry* (Chicago: University of Chicago Press, 1983); Robert Sklar, *Movie-Made America: A Cultural History of American Movies* (New York: Vintage, 1994); Steven Ross, *Working-Class Hollywood: Silent Film and the Shaping of Class in America* (Princeton, N.J.: Princeton University Press, 1998); Maggie Valentine, *The Show Starts on the Sidewalk: An Architectural History of the Movie Theater* (New Haven, Conn.: Yale University Press, 1996); Michael Putnam, *Silent Screens: The Decline and Transformation of the American Movie Theater* (Baltimore: Johns Hopkins University Press, 2000). On United's passé image, see Leo Burnett Advertising Agency for United Airlines, "Something Special about United," United Airlines Archives,

Chicago. Mary Wells also considered TWA's image passé in the 1960s, when she took the account. Lawrence, *A Big Life (in Advertising)*, 100.

46. Burnett, "Notes on Rationale for 'Courageous Candor' or 'No Hogwash' Series," United Airlines Campaign in the 1960s "Friendly Skies" Campaign Collection, Special Collections, Leo Burnett Advertising Agency Corporate Archives, Chicago.

47. Burnett, "New Horizons in Advertising for United Airlines," United Airlines Archives, Chicago; Stanwood, interview by the author, June 23, 2005; Leo Burnett to Sydney Harris, August 23, 1965, United Airlines Campaign in the 1960s "Friendly Skies" Campaign Collection, Special Collections, Leo Burnett Advertising Agency Corporate Archives, Chicago. John Kinsella, a Burnett executive during the early 1960s, said, "Friendly skies campaign was never put forth as a euphemism for [sexually] available. That kind of approach wouldn't be sanctioned by the agency or any of our clients." John Kinsella, interview by the author, September 15, 2011. Smith, who worked on the United Airlines campaign, also said the campaign was "not at all sexual." Jack Smith, interview by the author, May 3, 2010.

48. Burnett, "New Horizons in Advertising for United Airlines," 17, United Airlines Archives, Chicago.

49. Pan Am's strategy for creating "warmth" hinged on stewardesses. *Roses for Routine*, a Pan Am stewardess training film of 1958, depicted stewardesses offering passengers personalized service—for example, a stewardess notices that an elderly woman is cold and kindly brings her a blanket. The film concluded with a monologue addressing new stewardesses: "You are important in this mechanized, scientifically oriented world. . . . How you make us feel about the equipment every second of the flight. The warmth of a smile . . . the real interest in a fellow human being, the caring . . . words can be misunderstood, but a look, a feeling [*sic*]." Jerome Alden, *Roses for Routine*, training video, 1958, Tori Johnson, personal collection. The United ad campaign in 1966 depicted a stewardess pinning a rose on a passenger's lapel to show "extra care." "Come Back Soon," print advertisement for United Airlines, 1966, United Airlines Campaign in the 1960s "Friendly Skies" Campaign Collection, Special Collections, Leo Burnett Advertising Agency Corporate Archives, Chicago.

50. Stanwood, interview by the author, June 23, 2005. Pan Am also hired younger stewardesses. From 1945 to 1957, 40 percent of the stewardesses Pan Am had hired were twenty-one to twenty-four years old (and 54 percent of the stewardesses).From 1958 to 1969, almost 85 percent of the airline's stewardess hires were twenty-one to twenty-four years old. Statistics based on Pan Am Airways personnel records, calculated for this book by Lynne Pinkerton, National Institute of Occupational Safety and Health, Atlanta, Ga., 2005.

51. Airline advertising teams began fixating on creating images of personalized attention in the late 1950s (with the advent of jets) and the 1960s (with the coming of jumbo jets), in part because airlines faced a contradiction between the promise of personalized service and the new reality of larger planes and larger markets.

52. David Reisman, *The Lonely Crowd* (New Haven, Conn.: Yale University Press, 1950); William Whyte, *The Organization Man* (New York: Simon and Schuster, 1956); Suzanne Lee Kolm, "Women's Labor Aloft: A Cultural History of Airline Flight Attendants in the United States, 1930–1978" (Ph.D. diss., Brown University, 1995), 201; Daniel Boorstin, *The Image: A Guide to Pseudo-Events in America* (New York: Vintage, 1961); Fox, *The Mirror Makers*, 218.

53. Sydney Harris to Leo Burnett, September 13, 1965, United Airlines Campaign in the 1960s "Friendly Skies" Campaign Collection, Special Collections, Leo Burnett Advertising Agency Corporate Archives, Chicago.

54. See the following documents in the J. Walter Thompson Collection, John W. Hartman Center for Sales, Advertising and Marketing History, Duke University, Durham, N.C.: "Pan Am World Airways Script for System Sales Meeting," meeting agenda, December 1956, Review Board Records, Box 23; "Advertising Plan for 1957," meeting minutes, 1957, Meetings Pan Am Minutes 1957, Box 23; "Confidential Agreement on Advertising Strategy for Pan Am," meeting minutes, August 1964, Meetings, John Monsarrat Chairman: Pan Am Minutes 1964.

55. The Burnett team wanted to eliminate the feeling that flying was exclusively for the wealthy, while presenting air travel as a way for middle-class travelers to feel like elite members of the jet set. "Big Pitch," June 14, 1963, United Airlines Campaign in the 1960s "Friendly Skies" Campaign Collection, Special Collections, Leo Burnett Advertising Agency Corporate Archives, Chicago. See also "Program for Personal Travel," American Airlines Collection, Special Collections, C. R. Smith Museum, Fort Worth, Tex. For more on this theme, see Frank, *The Conquest of Cool*, 151.

56. This was not an uncommon strategy in the late 1950s and the 1960s. See Warlaumont, *Advertising in the 60s*, 112–13.

57. The historian K. A. Cuordileone shows how the terms "hard" and "soft" were used to express a larger cultural anxiety over masculinity during the Cold War, which put a premium on masculine toughness and rendered feminine softness in men a potential threat to the nation. Similarly, airlines used masculinized descriptions of aircraft (and pilots) to connect commercial aviation to Cold War visions of virile masculinity. United linked its corporate image to U.S. military strength and technological prowess. For more on the relationship between gender and technology, see Paul Edwards, "Industrial Genders: Soft/Hard," in *Gender and Technology: A Reader*, ed. Nina Lerman (Baltimore: Johns Hopkins University Press, 2003).

58. Leo Burnett, memo, August 19, 1967, United Airlines Campaign in the 1960s "Friendly Skies" Campaign Collection, Special Collections, Leo Burnett Advertising Agency Corporate Archives, Chicago.

59. Jack Smith, interview by the author, May 3, 2010.

60. Mark Tungate, *Ad Land: A Global History of Advertising* (Philadelphia: Kogan Page Press, 2007), 75.

61. Don Reed, memo, September 20, 1967, United Airlines Campaign in the 1960s "Friendly Skies" Campaign Collection, Special Collections, Leo Burnett Advertising Agency Corporate Archives, Chicago.

62. Stanwood, interview by the author, June 23, 2005.

63. Quant won the *Sunday Times* Fashion award and was voted Woman of the Year in 1965. Jennifer Craik, *The Face of Fashion: Cultural Studies in Fashion* (New York: Routledge, 1994), 81. This new trend in American stewardess uniforms made stewardesses look hip and young, but it also revealed more of their bodies.

64. Frank, *The Conquest of Cool*, 191.

65. "United Has the Most Nonstop Jets to Atlanta," print advertisement for United Airlines, 1967, United Airlines Campaign in the 1960s "Friendly Skies" Campaign

Collection, Special Collections, Leo Burnett Advertising Agency Corporate Archives, Chicago.

66. "See a Fashion Show on Your Way to California," print advertisement for United Airlines, 1968, United Airlines Campaign in the 1960s "Friendly Skies" Campaign Collection, Special Collections, Leo Burnett Advertising Agency Corporate Archives, Chicago.

67. Stewardess weight requirement charts for different heights ranged from 116 pounds at 5'2" to 140 pounds at 5'9". See "Flight Service Manual (1967)," training manual, September 1, 1967, 17, Box 25, Folder 244, World Wings International Collection, Otto Richter Library, University of Miami, Coral Gables, Fla. The stewardess application for Eastern Airlines in 1967 also requested height, weight, bust, waist, and hip measurements. Johni Smith, *How to Be a Flight Stewardess: A Handbook and Training Manual for Airline Hostesses*, 2nd ed. (North Hollywood: Pan American Navigation Service, 1970). See also "Trans Caribbean Operations Manual," training manual, March 1968, American Airlines Collection, Special Collections, C. R. Smith Museum, Fort Worth, Tex.

68. Many airlines began allowing "natural-looking hair dyes." In 1960, Pan Am began allowing limited hair dying among stewardesses, but required stewardesses to get permission from a grooming supervisor. "Flight Service Manual," training manual, July 18, 1966, 1966 Box 438, Pan Am World Airways Collection, Otto Richter Library, University of Miami, Coral Gables, Fla. The airline TWA modified its hair-coloring rule to allow some color: "The use of tints of rinses is permitted provided they achieve naturalness in color, complement the natural skin color and enhance the appearance in uniform. Dyes, bleaches, stripping, streaking, frosting or extreme colors such as platinum, silver, brassy yellow blondes, pink or orange reds, intense blacks or brown, etc. are not acceptable." Marci Nelson and Shirley Motter Linde, eds., *Airline Stewardess Handbook* (Careers Research, 1968), 60. See also "Look of the Leader for Stewardesses," training manual, 1965, 4, and "Trans Caribbean Operations Manual," 16, both in American Airlines Collection, Special Collections, C. R. Smith Museum, Fort Worth, Tex.; Johni Smith, *How to Be a Flight Stewardess*, 2nd ed.; Johni Smith, *How to Be a Flight Stewardess: A Handbook and Training Manual for Airline Hostesses*, 1st ed. (North Hollywood: Pan American Navigation Service, 1966), 23.

69. See, for example, "I Always Feel Like I'm Sort of Giving a Party," print advertisement for American Airlines, 1968, American Airlines Files, J. Walter Thompson Collection, John W. Hartman Center for Sales, Advertising and Marketing History, Duke University, Durham, N.C.

70. "T.W.A. 'Foreign Accent' Hostesses Dressed for Work," print advertisement, 1968, Box 38, J. Walter Thompson Collection, John W. Hartman Center for Sales, Advertising and Marketing History, Duke University, Durham, N.C.

71. Clare Christiansen, interview by the author, October 31, 2011.

72. Frank, *The Conquest of Cool*, 43, 110; Warlaumont, *Advertising in the 60s*, 105.

73. "Flight Service Manual," 1966 Box 438, Pan Am Airways Collection, Otto Richter Library, University of Miami, Coral Gables, Fla.; "What Do They Have in Common?," *Redbook* (February 1966): 74-77, 116, 117; "Pan Am Tells Marines—No Wigs, False Eyelashes," *Clipper*, May 1, 1967, Box 291, Folder 1, Pan Am World Airways Collection, Otto Richter Library, University of Miami, Coral Gables, Fla.; "Pan American Airlines Overseas Divi-

sion Manual," training manual, 1960, Box 28, Folder 278, Roiz Logan Papers, World Wings International Collection, Otto Richter Library, University of Miami, Coral Gables, Fla.

74. "Ladies Bridge Club Cindy's Cup of Tea," *Pan Am Clipper*, November 15, 1966, Special Collections, SFO Library, San Francisco Airport Museum, San Francisco, Calif. See also "Aviation's One World in the Jet Age," publicity brochure, 1968, 12, Pan American Airlines File, National Air and Space Museum, Washington, D.C.

75. "Pssst, Stewardess Watchers: P.S.A.'s New Lockheed 1011 Tristar Jetliners Will Each Carry 8 Lovely Stewardesses (and up to 300 Happy Passengers)," print advertisement for Pacific Southwest Airlines, 1970, Pacific Southwest Airlines File, National Air and Space Museum, Washington, D.C.

76. "I'm Cheryl. Fly Me," print advertisement for National Airlines, 1972, National Airlines File, National Air and Space Museum, Washington, D.C.

77. Richard Branson, the owner of Virgin Atlantic, claimed that he joined the mile high club at the age of nineteen (around 1969) in an airplane lavatory. The origins of the mile-high club are elusive. Agence France-Presse, July 29, 2007.

78. Trudy Baker and Rachel Jones, *Coffee, Tea, or Me?* (n.p.: Bartholomew House, 1967), 62.

79. Cornelius Wohl and Bill Wenzel, *How to Make a Good Airline Stewardess* (New York: Fawcett Books, 1972); Kathryn Leigh Scott, *The Bunny Years* (Los Angeles: Pomegranate Press, 1998).

80. Critics have often painted advertising (and popular culture generally) as a top-down product created by powerful corporations that inject dominant ideologies in the unwitting masses. See Theodor Adorno and Max Horkheimer, *Dialectic of Enlightenment* (New York: Herder and Herder, 1972); Leo Lowenthal, *Literature, Popular Culture and Society* (Englewood Cliffs, N.J.: Prentice-Hall, 1961). This approach implicitly assumes that viewers mindlessly ingest and internalize media messages. In this view, mass media convert audiences into passive zombies—too hypnotized to think for themselves or to formulate any opposition to the status quo. Recent studies of popular culture have questioned this analysis, insisting on reading popular culture as an arena where meanings are contested and negotiated. Some recent scholars have turned this media criticism on its head by showing how consumers give their own meanings to products of mass culture; this approach considers audiences creators who use mass-produced cultural texts to create their own alternative, potentially radical, meanings. See, for example, Lorraine Gamman and Margaret Marshment, *The Female Gaze: Women as Viewers of Popular Culture* (London: Women's Press, 1988), 1; Susan Douglas, *Where the Girls Are: Growing up Female with the Mass Media* (New York: Random House, 1994); Tania Modleski, *Loving with a Vengeance: Mass-Produced Fantasies for Women* (Harden, Conn.: Archon Books, 1982); John Storey, *An Introduction to Cultural Theory and Popular Culture* (Athens: University of Georgia Press, 1998).

Chapter 7

1. Patricia O'Neill, "Stewardess Questionnaire," author's unpublished form, Summer 2004. Similarly, other stewardesses who were considered stellar in terms of service, per-

sonality, and intelligence were criticized for their weights. See, for example, "Evaluation Report of Stewardess Gayla Kanaster," 1960, Gayla Kanaster, personal collection.

2. Fran McDowell, interview by the author, August 15, 2009.

3. Training evaluation form for Patricia O'Neill, March 6, 1964, O'Neill File, Pan Am Airways Personnel Records, National Institute of Occupational Safety and Health, Atlanta, Ga.

4. Patricia O'Neill, interview by the author, April 3, 2011.

5. Letter regarding flight on September 23, 1969 from Conrad Jacoby to Patricia O'Neill, O'Neill File, Pan Am Airways Personnel Records, National Institute of Occupational Safety and Health, Atlanta, Ga.

6. O'Neill cleverly managed to finagle an increase in her official height to 5′7″, which allowed her to weigh a few more pounds. At the same time, Pan Am lowered its weight limits for stewardesses. Now, at 5′6½″, she was allowed to weigh only 134½ pounds. In September 1966, another grooming supervisor wrote that O'Neill was 8½ pounds overweight at 143 pounds. O'Neill received a letter December 29, 1966 requiring her to report to the medical department for a weight check. Grooming chart for Patricia O'Neill, September 1, 1966, and letter to Patricia O'Neill, December 29, 1966, both in O'Neill File, Pan Am Airways Personnel Records, National Institute of Occupational Safety and Health, Atlanta, Ga.

7. See the following grooming discrepancy reports in the O'Neill File, Pan Am Airways Personnel Records, National Institute of Occupational Safety and Health, Atlanta, Ga.: "July 16 Grooming Discrepancy Report [1968]," "June 10 Grooming Discrepancy Report [1967]," "November 21 Grooming Discrepancy Report [1967]," "February 28, 1968 Grooming Discrepancy Report," "October 20, 1968 Grooming Discrepancy Report."

8. G. Vargas (Pan Am's base supervisor) to Patricia O'Neill, November 13, 1968, and letter from Patricia O'Neill to her supervisor, October 26, 1968, both in O'Neill File, Pan Am Airways Personnel Records, National Institute of Occupational Safety and Health, Atlanta, Ga.

9. These elite white-collar women workers organized for higher wages, better working conditions, and job security, but most stewardesses expected to get married and they expected to marry men who could support them financially so they were not overly concerned with whether the position offered financial security. Kathleen Barry suggests that stewardesses mobilized based on their discontent about wages and work conditions, but the intimate sources I found reveal that stewardesses' core motivation for unionization was their love of flying and their desire to keep the jobs they loved. Kathleen Barry, *Femininity in Flight: A History of Flight Attendants* (Durham, N.C.: Duke University Press, 2007), 143.

10. O'Neill, interview by the author, April 3, 2011.

11. She also noted that airlines were fair about how they doled out trips—it was merely a matter of seniority, rather than sleeping with a supervisor or a pilot to get a better trip. McDowell, interview by the author, August 15, 2009. On feeling free from sexual harassment, see also Patricia Patterson Dudley, interview by the author, August 31, 2011.

12. Marjorie Johansen, "Stewardess Questionnaire," author's unpublished form, Summer 2004.

13. Ibid.

14. Sonia Coyle, "Stewardess Questionnaire," author's unpublished form, Summer 2004.

15. Anne Sweeney, interview by the author, February 14, 2012.

16. Peggy Lee Baranowski, "Stewardess Questionnaire," author's unpublished form, Summer 2004. In a letter home in 1961, a new stewardess recruit expressed her enthusiasm about fellow stewardesses: "Really mother, these girls are even better and greater than I had ever even hoped for. They're wonderful people." Helene Hills, personal letters to her mother, 1961–62, Helene Hills, personal collection. See also Carolyn Richter Goff, "Stewardess Questionnaire," author's unpublished form, Summer 2004.

17. Peggy Casserta and her lover worked as stewardesses prior to 1964. Alice Echols, *Scars of Sweet Paradise: The Life and Times of Janice Joplin* (New York: Henry Holt, 1999), 142. For example, the United stewardess Connie Bosza and her coworker were so inseparable that they were nicknamed "Ham 'n Eggs." They lived together as a duo for years, spent most of their free time together, and owned a car together. Stewardesses, rather than male dates, formed the core of Bosza's social life. Connie Bosza, "21 Seats and a Head—How to Toss Your Cookies" (unpublished memoir, 1952), 174, Connie Bosza, personal collection.

18. Linda Lowrey Peddy, "Stewardess Questionnaire," author's unpublished form, Summer 2004; Maureen Swaney, "Stewardess Questionnaire," author's unpublished form, Summer 2004. "We treated each other as a family. Our schedules were fifteen to twenty days together so . . . we took care of each other," said a former Pan Am stewardess. Leona Tiede, "Stewardess Questionnaire," author's unpublished form, Summer 2004. See also Bev Bennis, "Stewardess Questionnaire," author's unpublished form, Summer 2004; Sylvia Griffin, "Stewardess Questionnaire," author's unpublished form, Summer 2004; Johansen, "Questionnaire"; Diane Johnson, "Stewardess Questionnaire," author's unpublished form, Summer 2004.

19. Sherry Waterman, *From Another Island: Adventures and Misadventures of an Airline Stewardess*, 2nd ed. (New York: Chilton, 1962), 34. Stewardesses considered their work a serious "career" (they used this term in their writings) and viewed themselves as career-oriented professionals—an unorthodox way for women to see themselves at the time. See, for example, Eva Kidney Crabtree, "Stewardess Questionnaire," author's unpublished form, Summer 2004. In fact, some stewardesses were so intent on working once married that they managed to circumvent marriage restrictions. When Lynne Mertes was a child, she saved up four hundred dollars for a private pilot's license, but her parents refused to let her take the family car to the field. She left her hometown in upstate New York to move to New York City and landed a job as a National Airlines stewardess in 1947. Three years later she got married and was required to resign. But Mertes was too in love with flying to quit. She tenaciously maneuvered her way into stewardess positions with eight different nonscheduled airlines (like charter services such as Mackey Airlines). Some of these airlines made exceptions by allowing her to work even though she was married; she lied about her marital status to others. As each of these airlines merged or went bankrupt, Mertes found another stewardess job. She flew for twenty years until she could no longer find an airline to hire her.

20. Waterman continued: "[It is] grossly unjust that only engagements and weddings rated newsworthy items in a girl's social life. What about the girl who might be leading a far more interesting existence and turning down marriage proposals right and left? Didn't she rate a column every now and then to let her contemporaries know that she

wasn't exactly sitting on her hands while they copped all the headlines?" Waterman, *From Another Island*, 34.

21. Bosza felt pressured to choose marriage over her stewardess position and considered herself an unusual woman for wanting career achievements, rather than solely wanting to get married and have children. She defended flying as an opportunity to accomplish something outside of family life in her unpublished memoir written in 1952. "I would no more be stuck in one place and wait for a fellow to come along with a proposal and find myself tied down than I would go to work in a salt mine. I can't understand girls who don't want to accomplish little else than hooking a man and getting married. That's all girls ever think of anymore. If that's what they want, let them go to it. But it's not for me." Bosza, "21 Seats and a Head—How to Toss Your Cookies," 38, 50, 70, 159.

22. American stewardesses were not the only voices endorsing working women during this era. In the global propaganda war, Soviet politicians promoted Soviet women's participation in the workforce as a testament to women's equality under Communism. Although the American press generally criticized Soviet working women, discussions about Soviet working women in the U.S. press also allowed the possibility of working women to seep into the American imagination and stir up feminist ideas about women and work that would eventually blossom in America. See Chapter 5, "Vodka, Tea, or Me?," for more on this subject.

23. Bosza, "21 Seats and a Head—How to Toss Your Cookies," 136, 1.

24. Ibid., 136.

25. See, for example, Katherine Milner (former TWA stewardess), interview by Mauree Jane Perry, May 14, 1999, Oral History Program, Special Collections, SFO Library, San Francisco Airport Museum, San Francisco, Calif.

26. Edith Lauterbach, interview by Barbara Hanson, April 16, 2002, United Airlines, Oral History Program, United Airlines Archives, Chicago; Daniel Horowitz, *Betty Friedan and the Making of the Feminine Mystique: The American Left, the Cold War, and Modern Feminism* (Amherst: University of Massachusetts Press, 1998).

27. While pink-collar activism did exist during the first half of the twentieth century (that is, by teachers), by the postwar era few women were union members. In 1946, the U.S. workforce had 16.7 million female wage earners, but only 3.5 million women belonged to unions. Barry, *Femininity in Flight*, 66.

28. Lauterbach, 33, United Airlines, Oral History Program, United Airlines Archives, Chicago.

29. Ibid.

30. Barry, *Femininity in Flight*, 64; Georgia Nielsen, *From Sky Girl to Flight Attendant: Women and the Making of a Union* (New York: Cornell University Press, 1982), 35–41.

31. Founded in 1931, the ALPA was an affiliate of the American Federation of Labor (AFL), but the ALPA made no efforts to assist other airline employees. It became interested in chartering stewardess unions after stewardesses began organizing on their own—the leaders of the ALPA wanted to gain control over emerging unions in the airline industry. The ALPA then chartered several unions, including the Air Line Stewards and Stewardesses Association (ALSSA), which was established in 1946. The ALSSA was subsidized by the ALPA and was, therefore, better funded than United's stewardess union, the ALSA. In

1949 Brown's independent stewardess union, the ALSA, merged with the ALSSA. Barry, *Femininity in Flight*, 68.

32. Ibid., 72.

33. William Coughlin, "Is 32 the 'Witching' Age? A Hostess Says 'No!,'" *Aviation Week*, April 5, 1954, 26; Barry, *Femininity in Flight*.

34. "Hair Pulling," *Newsweek*, June 11, 1962, 77.

35. Laurie Pintar, "Off Screen Realities: A History of Hollywood Labor Activism, 1933–47" (Ph.D. diss., University of Southern California, 1996); Shirli Brautbar, "Not Just 'Ladies That Lunch': Hadassah and the Formation of an American Jewish Women's Identity" (Ph.D. diss., University of Southern California, 2005); Jill Fields, *An Intimate Affair: Women, Lingerie, and Sexuality* (Berkeley: University of California Press, 2007).

36. McDowell, interview by the author, August 15, 2009.

37. For example, in 1956, the stewardess union, the ALSSA, cosponsored the first Miss Skyway contest, a beauty pageant exclusively for American stewardesses. Coverage of this event was featured alongside bargaining news in the union newsletter.

38. Sweeney, interview by the author, February 14, 2012.

39. A stewardess who flew with Pan Am from 1955 to 1966 was two inches too tall for a stewardess position, so when she was measured she bent her knees and passed. Betty Lou Ruble Snyder, "Stewardess Questionnaire," author's unpublished form, Summer 2004. Clare Christiansen, "Stewardess Questionnaire," author's unpublished form, Summer 2004; Bosza, "21 Seats and a Head—How to Toss Your Cookies," 160.

40. Barry, *Femininity in Flight*, 77. Throughout the 1950s, pilots had failed to support stewardesses on major issues. For instance, the pilots' union leaders had undermined stewardesses' efforts for safety certification because pilots feared that if stewardesses were certified and they walked off the job, then pilots would have to stop work too. Ibid., 79.

41. Barry, *Femininity in Flight*, 87.

42. Mary Laffey Inman, interview by the author, November 14, 2007.

43. "Stewardess Keeps Job—and a Husband," *AFL-CIO News*, October 2, 1965, 1.

44. McDowell, interview by the author, August 15, 2009.

45. See Phil Tiemeyer, "Male Stewardesses: Male Flight Attendants as a Queer Miscarriage of Justice," *Genders* 45 (2007).

46. Anne Sweeney also became very active in NOW during the late 1960s and the early 1970s.

47. McDowell, interview by the author, August 15, 2009.

48. Sweeney, interview by the author, February 14, 2012.

49. Ibid.

50. Inman, interview by the author, November 14, 2007.

51. The EEOC ruled that sex was not a bona fide occupational qualification for the flight attendant job. Shortly thereafter, the EEOC granted a few men permission to pursue their grievances in federal court. See Tiemeyer, "Male Stewardesses."

52. Inman, interview by the author, November 14, 2007; Barry, *Femininity in Flight*, 133.

53. Mary Dana, "Stewardess Questionnaire," author's unpublished form, Summer 2004. Stewardesses increasingly hid their marriages and pregnancies from airline management in efforts to keep their jobs. Caroline Jessup, for example, who flew with Eastern Airlines

from 1957 to 1967, continued flying until her pregnancy became obvious. Caroline Jessup, "Stewardess Questionnaire," author's unpublished form, Summer 2004. "People did not quit, they secretly married," said Mary Laffey Inman, who worked as a stewardess for Northwest from 1958 to 2000 and served as the master executive chairman of the ALSSA from 1966 to 1968. Inman, interview by the author, November 14, 2007. Carol Gurdak had been a stewardess with United Airlines for four years when she got married in June 1968. Gurdak loved flying so instead of submitting her resignation she went to great pains to keep her marriage a secret from the airlines. "I never told anyone I was married and we had two mailboxes and separate phone lines with my maiden name," Gurdak said. "I knew many stewardesses that were fired for being married." Carol Armstrong Gurdak, "Stewardess Questionnaire," author's unpublished form, Summer 2004. For months, Gurdak feared that her marriage would be discovered and her career would be abruptly cut short. Gurdak, who had been hiding her marriage for five months, was relieved to hear that United had changed its policy. She no longer had to conceal her marriage and went on to work as a stewardess for thirty-eight years. Inman, interview by the author, November 14, 2007.

54. Memo, November 8, 1968, Carol Armstrong Gurdak, personal collection.

55. In 1970, *Sprogis v. United*, stewardesses won.

56. Inman, interview by the author, November 14, 2007.

57. Conrad Jacoby (superintendent for the flight service bases) to Patricia O'Neill, May 2, 1970, O'Neill File, Pan Am Airways Personnel Records, National Institute of Occupational Safety and Health, Atlanta, Ga.

58. Barry, *Femininity in Flight*, 205.

59. Ibid., 197.

60. The same year, Paula Kane, a former stewardess and a member of SFWR, published her memoir, *Sex Objects in the Sky: A Personal Account of the Stewardess Rebellion* (Follett Publishing Company, 1974), which described her feminist awakening to the discrimination in the airline industry.

61. Drew Whitelegg, *Working the Skies: The Fast-Paced, Disorienting World of the Flight Attendant* (New York: New York University Press, 2007), 133.

62. Inman, interview by the author, November 14, 2007.

63. O'Neill, interview by the author, April 3, 2011.

64. Ibid.

65. *Patricia Griffith v. Pan Am Memorandum*, August 1976, U.S. District Court, O'Neill File, Pan Am Airways Personnel Records, National Institute of Occupational Safety and Health, Atlanta, Ga. Griffith was O'Neill's maiden name.

66. Even though beauty had become an increasingly central feature of women's lives in the twentieth century, gender historians have not paid much attention to fashion, appearance, and beauty—with the exception of a few foundational works, such as Lois W. Banner, *American Beauty: A Social History through Two Centuries of the American Idea, Ideal, and Image of the Beautiful Woman* (New York: Alfred A. Knopf, 1983); Kathy Peiss, *Hope in a Jar: The Making of America's Beauty Culture* (New York: Henry Holt, 1998). For more on the bifurcated role of glamour in women's experiences, see Liz Willis, "Hollywood Glamour: Sex, Power, and Photography, 1925–1939" (Ph.D. diss., University of Southern California, 2007); Brautbar, "Not Just 'Ladies That Lunch'"; Pintar, "Off Screen Realities."

The complex relationship between beauty and feminism, work, and unionization has not yet been fully explored. For feminist debate on beauty and glamour, see Jennifer Craik, *The Face of Fashion: Cultural Studies in Fashion* (New York: Routledge, 1994), 153; Susan Bordo, *Unbearable Weight: Feminism, Western Culture, and the Body* (Berkeley: University of California Press, 1993). For more on glamour, see also Stephen Gundle, "Hollywood Glamour and Mass Consumption in Postwar Italy," *Journal of Cold War Studies* 4, no. 3 (2002): 95–118; Peter Bailey, "Parasexuality and Glamour: The Victorian Barmaid as Cultural Prototype," *Gender and History* 2, no. 2 (1990): 148–72.

67. Pan American World Airways, Inc., Maternity Leave Practices and Flight Attendant Weight Program Litigation, *Justia US Law*, July 13, 1990.

68. O'Neill, interview by the author, April 3, 2011.

69. Louise Howe, "No More Stewardesses—We're Flight Attendants," *Redbook* (January 1979): 75; Letty Pogrebin, "The Working Woman," *Ladies' Home Journal* (November 1976): 86. For more on *Diaz v. Pan American Airways*, see Cathleen Marie Dooley, "Battle in the Sky: A Cultural and Legal History of Sex Discrimination in the United States Airline Industry, 1930–1980" (Ph.D. diss., University of Arizona, 2001), 178–88. Male stewards, however, were not subject to the same grooming and weight policies as female stewardesses.

70. American Airlines settled lawsuits in 1991, agreeing to relax its weight standards, to increase the weight limits with age, and to reinstate some stewardesses who had been dismissed because of their weights. In the early 1990s, United Airlines stewardesses and their union refused to join an employee buyout of the airline unless United eliminated weight restrictions. Tamar Lewin, "U.S. Air Agrees to Lift Rules on the Weight of Flight Attendants," *New York Times*, April 8 1994.

71. Although precise numbers do not exist, there are dozens of former stewardess associations—at least one for each airline—and they all have very active communities, even Pan Am and Eastern Airlines, both of which went out of business more than twenty years ago.

72. Lynn Mertes, "Stewardess Questionnaire," author's unpublished form, Summer 2004.

73. See also Anne Thomas, scrapbook, Anne Thomas, personal collection.

74. O'Neill, "Questionnaire."

INDEX

advertising: creative revolution in, 156–57, 159, 170; the girl next door in 1940s, 35, 51–52; glamour in 1950s, 170; 1960s trends in, 159, 173; 1960s use of color in, 166; sexual images in, 155, 168; youth counterculture and, 157, 158, 159; youth market and, 157, 175. *See also* airline advertising; Doyle Dane Bernbach; J. Walter Thompson Agency; Leo Burnett Advertising Agency; Wells Rich Greene

aerial couriers, 13. *See also* first flight attendants

Aeroflot, 103, 125; age ceilings at, 147–48; appearance requirements at, 140, 148; Cold War propaganda and, 127; expansion of international routes of, 141, 142, 143, 146; foreign language requirement at, 148; marriage and maternity policy at, 138–39; Moscow-to-New York flight of, 125; salaries at, 144; training at, 139–40, 141–42, 144; uniforms at, 127, 140–41, 146–47

Aeroflot stewardesses, 138–49 passim; American press representation of, 127, 144; in Soviet propaganda, 5, 128, 138, 139

African American railroad porters, 65

African American stewardesses, 59–90 passim; *Ebony* and, 81–82; in the jet age, 109; typical American girl and, 60, 211

Afro (hairstyle), 86, 89

age ceilings, 3, 190, 211; in the 1930s, 17; in the 1940s, 29; in the 1950s, 42, 197–98; in the jet age, 104; resistance against,

201, 204, 205. *See also under* American Airlines

air hostess, 40

airline advertising: in the 1930s, 20–22; in the 1940s, 52–54; in the 1960s, 155; in the jet age, 96, 99–100, 101–102, 122; personal travel market and, 162–63; in postwar era, 33–35; protests against, 208; sexual innuendo in, 180; sexualized stewardess in, 183, 185; targeting African American consumers, 85; youth market and, 163–64, 171, 175

Airline Deregulation Act, 212

airline industry: in the 1920s, 11–13; Airline Deregulation Act and, 212; jet-age changes of, 91, 96, 97, 98; mass transportation and, 97, 100, 111, 161–62, 173, 208; postwar changes of, 32–35; publicity of, 12–13, 29, 30–31, 52–54, 108–9, 122

airline marketing: African Americans and, 65, 85; glamour and, 101; middle class and, 97–101, 171, 174, 185; patriotism and, 35, 37; women and, 107, 171; youth and, 163–64, 171, 173, 175

Air Line Pilots Association (ALPA), 17, 197, 200

Air Line Stewardess Association (ALSA), 196–97

Air Line Stewards and Stewardesses Association (ALSSA), 197–202, 204, 205; African American stewardesses and, 60, 89, 109; all-American girl, 27, 29, 48, 52–57, 105, 210

NOTES ON SOURCES

My research on postwar stewardesses led me into unexpected nooks from Kansas City to Moscow. As I chased clues, I found myself sipping tea with a psychologist for Aeroflot stewardesses in the suburbs of Moscow, gently flipping through brittle *Playboy* magazines from the 1950s in the rare books collection at the Library of Congress, and admiring TWA's disposable paper uniforms in their only institutionally preserved home, the British Airways archives in London. Thanks to generous support from NASA, the Guggenheim Foundation, the Smithsonian Institution, the University of Southern California, Duke University, and the Center for Feminist Research, I was able to devote eight years to exploring archival collections across the country and overseas. I could not have gallivanted around the world to scour through stewardess papers without this kind support—it was all a nerd could ever hope for.

This international hunt turned up a range of rich, unique sources that had never before been seen by scholars—stewardess diaries, ad campaigns, airline records, and stewardess training manuals, from both the United States and Russia. This broad array of original sources allowed me to view the stewardess from multiple perspectives. I considered prescriptive sources, which stated who the stewardess was supposed to be, as well as sources produced by stewardesses themselves. Exploring the stewardess as an icon crafted by the airline industry, advertising agencies, and the popular media, I also drew on popular cultural texts (such as magazines, newspapers, and novels) as well as sources within the airline industry, including supervisor manuals, thousands of print ads, corporate airline collections, advertising agency records, and press releases.

One interesting collection used in this book was the confidential personnel files and medical records of Pan Am stewardesses; currently the collection is in the custody of the National Institute of Occupational Safety and Health (NIOSH). After I obtained signed permission slips and death certificates from former Pan Am stewardesses through a thorny two-year process, NIOSH granted me access to these records. The records contained detailed documentation of disciplinary procedures for stewardesses' beauty violations, stewardess employment applications, supervisor evaluations, and personal information for stewardesses. The researchers at NIOSH also kindly calculated invaluable statistics for my work; these statistics offer the only existing demographic information on stewardesses from this era.

Luckily, some of the women who worked during the glamorous era of air travel were still around to tell their stories. My quest to piece together the world of stewardesses led me on a cross-country adventure to find these women. Associations of former stewardesses (such as World Wings International [Pan Am], Clipped Wings [United], the Silverliners [Eastern], and the Kiwi Club [American]) helped track down hundreds of former stewardesses, who generously shared their intimate collections, including personal diaries, letters to their parents, unpublished memoirs, and scrapbooks. These organizations also welcomed me at their conventions, where I met ex-stewardesses. At a Miami Hilton, I listened to former stewardesses reminisce about the golden days of air travel and watched them model their old uniforms in a makeshift fashion show. Former stewardesses also invited me into their homes and spent hours talking with me about their experiences. One retired stewardess in rural North Carolina, for example, allowed me to dig through crumbling letters that she had written home sixty years earlier. I also emailed, interviewed, and sent questionnaires to hundreds of former stewardesses using contact lists that stewardess organizations were kind enough to share with me. These sources provide deeply personal insight into these women's experiences—particularly, how they navigated gender roles; how they wrestled with airline policies; and how they defined themselves as women, professionals, and Americans.

I was also fortunate to gain access to corporate airline and advertising records that had previously been closed to scholars. In the wake of severe financial distress over the past few years, several airline industry archives

282

I examined have since closed down. These corporate records from several major airlines and ad agencies reveal the complex, behind-the-scenes business side of the stewardess image. They offer insight into how airlines selected, trained, and disciplined stewardesses, as well as how they crafted the stewardess image and why that image changed dramatically over the years.

Several archival collections contributed to my understanding of how race operated in the airlines, including airline corporate records on discrimination lawsuits at the Minnesota Historical Society, court transcripts for stewardess discrimination cases, and the Fair Employment Practices Commission's records. In addition, the Black Flight Attendants of America helped me track down the nation's first black stewardess for a major airline, who shared her personal letters and spoke with me about her battle to fly.

I also used internal advertising records from several major advertising agencies, including the Leo Burnett Agency in Chicago, the N. Y. Ayer Agency at the National Museum of American History in Washington, D.C., and the J. W. Thompson Agency in Durham, N.C. I reviewed several thousand print advertisements for major airlines of this era, as well as internal corporate memos and records produced by advertising teams and airline executives. These sources reveal the production side of the stewardess image—particularly why airlines created each incarnation of it.

Uncovering sources on Soviet stewardesses was trickier. By exchanging faxes and phone calls with archivists and Aeroflot employees in Russia for several months, I learned that Aeroflot's records might exist somewhere in Moscow, but no one was sure exactly where or whether I would be granted access if they were located. I flew to Moscow, learned rudimentary Russian (just enough to read and pronounce the word for "stewardess"), and set out to find these elusive Aeroflot records. After meeting with dozens of aviation officials, archivists, and Aeroflot employees for weeks, we located the Aeroflot records at the Russian State Economic Archives. But the archive's director was on an extended vacation and I could not be admitted without his permission. After extensive paperwork and numerous cups of tea, I was granted permission to explore the records at the Ministry of Civil Aviation; these turned out to be massive piles of boxes—most of them unlabeled. With a determined translator by my side, I rummaged through mounds of documents in a dark hallway at the archives, hoping to hit pay dirt. Ultimately,

Sources

I discovered invaluable aviation records from the Cold War era, including Aeroflot stewardess training manuals from the 1950s. I also found materials at the Aeroflot museum and interviewed former Aeroflot stewardesses who worked the first flights between New York and Moscow in the late 1960s. The sources from this research journey formed the basis of this book.

ACKNOWLEDGMENTS

In the time that I've worked on this book, I have incurred many debts. Several organizations supported this project with grants and fellowships, including the Guggenheim Foundation, the Smithsonian Institution's National Air and Space Museum, NASA, the University of Southern California and its Center for Feminist Research, Hedgebrook, and Duke University. These organizations generously provided the funding and support I needed to research and write this book.

I am indebted to the archivists at the Leo Burnett Agency, the Minnesota Historical Society, the Hartman Center for Advertising, the University of Miami's Richter Library, the Historical Museum of Southern Florida, the San Francisco Airport Museum, the Boeing Corporation, the Schomburg Center, the UCLA Film and Television Library, the National Institute of Occupational Safety and Health, Aeroflot, and the Russian State Economic Archives. Harry Leich at the Library of Congress was especially helpful for finding Russian aviation magazines. The archivists at American Airlines, United Airlines, and Delta Airlines kindly granted me access to their collections before they closed down. Several organizations of former stewardesses also offered an enormous amount of help—especially World Wings International, the Kiwi Club, the Silverliners, and Clipped Wings. These associations welcomed me warmly at their conventions and helped me find original sources that I otherwise would never have seen.

My agents, Jill Marr and Sandy Dijkstra, have offered invaluable advice and enthusiasm. I am also deeply grateful to everyone at the University of Pennsylvania Press and especially to my editor, Robert Lockhart, for believing in this project from the beginning, for thoughtfully reading various drafts, and for offering insight and encouragement along the way.

Acknowledgments

I am thankful to everyone at the National Air and Space Museum, especially Dom Pisano, who offered guidance in navigating the museum's immense collections and friendship while I was living in Washington. Ron Davies also shared his wonderful collection of airline binders and immense knowledge about flying.

I am especially grateful to everyone in the University of Southern California history department for all of the support over the years. Historians Lois Banner and Steve Ross were always demanding critics and enthusiastic supporters. I am thankful to Lois for engaging me in long discussions about hair color in the 1950s, for thoughtful criticisms, and for long walks. I'm grateful to Steve for tirelessly asking big-picture questions (why should trees die for this book?). I am thankful to Stephanie Schnorbus, who patiently explained the proper usage of the mysterious "en dash" in the wee hours of the morning and miraculously transformed an enormous, unwieldy mass of citations into readable endnotes with the patience of a saint and the brain of a supercomputer. I am also indebted to Sarah Winfrey, Erin Barnes, Kim Blake, and Anne Albrecht for help with the notes and images. My friend Wendy Call acted as my consulting editor—she helped me see this book with a fresh outlook and inspired me to approach revisions with gusto. Her storytelling skills and her ability to digest academic material helped me transform my research into a book. I'm grateful to her for so many reasons. I also want to thank my sister for decoding the mysterious legal language in stewardess discrimination lawsuits. I would have been adrift without her legal expertise.

I am thankful to my family—Paul, Fran, Monica, Kilian, the Krushies, the Tippens, West—and to my friends—especially Mo, Tone, Mademod, Karen, Philip, Leigh, and the members of the infamous Map and Touring Club. I am also deeply grateful to my partner, Misha Collins, for surprising me with writing-break field trips to the Los Angeles river during rainstorms, for offering insightful comments on seemingly countless drafts, for fixing the printer on a near daily basis, for building a beautiful place for me to work, for making me laugh when I thought I couldn't, and for sustaining me when I got discouraged. His patience, love, and support have meant everything to me.

I am also grateful to the hundreds of former stewardesses who were kind enough to share their treasured memorabilia as well as personal diaries, letters to their loved ones, scrapbooks, and other intimate sources. Many of these women spent hours talking with me about their experiences. Their generosity made it possible for me to gain a deeper understanding of the world of stewardesses. Without these amazing women, this book would not have been possible—and, with gratitude, I dedicate this book to them.